Rethinking Capitalism

Routledge Studies in Business Ethics

1. Rethinking Capitalism
Community and Responsibility
in Business
Rogene A. Buchholz

Rethinking Capitalism

Community and Responsibility in Business

Rogene A. Buchholz

Routledge
Taylor & Francis Group
New York   London

First published 2009
by Routledge
270 Madison Ave, New York, NY 10016

Simultaneously published in the UK
by Routledge
2 Park Square, Milton Park, Abingdon, Oxon OX14 4RN

Routledge is an imprint of the Taylor & Francis Group, an informa business

© 2009 Taylor & Francis

Typeset in Sabon by IBT Global.
Printed and bound in the United States of America on acid-free paper by IBT Global.

Library of Congress Cataloging in Publication Data
Buchholz, Rogene A.
   Rethinking capitalism : community and responsibility in business / Rogene A. Buchholz.
      p. cm. — (Routledge studies in business ethics ; 1)
   Includes bibliographical references and index.
   1. Capitalism — Moral and ethical aspects.   2. Social responsibility of business.   I. Title.
   HB501.B8456 2009
   174 — dc22
   2008036867

ISBN10: 0-415-99721-6 (hbk)
ISBN10: 0-203-88173-7 (ebk)

ISBN13: 978-0-415-99721-8 (hbk)
ISBN13: 978-0-203-88173-6 (ebk)

This book is dedicated to William C. Frederick, who introduced me to the field of Business and Society and has been a continual inspiration to all of us interested in social responsibility and business ethics

Contents

Part III: Implications of the Framework for the Corporation

Acknowledgments

This book would not have been possible were it not for the person to whom the book is dedicated. William C. Frederick was my mentor while I was studying for my doctorate at the University of Pittsburgh and has been a continual source for new insights into the nature of corporate social responsibility and business ethics. He guided me through the doctoral program and has been continually supportive of my efforts to contribute to the development of the field. Without his leadership in establishing the field at the University of Pittsburgh and instituting a doctoral program, I might have never have gotten into the field, a field which has proven to be such a marvelous career for someone with my interests.

This book would also not have been possible without the input of my wife, Sandra B. Rosenthal, who introduced me to classical American pragmatism and provided a different way of looking at the capitalistic system and its relationship to human well-being. We collaborated on a book published by Oxford University Press as part of the Ruffin Series in Business Ethics, from which I rewrote some material for some of the more theoretical portions of this book. American pragmatism provided the intellectual foundations for community and responsibility, which form the basis for a rethinking of capitalism and the business system. My wife also read all the chapters and made many suggestions for improvement of the content as well as helping with the title of the book and chapter headings.

In addition, I would also like to thank Warren Bennis and James O'Toole for writing their article that appeared in the *Harvard Business Review* that criticized management education for a wholesale adoption of the scientific model and advocated the adoption of a more professional approach to business education. This article set me to thinking about management as a profession and what it would take to implement this vision. Thus I came to the realization that it would take no less than a rethinking of capitalism for management to become a profession in the best sense of the word, which provided the motivation for writing this book.

Since I retired, I have been auditing philosophy classes at the University of Colorado at Denver, which has broadened my horizons and introduced me to new ways of thinking. In particular, I would like to thank Myra

x *Acknowledgments*

Bookman, Maria Talero, and Michael Boring, who taught classes that I audited, which gave me new ideas about capitalism and introduced me to philosophical writings that were relevant to this book. It has been great fun to audit these courses and have the privilege of interacting with these faculty and the students in the classes I audited. It is like going back to school without having to write papers or take exams, the best of all possible worlds.

Robert W. Kolb, the Frank W. Considine Chair in Applied Ethics at Loyola University in Chicago, is owed a great many thanks for introducing me to Laura D. H. Stearns, my editor at Routledge Research of the Taylor & Francis Group, who took an interest in the book and guided it through the review process. She was a great pleasure to work with and deserves many thanks for her efforts. Thanks are also due to Nicholas Mendoza, Editorial Assistant at Routledge Research, for guiding the book through the production process, as well as Caroline Cautley and Sarah Stone from the production department, and Carey Nershi and Terence James Johnson from IBT, who were also involved in production and printing.

Finally, I would like to thank Diane L. Swanson, The vonWadden Business Administration Professor and Chair of the Ethics Initiative at the School of Business at Kansas State University, Jeffrey Lenn, Associate Vice-President for Academic Operations and Professor of Strategic Management at George Washington University, Kenneth Stikkers, Professor in the Philosophy Department at Southern Illinois University at Carbondale, and Kimberly Garchar at Kent State University, all of whom gave the book a positive response and made many suggestions for improvement that were taken into account in a revision and reorganization of the book. Their efforts are greatly appreciated and their suggestions made for a much better book.

Excerpts were rewritten from the following publications with kind permission from Springer Science+Business Media:

Journal of Business Ethics, Stakeholder Theory and Public Policy: How Governments Matter, 2004, 143–153, Rogene A. Buchholz and Sandra B. Rosenthal, Copyright Kluwer Academic Publishers.
Journal of Business Ethics, Toward A Contemporary Conceptual Framework for Stakeholder Theory, 2005, 137–148, Rogene A. Buchholz and Sandra B. Rosenthal, Copyright Springer.
Journal of Business Ethics, The Unholy Alliance of Business and Science, 2008, 199–206, Rogene A. Buchholz and Sandra B. Rosenthal, Copyright Springer.

Excerpts were also rewritten from the following book with the kind permission of Oxford University Press.

Sandra B. Rosenthal and Rogene A. Buchholz, *Rethinking Business Ethics*. New York: Oxford University Press, 2000.

Introduction

This book grew out of an article that appeared in the *Harvard Business Review* in 2005 in which Warren Bennis and James O'Toole, two management professors at the University of Southern California, analyze the reasons for the alleged failure of business schools to adequately prepare their graduates for the world of business.[1] This article prompted me to write a response in the form of a paper that I presented at a conference and that was subsequently published in *The Journal of Business Ethics*.[2] In the course of writing this paper I came to some new thoughts about management and the role of business organizations in society and I thought a book might be in order to explore the implications of this thinking.

In the beginning of the article Bennis and O'Toole enumerate recent criticisms of MBA programs that include failing to impart useful skills, failing to prepare leaders, failing to instill norms of ethical behavior, and even failing to lead graduates to corporate jobs. These criticisms came from many different groups including students, employers, the media, and deans of some of the country's most prestigious business schools. Attempts to address these problems resulted in many efforts to revise the curriculum to be more relevant to the business world, however Bennis and O'Toole believe that the curriculum is the effect, and not the cause, of what ails the modern business school.

The actual cause of today's crisis in management education, they believe, can be traced to a dramatic shift in the culture of business schools that has taken place over the past several decades as many leading business schools have come to measure their success solely by the rigor of their scientific research rather than in terms of the competence of their graduates or how well faculties understand the important drivers of business performance. Bennis and O'Toole argue that this scientific model is predicated on the faulty assumption that business is an academic discipline like chemistry or geology, when in fact it is a profession akin to medicine and the law. Business schools should be professional schools, and this distinction between a profession and an academic discipline is crucial. No curricular reforms will work, in their opinion, until the scientific model is replaced by a model that is more appropriate for the special requirements of a profession.

The rest of the article discusses how business schools came to embrace the scientific model of physicists and economists rather than the professional model of doctors and lawyers. The problem is not that business schools have embraced scientific rigor, but rather that they have forsaken other forms of knowledge that are relevant to business organizations. According to Bennis and O'Toole, in order to regain relevance, business schools must realize that business management is not a scientific discipline, but a profession, and they must deal with the things a professional education requires. There must be a balance between rigor and relevance.

This argument caused me to think once again about management as a profession, and whether it is indeed a profession akin to medicine and the legal profession or even to my own chosen profession as a college educator. In what sense can business management be considered a profession? Since I taught for twenty-eight years in various schools of business and management throughout the country in the areas of social responsibility and business ethics, this question came up every now and then. But it was not until I wrote a paper in response to Bennis and O'Toole that I began to see the profound implications of this question and its relevance to the economic system in which business functions.

Citing an associate professor at Harvard Business School, Bennis and O'Toole point out that the professions have at least four key elements: (1) an accepted body of knowledge, (2) a system for certifying that individuals have mastered that body of knowledge before they are allowed to practice, (3) a commitment to the public good, and (4) an enforceable code of ethics.[3] Professions are oriented toward practice and focused on client needs, and above all integrate knowledge and practice. While not proposing making management a gated profession requiring credentialing and licensing, they do believe these elements of a profession are critical to business school education.

The profession model they propose raises some profound questions about the activity of business management and whether it is indeed a profession akin to law and medicine. Taking the criteria they mention as important elements of a profession and applying them to the practice of management is problematic. For one thing, is there an accepted body of knowledge that has to be mastered before one can enter business? The MBA. degree is not like a law degree or a degree from a medical school. One does not need it in order to start a business or even get a job in a business organization. There are hundreds of people like Bill Gates who are college dropouts or who never went to college and majored in business who went on to be an enormous success in business. This in itself constitutes an important and crucial difference between business management and the more traditional professions of law and medicine.

Regarding a code of ethics, there is no code of ethics for management as there is for the practice of law and medicine. What codes of ethics *do* exist are related to particular business organizations and not to the practice of management as a whole. This alone suggests that there is no such thing as a management profession, but that the focus of business is on organizations where some people are managers who control the behavior of others in the organization. These codes of ethics are meant to express the values of the organization and what it stands for in terms of acceptable and unacceptable behavior and do not necessarily reflect the values of management as a profession.

The traditional professions of law and medicine also have no home discipline, so to speak, that provides them with the rationale and justification for their existence. They are strictly practical activities that need no other justification beyond their duty to serve their clients' interests. Business and management, however, do have a home discipline in economics that prescribes the role business is to play in society, and describes how the firm functions to create economic wealth. While it could be argued that certain courses such as organizational behavior have their home in sociology, this emphasis is subservient to the larger economic purpose and role of the business enterprise as prescribed in economics.

This brings us to the final element of a profession that is the most important criterion for purposes of this book, and perhaps for a profession in general, namely, commitment to the public good. What does this mean in a business context and what implications does this criterion have for management education? Is it possible for business management to be committed to the public good, or is this something that is more akin to the traditional professions that have an obligation to focus on their clients' needs? What is expected of management in our society in the kind of economic system in which business functions? What does it mean for business management to be a profession in the context of a free enterprise or capitalistic system?

According to Albert William Levi writing in an article entitled "Ethical Confusion and the Business Community," the aim of a profession is the performance of a service and the true professional keeps his or her eye on the activity. On the one hand, commitment and responsibility are thus a mark of the profession. The aim of business, on the other hand, is profit and the true businessman keeps his eye on the reward. This is a logical distinction according to Levi, and calls attention to the diametrically opposed point of view between a "business" and a "profession" as ordinarily understood. The major problem with a professional model for business is the conflict between the professional demand for service and the exclusively business demand for profits.[4]

This distinction is largely a matter of emphasis, according to Levi, as if a doctor thinks more of his fee than of the welfare of the patient, he is a businessman even if he spent six years in the best medical school in the country. Likewise, if the owner of a bakery takes pride in his bread and is less interested in the volume of his yearly profit than in the quality and reputation of his merchandise, he is a professional man even if he has never graduated from college. Levi recognizes this distinction may sound "utopian" to many people and square badly with the practice of many fee-hungry doctors and lawyers. But this does not impair the logic of the position, and only indicates the falling off which results when business mentality at its worst corrupts the traditional professions.

For business to become a profession, then, methods must be devised whereby emphasis upon the activity, commitment, and responsibility become the common property of members of the business community. But this change of emphasis in business goes against the grain of the mentality of Western civilization and requires a psychological re-orientation of business mentality, a rethinking of the purpose of business, and a rethinking of society itself. As Levi states, "The ethical behavior of any segment within society is generally not without roots in the more general aspirations of that society as a whole".[5] And our society is infused with a philosophy of individualism and rights that forms the basis for our understanding of modern capitalism. It is this philosophy that must be broadened to include community and responsibility in order for management to be considered a profession.

In Chapter 1, I show how this philosophy of individualism and rights is contained in the works of Adam Smith and John Locke and how their ideas were critical in the development of our modern understanding of capitalism. Individualism is the idea that individuals are the basic building blocks of society and that a society is nothing more than the sum of the individuals that comprise that society. Rights inhere in the individual and are not in any way a social product. These ideas support what is said to be a system of natural liberty in which people are free to pursue their own interests and use their property as they see fit, quite apart from any obligation to the larger society in which they function. Efforts to broaden the responsibilities of business that contain some notion of community such as social responsibility, stakeholder theory, public policy, and ethics have floundered on the shoals of this philosophy. The remaining chapters in Part I describe these efforts and the problems they have encountered because of this individualistic philosophy.

Part II deals with a new theoretical framework for capitalism based on a philosophy of community and responsibility that comes from classical American pragmatism, particularly the writings of John Dewey, George Herbert Mead, and William James. These writings provide a theory of the self that is social in nature and inextricably tied to the community in which the self develops. This understanding of self and community leads to a different understanding of rights and how they develop and function in the context of community, and emphasizes the responsibilities of individuals to the larger community. This framework leads to a different way to interpret and understand the capitalistic system, the market system, and the natural environment, and points toward a reorientation of our thinking about capitalistic economic activity.

Part III of the book has a more practical and institutional focus in dealing with the implications of this new philosophy for various aspects of the corporation. The corporation itself is understood as a community rather than a voluntary organization of individuals who band together for self-interested purposes. This notion of community is extended into the global arena which entails a whole different set of responsibilities. Science and technology are seen in the context of community rather than as serving private interests. Corporate governance deals with the issue of who controls the modern corporation and the argument is made in Chapter 13 that it is management that largely controls corporate activities, making the final chapter, Chapter 14, on the professionalization of management and a commitment to service of critical importance in this new philosophy.

Part I

The Problem with Contemporary Capitalism

1 Individualism and Rights
The Basis of the Problem

Modern capitalism is based upon a philosophy of individualism rather than community, and the moral basis of society is to be found in rights and not in responsibilities. Individuals have a "natural right" to use their property as they see fit and follow their economic self-interest, independent of any obligation or duty to serve society. These rights are possessed by individuals quite apart from any obligation to contribute to the general happiness of society or to an overarching social purpose or public good. It was Adam Smith who, whether intended or not, made this feature of capitalistic societies into a virtue with the claim that the pursuit of economic self-interest led to the public good by increasing the wealth of nations through the production of more and more goods and services.[1]

> From the time Adam Smith published The Wealth of Nations, which examined the origins of wealth creation, the liberal free market he espoused has been seen to deliver an indefinite augmentation of wealth and living standards. Such economic growth has succeeded in making belief in perpetual progress in welfare, if not happiness, the dominant faith of modern man. Moreover, the modern liberal economy has seemed not only to promise the morally attractive outcome of maximizing the welfare of society as a whole, but to do so without even requiring individuals to have consciously moral or social intentions. For the 'invisible hand' of the market is seen to lead to the most efficient satisfaction of the wants of different market participants, and in this sense to maximize the social good, merely by harnessing the selfish desires to individuals to further their own ends.[2]

Smith, however, did not advocate the pursuit of self-interest in a moral vacuum. In *The Theory of Moral Sentiments*, he stressed the role of sympathy and benevolence in creating a cohesive society, and it seems clear that Smith assumed that the free pursuit by individuals of their own self-interest would serve the public good only if it occurred in a society that was morally disciplined in this regard. In this moral context, social cooperation and cohesiveness would be further advanced by the pursuit of self-interest. Given the division of labor and the enhancement of productivity this division brought about, it would be in everyone's self-interest to engage in mutually advantageous cooperative economic transactions. Thus self-interest was viewed in the context of certain background moral conditions that would direct it in the interests of the whole.[3] One could even argue that there was an implicit view of community in this view, but if so, it was undermined by other passages such as the following:

> As every *individual*, therefore, endeavours as much as he can both to employ his capital in the support of domestic industry, and so to direct that industry that its produce may be of the greatest value; every individual necessarily labours to render the annual revenue of the society as great as he can. He generally, indeed, neither intends to promote the public interest, nor knows how much he is promoting it. By preferring the support of domestic to that of foreign industry, he intends only his own security; and by directing that industry in such a manner as its produce may be of the greatest value, he intends only his own gain, and he is in this, as in many other cases, led by an invisible hand to promote an end which was no part of this intention. Nor is it always the worse for society that it was no part of it. By pursuing his own interest he frequently promotes that of the society more effectually than when he really intends to promote it.[4]

This image of the "invisible hand" is a metaphor for the socially positive unintended consequences of the market, through which the economic self-interest of individuals is channeled into collective benefits for the society as a whole. Over time, this view of the market as a mechanism for directing self-interest for the social good took precedence over his view of moral sentiments as necessary background conditions for this to take place. When taken out of context, the market itself offered individuals that their own self-interest expressed in a system of free and open competition would be sufficient to further the economic interests of society as a whole. The invisible hand of the free market could, on its own, ensure an outcome that exploited the benefits of market exchange to the mutual advantage of all the participants in the market.

This proved to be a morally attractive outcome that was brought about by individual freedom, without the need for government intervention and the explicit need for moral motives. Self-interest and competition were shown to be positively beneficial, and a system of natural liberty for individuals to pursue their own interests was shown to be compatible with the good of society as a whole. One did not need to worry about the outcome of these self-interested actions nor did anyone need to concern themselves with the moral implications of these actions. This was indeed a system that captured the imagination of people and warranted their allegiance. While *The Theory of Moral Sentiments* emphasizes the role of sympathy, imagination, desire for approval and benevolence in forming socializing attitudes and creating a cohesive society, *The Wealth of Nations* stresses the importance of self-interest as the driving force behind the development of cooperation and mutual dependence in society. Perhaps it is not surprising that the latter view won the hearts and minds of people in industrial societies.[5]

Consistent with this view of capitalism is the notion of property rights as developed by John Locke, who formulated an individualistic political theory that contained a strong defense of property rights, among other things.[6] The key elements in this political theory are natural rights, social contract, government by consent, and the right of revolution. Locke derived his theory of property rights from natural law, which he believed provided the basis for a claim to innate, indefeasible rights inherent in each individual. According to Locke, the true end of government is to protect property, and the right of property provided an effective limitation upon the powers of the government.

Human life begins in a hypothetical state of nature, where each individual is perfectly equal with every other and all have the absolute liberty to act as they will without interference from any other. The earth and everything in it belongs to everyone in common and each individual has the same right to make use of whatever he or she can find and use for themselves, except that each individual has an exclusive right to his/her own body and its actions. Everyone has a right to draw subsistence from whatever is offered in nature, and when things are taken out of a state of nature for this purpose and individual actions are applied to natural objects, an individual's labor is mixed with natural objects.

This mixture of nature and labor provided a clear moral basis for appropriating nature as an extension of our own personal property. Everyone has a natural right to that with which he has "mixed" the labor of his body. By expending energy to make natural objects useful, people make them a part of themselves. Individuals who plow the land and take it out of a state of nature, for example, and improve its productivity by spending their own time and effort on its cultivation, acquire a property interest in the result. The plowed field is worth more than the virgin prairie because someone has invested labor in plowing it, so even if the prairie was originally held in common by all, the plowed field belongs to the person who expended the energy to make it productive.

Society does not create this right to property; it is a natural right that each person brings to society in his or her own person. This right can be regulated only to the extent necessary to make effective the equally valid claims of another individual to the same rights. The legitimacy of political power is derived from this individual right of each person to protect his or her property. The creation of government is justified because it is a better way of protecting this natural right to property than the self-help to which each individual is naturally entitled. The power of the government, however, cannot be exercised in an arbitrary manner, and property cannot be taken from individuals without their consent. Government exists to protect the prior right to private property.

Locke's theory of property dovetails nicely with the views of Adam Smith, and together they provide a philosophical basis for the use of private property for self-interested purposes that are rooted in a conception of natural rights and natural liberty inherent in individuals. It is individualism and rights that are at the core of this philosophy and provide an understanding of how individuals relate to each other in economic, social, and political institutions. These institutions are to promote and support this natural right to liberty and the natural right to property, and any interference with these natural rights goes against the laws of nature. This is a powerful philosophy that has captured the imagination of people for many years and provides the moral basis for our modern understanding of capitalism.

INDIVIDUALISM AND RIGHTS EXAMINED

Individualism has been a key idea in Western societies for many centuries and is one of those unexamined assumptions about the way the world is constituted. Individualism is the idea that people are individual selves that are quite distinguishable from other selves and can be defined apart from any social context. The individual is held to be the primary unit of reality and the ultimate standard of value. Every person is an end in himself or herself and no person should be sacrificed for the sake of another in some utilitarian context where the greater good would override individual interests. While societies and other collective entities such as business organizations exist, they are nothing more than a collection of the individuals in them, not something over and above them. Organizations thus derive their being from the individuals who choose to become part of them and comprise their membership.

We are thought to be like atoms that are traveling around the world bumping up against other atoms or individuals in the course of our existence. As individual selves, we are by and large alone in the world and in competition with other selves for the resources of society. We create institutions such as business and enter into contracts in order to survive and provide for our needs through some form of cooperative endeavor. But most of these institutional and contractual relationships are instrumental in that we relate to other people who can do something for us and provide us with something we need for our existence. We are not linked to people except through external ties that can never lead to a true community.

Within this philosophy of individualism, there is nothing but these external links to bind people and institutions together. Self-interested individuals and institutions that have separate wills and desires are constantly colliding like atoms in space, hence this philosophy of individualism is sometimes called atomic individualism. To minimize the collisions and reduce conflict, people and institutions may come together on occasion to work out these differences and establish some sort of relationship. But while peripheral ties may be established when antecedent individuals enter into contract with one another or come together to more readily secure their own individualistic goals, these kinds of bonds cannot root them in any ongoing endeavor that is more than the sum of their separate selves, separate wills, and separate egoistic desires. There is never any possibility of developing a true community or society based upon a sense of responsibility for each other.

If the community is seen as nothing more than the sum of its parts, society bounces back and forth between an emphasis on individual rights and community needs, between a celebration of diversity and the need for common goals and interests. Once the individual is taken as an isolatable unit, the individual and the community become pitted against each other in an ultimately irreconcilable tension. This tension between the individual and community causes a great deal of difficulty in arriving at mutually satisfactory solutions to social and political problems. Nothing binds individuals and institutions together except self-interest, and if one starts with individual and separate atomic bits of this sort, there is no way to get to a true community. True unity can arise only in a form of action and thinking that does not attempt to fragment the whole of reality.[7]

Thomas Michael Power argues that this view of the atomic self permeates our understanding of the economy and the functioning of the economic system.[8] Economics assumes that society is nothing but the aggregation of atomistic individuals so that there are no social objectives to individual decisions. The economy and economic activity are envisioned as separate realms of human activity that can be studied outside of their social and political contexts and have an existence separate from the rest of people's existence. Thus one of the important accomplishments of economics, according to Power, has been to distinguish the economy as a separate realm of human activity and then see it as managed by an automatic mechanism that is both self-adjusting and socially rational, even though no rational thought is involved in its operation. Conscious direction of the economy is not only unnecessary but inappropriate and destructive. Through the competition among self-interested parties, the narrow self-seeking that motivates these individuals is cancelled out, and an outcome intended by none of these participants emerges. This outcome is supposedly rational in the sense of minimizing costs and using scarce resources efficiently in satisfying the aggregate preferences of the population.

Consistent with this view of individualism is the notion that rights inhere in individuals who are born with certain inalienable rights that are part and parcel of our being. These rights do not come from outside or in any sense belong to a community, but are inherent in each individual in some sense when he or she is born. Our Declaration of Independence is based on this notion of rights, as is the Bill of Rights spelled out in the first ten amendments to our Constitution. The former states that certain truths are held to be self-evident and that men are endowed by their creator with certain unalienable rights. This notion of rights is more or less universal, as nations all over the world insist they have a right to do whatever they deem appropriate for their survival.

Rights have been used throughout history to overthrow systems of governance and establish new forms of social and economic power. In the Middle Ages, kings claimed a divine right to govern their subjects in order to throw off the shackles of the church, and then went on to claim ever more extensive powers over the subjects they came to dominate. Fledging democracies such as our own claimed a natural right to liberty in order to overthrow this order and establish a new system of government based on the sovereignty of the people. The notion of natural rights arises out of a need to check the sovereign power of kings, as was the case in the establishment of our country. Such rights can also be used to put a check on the sovereign power of the state, as in Locke's view of property rights.

The Declaration of Independence refers to certain basic rights that are believed to be self-evident. This notion seems to be based on some kind of a natural law concept and assumes that there is an ideal standard of justice fixed by nature that is binding on all persons. This standard takes precedence over the particular laws and standards created by social convention. The concept of natural rights provides absolute standards against which the laws and policies of particular states and institutions are to be measured. These rights are considered to be fundamental regardless of merit, due to be respected because they are rooted in a knowledge of certain universal regularities in nature. They refer to a proper ordering of the universe. Knowledge of this structure was believed to be accessible to all people by virtue of the reason they possessed.[9]

Thus a right is an individual's entitlement to something. A person has a right when that person is entitled to act in a certain way or have others act in a certain way toward him or her. This entitlement may derive from a legal system that permits or empowers the person to act in a specified way or that requires others to act in certain ways toward that person. Legal rights are derived from political constitutions, legislative enactments, case law, and executive orders of the highest state official. They can be eliminated by lawful amendments or other political actions and are limited to the particular jurisdiction within which the legal system is in force.

Entitlements can also be derived from a system of moral standards independently of any particular legal system and cannot be eroded or banished by political votes, powers, or amendments. They can be based on moral norms or principles that specify that all human beings are permitted or empowered to do something or are entitled to have something done for them. Moral rights provide individuals with autonomy and/or equality in the free pursuit of their interests. These rights identify activities or interests that people must be left free to pursue or not to pursue as they themselves choose, and whose pursuit must not be subordinated to the interests of others except for special and exceptionally weighty reasons. Moral rights provide a basis for justifying one's actions and for invoking the protection or aid of others. They express the requirements of morality from the point of view of the individual instead of society as a whole, and promote individual welfare and protect individual choices against encroachment by society.

Utilitarian considerations promote society's aggregate utility and are indifferent to individual welfare except insofar as it affects this social aggregate. Moral rights, however, limit the validity of appeals to social benefits. If a person has a right to do something, then it is wrong for anyone or any institution to interfere with this right, even though a large number of people might gain much more utility from such interference. If utilitarian benefits or losses imposed on society become great enough, they may be sufficient, in some cases, to breach the wall of rights set to protect a person's freedom to pursue his or her interests.

Negative rights can be considered to be duties others have not to interfere in certain activities of individuals. A negative right is a right to be free to hold and practice a belief, to pursue an action, or enjoy a state of affairs without outside interference. Negative rights protect an individual from interference from the state and from other people. The state is to protect this basic right to be left alone and is not to encroach on this right itself. Positive rights, on the other hand, mean some other agents have a positive duty of providing the holder of rights with whatever he or she needs to freely pursue his or her interests. Positive rights are rights to obtain goods and services, opportunities, or certain kinds of equal treatment.

Both kinds of rights entail some kinds of responsibilities on the part of certain persons and groups. Negative rights involve responsibilities that others have not to interfere in certain activities of a person and leave him or her alone. These rights are to be respected by other people as well as the institutions of society. Positive rights involve responsibilities some agents have to provide the rights holders with the things they have coming to them as a result of these rights. But these responsibilities are derived from rights in that they stem from the rights people hold to be left alone or to be provided with certain things. Rights are prior and responsibilities would not exist in the absence of rights.

Today we speak a good deal about human rights and attempt to promote such rights throughout the world. These rights are not derived from the operations of natural reason, but rather from ideas of what it means to be human. It is assumed that human beings have an essential nature that determines the fundamental obligations and rights that are to be respected by other people and social institutions. The rights that are asserted as fundamental to the development of human beings are believed to stem from knowledge of certain essential properties of human nature.

Thus people have a right to be treated equally in the workplace, to work and play in a smoke-free environment, to carry out their work-related activities in a safe workplace, and the right to a clean environment, among other things. These rights often clash with property rights, which still seem to be rooted in a system of natural liberty, that people have a natural right to use their property in their own interests. Affirmative action programs, job safety programs, pollution control programs, and similar measures sometimes override property rights and limit the freedoms of property owners. At other times, property rights take precedence. Rights clash because they are rooted in individualism, and these clashes have to be sorted out by whatever political system is in place.

TOWARD A NEW PHILOSOPHY

Thus we have the development over the years of an "acquisitive society," whose main preoccupation is the acquisition of economic wealth and which has enthroned money as the measure of success. The business organization is the engine that creates this economic wealth, and its primary purpose, if not its social responsibility, as Milton Friedman put it years ago, is to make as much money as possible while staying within the rules of the game.[10] The business school curriculum reflects this philosophy, as the maximization of shareholder wealth is still the stated or unstated purpose of most courses despite many years of social responsibility, ethics, and stakeholder management. There has been no significant change in the economic, social, and moral philosophy that undergirds the business enterprise.

What a professional model for schools of business and management would require is the formulation of a new moral, social, and economic philosophy for business, something that has not as yet been attempted on a large enough scale by scholars in business schools or in ethics for that matter. It would require a new vision of Western economic society based on the idea of community and responsibility rather than individualism and rights related to the use of property. Otherwise, "the hope of committing business to the canons of responsible professional behavior is only a dream, a moralist's vision without consequences in reality."[11]

In this book I want to make some suggestions regarding certain ideas that it may be useful to think about that could be a key part of this new philosophy. Ideas play a crucial role in how people understand themselves and their role in society. These ideas give rise to concepts that are the basis for knowledge. Certain key ideas become rooted in our minds over time and may not even be conscious until something happens to bring them to consciousness. They are basic assumptions that are like absolutes in that they are not questioned or examined.

This book, then, will focus on two key ideas, community and responsibility, and argue that these ideas could constitute the core of a new philosophy to undergird business organizations and the capitalistic system in which they function. These ideas do not necessarily necessitate a change in the system itself, but only a change of attitude or emphasis. Capitalism, or some form of it, has taken root worldwide with the collapse of socialistic states. It has proven to be the most efficient system to allocate resources to their best use as far as the production of private goods and services is concerned. But when it comes to dealing with the public good and addressing problems like global warming and global poverty, it is much less than adequate.

The following topics to be discussed in this first part of the book concern attempts to broaden the responsibilities of business that include some notion of community. There have been several attempts of this sort over the past decades that have largely failed because they floundered on the shoals of the traditional individualistic philosophy. These include the notion of corporate social responsibility, stakeholder theory, public policy, particularly in the form of social regulation, and ethics as it has been applied over the past several years to business activities. These efforts to extend the responsibilities of business beyond shareholders and have business serve values other than solely economic values have met with limited success because they run counter to the traditional philosophical framework that informs our understanding of capitalism and business.

2   Social Responsibility

These two ideas, individualism and rights, have permeated our understanding of capitalism and the role of business in society. Those concerned with some notion of the public good that goes beyond the immediate self-interest of corporations have had to fight an uphill battle. There have been several attempts to deal with this problem and argue that business has a broader set of relationships to society than stockholders alone and a broader set of responsibilities to the larger society. Many recognized that the pursuit of self-interest alone will not necessarily lead to the public good and argued that corporations must recognize that they function in a broader social context that involves more direct responsibility for their impacts on society. These efforts were trying to offer an alternative view of corporations and their role in society based on something more than individualism and rights, and contained within them some notion of community that went beyond individualism and a view of responsibilities that did not stem from individual rights.

The notion of social responsibility was the first such attempt and came about as a response to social problems that began to plague the society. It was argued that the market by itself failed to provide sufficient incentives for business organizations to address social problems such as equal opportunity, job safety, product safety, poverty, and a host of environmental concerns. Business must find ways to be more socially responsible, it was argued, and address these issues to make a better society. While the concept of corporate social responsibility may have had its origins in the 1930s, as some suggested, it really came to be important during the 1960s and 1970s as a response to the changing social values of society.[1]

The problems that advocates for social responsibility addressed, such as pollution and unsafe workplaces, were in large part created by the drive for economic efficiency in the workplace. These problems were becoming of increasing concern in society as they began to adversely affect the quality of life for large numbers of people. Thus it was argued that business needed to be viewed as a social as well as an economic institution that had social impacts that needed to be considered by management. Proponents of social responsibility developed various approaches to describe a broader relationship of business to society that dealt with the social responsibilities they believed corporations had to the society at large. Corporations needed to fulfill these responsibilities, it was argued, as well as their economic responsibilities.

Thus business executives began to talk about the social responsibilities of business and develop specific programs in response to problems of a social rather than economic nature. Some corporations began to develop programs to deal with poverty in their local communities, for example, and began to concern themselves with pollution from their factories in various parts of the country. Schools of business and management implemented new courses in business and society or in the social responsibilities of business. Because of these developments, there was a need to develop new justifications and rationales for business involvement in solving social problems. The discussion of these new efforts focused on the concept of social responsibility as a way to rationalize and justify this behavior.

There were many definitions of social responsibility, but in general the concept meant that (1) a private corporation has responsibilities to society that go beyond the production of goods and services at a profit, (2) a corporation has a broader constituency to serve than that of stockholders alone, (3) corporations relate to society through more than just the marketplace, and (4) they serve a wider range of human values than the traditional economic values that are dominant in the marketplace. Corporate social responsibility means that corporations are more than just economic institutions and have a responsibility to help society solve some of its most pressing social problems, many of which the corporations helped to cause, by devoting some of their resources to the solution of these problems.

Social responsibility received increasing attention over time because of the need for corporations to respond to the changing social environment of business. This change was often characterized as a change in the terms of the contract between business and society that reflected changing expectations regarding the social performance of business.[2] The old contract was based on the view that economic growth was the source of all progress, social as well as economic, and all wealth was economic in nature. The engine providing this growth and creating this wealth was considered to be the drive for profits by competitive private enterprise. The basic mission of business was thus to produce goods and services at a profit, and in doing so business was making its maximum contribution to society and, in fact, being socially responsible.[3]

The so-called new contract between business and society was based on the view that the single-minded pursuit of economic growth produced some detrimental side effects that imposed social costs on certain segments of society or on society as a whole. The pursuit of economic growth, it was argued, did not necessarily lead to social progress. In many cases, it led instead to a deteriorating physical environment, an unsafe workplace, needless exposure to toxic substances on the part of workers and consumers, discrimination against certain groups in society, urban decay, and other such social problems. This new contract between business and society involved the reduction of these social costs of business through impressing upon business the idea that it has an obligation to work for social as well as economic betterment.

This concept of social responsibility involved changing notions of human welfare and focused on a concern with the social dimensions of business activity that have a direct connection with the quality of life in society. It provided a way for business to concern itself with these social dimensions of its activities and pay some attention to its social impacts. The word social has do to with human beings and their living together in society, and thus implies some form of a community in which business functions. The word responsibility implies that business organizations have an obligation to the society in which they function to deal with social problems and base their operations on something more than just economic self-interest.

ARGUMENTS IN FAVOR OF SOCIAL RESPONSIBILITY

Keeping in tune with public expectations
Long-run self-interest
Gain a better public image
Balance of responsibility with power
Business has useful resources
Social problems can be seen as business opportunities
Avoid government regulation
Business has contributed to social problems

The debate about social responsibility was extensive particularly in the academic community, and involved many different points in favor of the concept as shown above. Proponents argued that if public expectations of business have changed, business has no choice but to accommodate itself to these changes. An institution such as business is allowed to exist only because it performs a useful function in society, and its so-called charter can be revoked at any time if it fails to live up to society's expectations. Thus if business wants to continue in existence, it must respond to changes in society and do what society demands. If society wants business to respond to social problems, it must do so or be threatened with extinction.

The notion of self-interest was also broadened, as it was advocated that business should view its profits over a longer time period. While expenditures to help solve social problems may reduce short-run profits, it is in the long-run self-interest of business to produce social conditions that are favorable for business survival and continued profitability. Business is dependent on its external environment for the resources that it uses to fulfill its economic role in society, such as an educated labor force and a stable political system. Thus enlightened or long-run self-interest dictates a business concern for social problems, as business cannot hope to remain a viable institution in a deteriorating society. Since the business community as a whole has a stake in a good, well-functioning society, the stockholder's long-run self-interest is best served by corporate policies that contribute to the development of the kind of society in which business can grow and prosper.[4]

Business may also be able to gain a better public image by being socially responsible. If the values of society have indeed changed, a company that is responsive to these changes should be more favorably thought of than one that is not responsive. This should mean more customers, more sales of products, better employees, better stock market performance, and easier access to capital markets to raise funds for expansion, provided all other things are equal. An example of this argument is the efforts of some business organizations to produce "green" products that will meet the needs of environmentally conscious consumers and to create an image of an environmentally responsible company through its advertising. A business organization that is seen to be socially responsible in this sense may gain a competitive advantage over its rivals that do not have as good an image in this respect with the public.

Another argument to support the notion of social responsibility relates business power to responsibility. Since business has a large amount of social power in that its activities affect the environment, consumers, employees, communities, and many other areas of society, it has an equal amount of responsibility for these effects. Responsibility is a necessary reciprocal of power, and any imbalance opens the door to irresponsible behavior that may negatively affect the welfare of society. Responsibilities thus arise from power, and if business insists on avoiding its responsibilities, then some of its power may gradually be taken away by other groups or institutions in society, such as government, which will then shape business behavior through group pressure or actual legislation and regulation.[5]

Business also has enormous resources that would be useful in solving social problems. Business has managerial talent, expertise in many technical areas, and physical and financial resources, all of which could be very useful in helping to alleviate society's problems. Business is also known for its innovational ability and its concern for efficient use of resources, which are also useful assets in the social realm. Business ought to be encouraged or perhaps even required to try its hand at solving social problems. The basic idea behind this argument is that if social problems can be privatized, society is likely to benefit from more efficient use of resources to deal with these problems than if they were left entirely to the government.

Closely related to this argument is the idea that social problems can be turned into profitable business opportunities, an especially intriguing idea for some business executives. A few corporations, such as Control Data in the 1970s, claimed this argument as their justification for social involvement.[6] They built plants in disadvantaged areas, for example, not necessarily out of a moral sense of doing good, but more out of a practical business sense of exploiting a profit-making opportunity. A lot of wasted talent could be put to good use in making products. Some companies also found that enough useful products could be made out of waste material to make a recycling program a profitable endeavor.

One of the most powerful arguments for social responsibility is simply that by being socially responsible business may be able to avoid government regulation. This argument is based on the belief that social issues or expectations go through some sort of evolutionary sequence. According to this view, if business does not respond properly to a change in social expectations, social issues will be picked up by the political system and eventually find their way into legislation, which if passed will result in regulation to force business to comply with social objectives. As an issue moves through this sequence, the options are narrowed to where they become more and more legal in nature. The best strategy for business is to get involved with an issue in the early stages of its development, and if business could make a proper response that effectively met social expectations, government regulation may be avoided altogether.

Finally, there is the moral argument that business has a moral obligation to help solve social problems because it helped create or at least perpetuate most of them in the first place. Business polluted the air and water, it failed to dispose of its toxic wastes properly, it created unsafe workplaces, and it helped perpetuate discrimination through its hiring and promotion policies. Therefore business has a moral responsibility to deal with these negative impacts on society rather than leaving them for someone else to solve. Many social problems are the direct result of business operations and these are quite properly the social responsibility of business.

ARGUMENTS AGAINST SOCIAL RESPONSIBILITY

> Difficult to define the concept
> Lack of accountability
> Increase of business power
> Dilutes responsibility to shareholders
> Lack of skills and incentives to deal with social problems
> Reduced international competitiveness
> Corporations are not moral agents
> Undermines the free enterprise system

Despite these supporting arguments, the concept of social responsibility had some serious problems raised by those who did not support the concept wholeheartedly or simply opposed it on ideological grounds. One such problem was the matter of definition. One author wrote that social responsibility "has been used in so many different contexts that it has lost all meaning. Devoid of an internal structure and content, it has come to mean all things to all people."[7] This diversity and fuzziness of meaning left concerned citizens, corporate executives, scholars, and public policy makers confused.

This definitional problem existed at both the conceptual and operational levels, but at the latter level it became a particularly crucial problem as corporations tried to be specific about their social responsibilities. How should a corporation's resources be allocated to help solve social problems? With what specific problems should the corporation concern itself? How much money should be spent? What priorities should be established? What technology should be employed? What goals or standards of performance are relevant? What measures are appropriate to determine adequate performance in solving social problems?

There is no market mechanism to answer these questions about resource allocation, as the market does not work in allocating resources for the provision of such social goods and services to meet social expectations. Preferences or desires for social goods and services are not revealed through market behavior, and thus the market offers little or no information to the manager that is useful in making decisions about solving social problems. For most corporations, there is no money to be made in pollution control, affirmative action programs, hiring the disadvantaged, or other social efforts. The measurement of long-run profits or the profits that might result from an improved corporate image has proven to be problematical.

In the absence of a market mechanism, management could presumably make these operational decisions on their own according to whatever criteria they deem appropriate. This, however, raises an accountability problem. What right do managers of private corporations have to determine social policy for the society as a whole?[8] When managers assume the right to make decisions about social investment, they are involved in the realm of public decision-making without being subject to any of the guidelines or limitations imposed by the market. Nor are they subject to any democratic political process that would serve as a check on their decision-making.

By being socially responsible, it was argued, business managers would in effect be imposing taxes on the public by using stockholders', consumers', and employees' money for a public purpose, as this money could have been used to pay dividends, lower prices, or pay higher wages and salaries. Furthermore, they would be making the decisions on how these funds should be spent. They would thus be spending someone else's money for a social interest and exercising governmental (political) power without any definite criteria for them to follow. This leaves the public with nothing more than business people's claim that their actions are in the public interest, a claim that has no clear meaning and thus cannot be challenged by the public whose interests are at stake. Social responsibility would, therefore, mean whatever corporate managers wanted it to mean and represents:

> . . . an invasion into the public domain by managers who are not elected through any public process, are not subject to annual reviews provided by elections, are not forced to engage in public dialogue with their constituents, are not required to justify the expenditures of corporate funds (involuntary taxes) before a budget committee of the Congress, and need not balance competing interests before coming to their decisions.[9]

Without some kind of accountability, a corporation's decisions can be arbitrary. A corporation may make philanthropic grants or hire disadvantaged people and incur extra costs for training. But the corporation, or more precisely its managers, would be deciding what causes are worthy of support and what people should be singled out as disadvantaged and deserving of attention. Corporate power used in this manner is not accountable and is not to be trusted. It is dangerous to assume that corporate managers know what is best for society, yet the social responsibility doctrine encourages nonelected corporate executives to impose their tastes and preferences on the society as a whole.

Related to this view is the observation that if business does take over activities that traditionally have been considered within the domain of other institutions or groups such as government or community agencies, it might substantially increase its power and influence over the other members and institutions of society and become a monolithic institution, being all things to all people. Business would thus provide for both our economic and social well-being. Such a concentration of power in one institution would lead to a breakdown of pluralism and pose a threat to individual freedoms of the American people.[10]

> Employing the standard self-interest assumption common to economic analysis, it can be seen that social responsibility would indeed be a popular idea among corporate executives, as apparently it is. It is, for whatever reasons, an opportunity to increase the power of corporate decision-makers. Just as with virtually all other goods, more power is usually preferred to less . . . such power carries with it few restrictions. In essence, the doctrine of corporate social responsibility suggests that corporate executives do what politicians have not done and offers fewer constraints to promote responsive behavior. The implication of this logic must be that corporate executives are simply better persons than our current (or past) public servants. If this is indeed true, great steps toward more responsive government can be made by replacing current politicians with corporate executives.
>
> If, on the other hand, corporate leaders are not fundamentally different from other men, the acceptance of the social responsibility

doctrine implies even more autonomy for "public" decision-makers than is currently possible. Such an arrangement should result in even more resources directed toward those uses which benefit the corporate leaders of special interest groups than is observed under existing arrangements. Furthermore, cooperation among corporate executives to facilitate efficient social investment would enhance their opportunities to form cartels and further other efforts to restrict competition.[11]

Then there is the traditional view that the sole responsibility of a corporation is to its shareholders. The manager of a corporation is only a salaried employee of the owners, and is legally and ethically bound to earn the highest return on their investment while staying within the rules of the game. Managers must abide by the principles of profit maximization. They have no legal or moral right to pursue any other objectives, social or otherwise. Business is strictly an economic institution that has the sole responsibility of creating economic wealth.[12]

Others questioned the ability of business to solve social problems. Business executives, by and large, have no experience in dealing with such problems. What do they know, for example, about building housing projects for low-income people? There is no reason to believe they will be any more effective, or even as effective, as other institutions that have more experience and expertise in dealing with these kinds of problems. There is not enough of an incentive for them to pursue social goals with the same vigor with which they pursue private goals, which would motivate them to develop the necessary expertise and gain needed experience.

Private efforts, it is argued, will be more efficient because corporations have demonstrated great efficiency in pursuing private goals. Unfortunately, such efficiency observed in the pursuit of private goals cannot necessarily be transferred to efforts directed toward public or social goals. The organizational structure of the corporation which delivers efficient production of private goods and services cannot be expected to pursue social goals with the same efficiency simply because the incentives for doing so are absent.[13]

Social responsibility must also be looked at in an international context. If business organizations in the U.S. spent significant sums of money to be socially responsible, this expenditure will increase their costs and undoubtedly be added to the cost of their products. If these firms are competing in an international marketplace with firms from other countries that do not have these costs added to their products, these foreign firms will enjoy an even greater competitive advantage than they already do because of lower wage scales and other factors. Thus U.S. firms are likely to have lower sales internationally, which will further contribute to our balance of trade problems. The consequences of this reduced competitiveness could be loss of jobs in the U.S., lower dividends for stockholders, higher prices for consumers, and other social and economic effects.

The claim is also made that social responsibility is fundamentally a moral concept, and it is difficult, if not impossible, for organizations such as business to respond to the moral imperatives inherent in such a concept. People have moral responsibilities, but not organizations, which are structured to attain certain practical objectives and are basically amoral in their operations. A moral concept such as social responsibility does not apply to organizations such as corporations because they are not moral agents that can act for moral reasons.[14]

Finally, it has been pointed out that the concept of social responsibility is a subversive doctrine that would undermine the principles upon which a free enterprise system is based. For managers to be held accountable for the use of corporate resources to solve social problems, people affected by these decisions would have to be represented at some point in the decision-making process. This could mean that consumers, minorities, women, environmentalists, and so on, would all have to be represented on the board of directors, for example. Such a diversity of interests means that decision-making in the corporation would be political rather than economic in nature. Decisions would reflect the political power of these various interests rather than the single objective of economic profitability. Moreover, the politicalization of decision-making in economic organizations mirrors the operation of a socialistic economy, thus social responsibility would subvert the principles of a free enterprise economy.[15]

> The view has been gaining widespread acceptance that corporate officials and labor leaders have a social responsibility that goes beyond serving the interests of their stockholders or their members. This view shows a fundamental misconception of the character and nature of a free economy. In such an economy, there is one and only one social responsibility of business—to use its resources and engage in activities designed to increase its profit so long as it stays within the rules of the game, which is to say, engages in open and free competition without deception or fraud . . . Few trends could so thoroughly undermine the very foundations of our free society as the acceptance by corporations of a social responsibility other than to make as much money for their stockholders as possible. This is a fundamentally subversive doctrine.[16]

CONSEQUENCES

This debate went on for some time and in some sense remains unresolved. Neither side was able to "win the day" and claim that its arguments carried more weight in the society than the others. Many corporations, however, instituted programs to address social issues and some even reported on these activities to shareholders and interested members of the public. There were many proposals regarding a social audit that companies could undertake to measure and report on their performance relative to these social programs. These reports included statistics on hiring and promotion of women and minorities, efforts expended to control the company's pollution, figures on fatalities and injuries in the workplace, and other such measures. One might look at these activities and conclude that social responsibility was widely accepted throughout corporate America and that a great deal of activity was taking place. While this notion did result in some changes in corporate behavior, it did not take root on a large enough scale to make a real difference in society.

There were many unresolved problems with the concept that limited its effectiveness. Besides the definitional problems mentioned earlier, it was recognized that the concept does not take into account the competitive environment in which corporations function. Many advocates of social responsibility treated the corporation as an isolated entity that had unlimited ability to engage in unilateral social action. But it was increasingly recognized that corporations are severely limited in their ability to respond to social problems. If a firm unilaterally engages in social action that increases its costs and prices, it will place itself at a competitive disadvantage relative to other firms in the industry that may not be concerned about being socially responsible. One scholar stated the problem in this manner:

> Every business is . . . in effect, "trapped" in the business system it has helped to create. It is incapable, as an individual unit, of transcending that system . . . the dream of the socially responsible corporation that, replicated over and over again can transform our society is illusory . . . Because their aggregate power is not unified, not truly collective, not organized, they [corporations] have no way, even if they wished, of redirecting that power to meet the most pressing needs of society . . . Such redirecting could only occur through the intermediate agency of government rewriting the rules under which all corporations operate.[17]

The debate about social responsibility never took this institutional context of corporations seriously. Concerted action to solve social problems is not feasible in a competitive system unless all competitors pursue roughly the same policy on the same problems. Since collusion among competitors is illegal, the only way such concerted action can occur is when some other institution such as government makes all competitors engage in the same activity and pursue the same policies with respect to social problems. And this is in fact what happened.

While the debate about social responsibility was continuing and corporate executives were asking for a definition of their social responsibilities, government was in fact rewriting the rules under which all corporations operate through a vast amount of legislation and regulation pertaining to the physical environment, occupational safety and health, equal opportunity, and various consumer concerns. These issues became matters of public policy as politicians seized on the public's concern about social issues and made them into political issues to be addressed by the government. Thus business was faced with a new kind of regulation, called social regulation, which created legal responsibilities for them to institute policies and programs to respond to social problems.

These actions on the part of government did make a difference, as corporations had to devote a considerable amount of resources to address these issues. These activities cost money and resulted in considerable expense to the society as a whole, but they also resulted in cleaner air and water, more responsible disposal of toxic wastes, hiring of more minorities and women and promotion of them to higher levels in the corporation, safer workplaces, and the provision of more information to consumers as well as safer products. It was these public policy measures, not social responsibility, that made business address these problems on anything like a large enough scale that could make a real difference in society.

The notion of social responsibility never had a theoretical underpinning that would provide an alternative philosophy for the traditional economic understanding of business and its role in society. While it did contain the notion of community in emphasizing that business related to society in ways not captured by an economic model and held that business has a broader constituency than just stockholders and rooted the notion of responsibility in this broader conception of a corporation's relationship to society, these ideas were not part of a new philosophy that would offer a challenge to the traditional philosophical understanding of capitalism with its emphasis on individualism and rights. In fact, the notion of social responsibility was infused with the same kind of individualism as in capitalism and was based on the notion that the corporation and society are isolatable entities that are somehow separable from each other.

> The notion of responsibility is very much a part of the . . . individualism that I am attacking as inadequate, and the classical arguments for "the social responsibilities of business" all too often fall in the trap of beginning with the assumption of the corporation as an autonomous, independent entity, which then needs to consider its obligations to the surrounding community. But corporations, like individuals, are part and parcel of the communities that created them, and the responsibilities that they bear are not products of argument or implicit contracts but intrinsic to their very existence as social entities.[18]

The proponents of social responsibility produced no clear and generally accepted moral principle that would impose upon business an obligation to work for social betterment. Ascribing social responsibility to corporations does not necessarily imply that they are moral agents that are then responsible for their social impacts. The various arguments that were used to try and impose this obligation, such as enlightened self-interest, responsible use of power, and the like, tried to link moral behavior to business performance. Little was accomplished, however, by way of developing acceptable moral support for the notion of social responsibility that was rooted in a new philosophy of capitalism.

The bottom line for business remained intact. Business had no other moral responsibility other than to make as much money as it could for individual shareholders, because they were the property owners. Business had no responsibility to help a collective entity such as society solve its social problems. Such a responsibility is not built into the system, it is not measurable, it is not something that business is required to report on to its shareholders. It became an illusion to think that the notion of social responsibility could make a significant difference in getting business to clean up its pollution, to hire minorities and women and treat them equally, and to have consumer protection in mind rather than profits.[19]

3 Stakeholder Theory

Another approach that attempts to broaden the responsibilities of business and prescribe a different model for understanding the relationship of business to society is the stakeholder approach. This stakeholder concept has been widely employed to describe and analyze the corporation's relationship to a broader constituency than that of stockholders. In 1995, Tom Donaldson and Lee Preston reported that there were about a dozen books and more than 100 articles with primary emphasis on the stakeholder concept.[1] Conferences have been held that dealt exclusively with the concept, and journals have published special issues that focused on stakeholder theory and related concerns.

While the stakeholder concept has been defined many different ways, as has social responsibility, each version generally stands for the same principle, namely that corporations should heed the needs, interests, and influence of those affected by their policies and operations.[2] A typical definition holds that a stakeholder may be thought of as "any individual or group who can affect or is affected by the actions, decisions, policies, or goals of the organization."[3] Another author describes a stakeholder as "those persons or interests that have a stake, something to gain or lose as a result of its [the corporation's] activities."[4] A stakeholder, then, is an individual or group that has some kind of stake in what a business does and may also be able to affect the organization in some fashion.

The typical stakeholders are considered to be consumers, suppliers, government, competitors, communities, employees, and of course, stockholders. These are considered to be the primary stakeholders, but the stakeholder map of a corporation with respect to a specific issue can become quite complicated.[5] Stakeholder management involves taking the interests and concerns of these various groups and individuals into account in arriving at a management decision so that they are all satisfied at least to some extent, or that the most important stakeholders with regard to a given issue are satisfied. The purpose of the firm is to serve and coordinate the interests of its various stakeholders, and it is the moral obligation of the firm's managers to strike an appropriate balance among stakeholder interests in directing the activities of the firm.

The "stakeholder model" has become the focus of an effort to "redefine" the corporation as an entity within the economy, polity, and society.[6] Those who advocate the stakeholder approach to corporate responsibility do not seek the demise of the modern corporation, but rather its transformation, to "rebuild the ship, plank by plank, while it remains afloat."[7] It is hoped that stakeholder capitalism can replace the traditional theory of capitalism, where stockholders are held to be the primary if not sole stakeholder. As one critic says: "among business ethicists there is a consensus favoring the stakeholder theory of the firm—a theory that seeks to redefine and reorient the purpose and activities of the firm. Far from providing an ethical foundation for capitalism, these business ethicists seek to change it dramatically."[8]

As with social responsibility, the stakeholder approach is considered to be something of an alternative to government regulation. Advocates hope that through stakeholder pressure, corporations will implement concerns related to product safety, truth in advertising, workplace safety, the physical environment, and other such issues that have been on the social agenda, and thus make government intervention unnecessary. In the words of R. Edward Freeman, who is credited with doing the seminal work on the stakeholder concept, "Implementation of stakeholder principles, in the long run, mitigates the need for industrial policy and an increasing role of government intervention and regulation."[9] Thus stakeholder advocates hope that government will matter less as stakeholder principles are implemented throughout corporate America.

PROBLEMS WITH STAKEHOLDER THEORY

Management Accountability

In the debate about social responsibility, criticisms were leveled at the role management played in deciding the meaning of the term and which social issues the corporation would address. The same can be said for stakeholder theory. Management plays the critical role in deciding which stakeholder interests get attention and what priorities to assign stakeholder concerns. This is a difficult enough task given the relatively simple stakeholder model most advocates propose, but the map of actual issues facing corporations can become hopelessly complicated, involving dozens or more stakeholders whose interests have to be taken into account. This is a monumental task for management under the best of circumstances.

> The task of management today is akin to that of King Solomon. The stakeholder theory does not give primacy to one stakeholder group over another, though there will surely be times when one group will benefit at the expense of others. In general, however, management must keep

the relationships among stakeholders in balance. When these relationships become imbalanced, the survival of the firm is in jeopardy.[10]

The stakeholder approach provides no formal process or means of balancing stakeholder interests, but is more in the nature of a political model of the corporation. It elevates nonshareholding interests to the level of shareholder interests in formulating business strategy and policy and seeks to free both the firm and the manager from exclusive attention to the concerns of shareholders so that they can focus on a broader set of interests. The theory thus involves a reorientation of corporate law toward the interests of stakeholders and the insulation of managers from the market as far as corporate control is concerned.[11] Managers are given almost unlimited power in the stakeholder model, as it is managers who have the ultimate responsibility to decide what stakeholder interests receive attention.

Managers are to weigh and balance stakeholder interests, trading off one against another in setting a course of action. But such a process provides little or no accountability for self-serving managerial decisions. Under stakeholder-oriented corporate law, such behavior would be difficult to detect as well as deter, as almost all managerial behavior would coincide with the interests of some stakeholder group, thus allowing the manager to point to the benefited and burdened stakeholders and make a case that his or her decision was the optimal way to balance competing stakeholder interests. Managers can play one stakeholder group against another and escape accountability. When a manager serves two or more masters, he or she is in some sense freed from accountability to all and is answerable to none.

Managerial action that is self-serving, even if detected, would be difficult to deter because stakeholder-oriented corporate law must provide protections to managers from being sued perpetually by shareholders, employees, customers, suppliers, or communities who believe their interests were not properly weighed and balanced. Stakeholder theory assumes that good-faith stakeholder-oriented managerial action will serve some interests and frustrate others in attaining some kind of overall balance of interests. Thus corporate law must provide adequate protection for managers if firms are to be managed without undue interference from stakeholder groups. Such stakeholder-oriented corporate law further erodes management accountability.[12]

Political Decision-making

In order to hold management accountable, stakeholder groups would have to have some representation in corporate decision-making, most likely at the board level. The stakeholder approach thus promises to have the boardroom populated by representatives of all stakeholder groups who believe they have an interest in the strategies and policies of the corporation. This will make decision-making and overall guidance for the firm more difficult, as decisions will most likely be the result of interest group politicking. With so many representatives of different interests, bureaucratic political maneuvering will surely increase, and corporate decision-making will more and more resemble the political practices that are the hallmark of democratic politics.

This problem was raised with respect to corporate social responsibility, where some critics believed that the concept was a subversive doctrine that would undermine the principles upon which free enterprise is based. Such a diversity of interests means that decision-making in the corporation would be political rather than economic in nature. Decisions would reflect the political power of these various interests rather than the single objective of economic profitability. This politicalization of decision-making in economic organizations would mirror the operation of a socialistic economy, in some sense, and lead to inefficiencies in the allocation of corporate resources.

The Role of Competition

Freeman does not include competitors in what he calls the narrow sense, "since strictly speaking they are not necessary for the survival and success of the firm; the stakeholder theory works equally well in monopoly contexts."[13] Is there an implication here that competition is not necessary in stakeholder capitalism because stakeholders would see to it that managers do not gouge the public with exorbitant prices and would maintain quality in their products even if they had a monopoly position? This claim, if implied, is one of the most serious, as competition is a key component of the capitalistic system, assuring that the power of any one corporation is limited. There is a problem here that is fundamental to the nature of stakeholder capitalism.

The marketplace in which business functions places severe restrictions on the ability of corporations to respond to stakeholder issues in an effective fashion, because to do so would put them at a competitive disadvantage. The same argument was made with respect to social responsibility. Thus in a competitive system, there is a need for someone like government to underwrite the rules of engagement, so to speak, to set rules related to not only competition but also for externalities such as environmental problems. However, Freeman has an answer to this problem, as he believes there is no reason trade associations and other multi-organizational groups cannot band together to solve common problems that have little do to with how to restrain trade. The interests of competitors, Freeman believes, are not always in conflict and thus agreements are possible.[14]

The questions are, however, whether such agreements can be sufficiently representative of the stakeholder interests, and whether these groups have the legitimacy necessary for these agreements to be accepted. Could a trade association for the drug industry develop the expertise and trust necessary to perform the work of the Food and Drug Administration (FDA) of establishing testing procedures that all drug companies would follow to assure the drugs placed on the market are safe and effective? The FDA was given this role because the public does not trust individual companies to do enough testing because of competitive pressures and the drive to make as much profit as possible.

Likewise, could some multi-organizational group set environmental standards for all business and have an enforcement mechanism that was effective enough to assure that all business organizations were in compliance? Could such groups speak for all stakeholders in setting and enforcing these standards such that the Environmental Protection Agency would be rendered unnecessary? And perhaps most important, could some industry group set and enforce standards related to competition itself, and police price fixing, tying arrangements, price discrimination, and the like, or would this be like sending the fox to guard the chicken coop?

STAKEHOLDER THEORY AND GOVERNMENT

In many stakeholder models, government is seen as just another stakeholder, analogous to the way in which some popular political models portray business as just another interest group competing for political favors. Although government is a stakeholder of sorts, it is far more than just another stakeholder because it is the major player in the public policy process and thus can rewrite the rules of the game for business. Similarly, while business is something of an interest group, it is far more than just another interest group because it is the major player in the free market process. Government and business are two of the major institutions in our society and relate to each other as much more than just a stakeholder and an interest group.

Some stakeholder advocates recognize the role that the government has played in attacking what they call the theory of managerial capitalism and circumscribing the interests of stockholders. This form of capitalism holds that while managers indeed control the modern corporation, they are bound to maximize the interests of stockholders. But managers can go astray, and these advocates are not oblivious to the need for a legal framework to circumscribe the power of management and make it accountable to stakeholders. However, they see this intervention of the law as just a temporary stage that will be unnecessary when stakeholder principles are fully implemented across the corporate world.

> In this century, however, the law has evolved to effectively constrain the pursuit of stakeholder interests at the expense of other claimants on the firm. It has, in effect, required that the claims of customers, suppliers,

local communities, and employees be taken into consideration . . . the results of such changes in the legal system can be viewed as giving some rights to those groups that have a claim on the firm, for example, customers suppliers, employees, local communities, stockholders, and management. It raises the question, at the core of a theory of the firm: in whose interest and for whose benefit should the firm be managed? The answer proposed by managerial capitalism is clearly "the stockholders," but I have argued that the law has been progressively circumscribing this answer . . . Externalities, moral hazards, and monopoly power have led to more external control on managerial capitalism.[15]

Yet government must create and pass enabling legislation to make stakeholder management work in the real world and play an active and continuing role in seeing that the rules of the game are followed by management as well as other stakeholders. Aggrieved stakeholders must be able to pursue their interests through the court system when all other avenues are closed. Government must use its power of coercion when necessary to see that the system is not undermined by self-serving managers or other stakeholders. And there must be a way to change the rules when they prove unworkable.

This presents something of a paradox for stakeholder theorists. Some authors note that stakeholder management requires simultaneous attention to the legitimate interests of all appropriate stakeholders—including government as one among the variety of types of stakeholder—and that the very foundation of the stakeholder model prohibits any undue attention to the interests of any one constituency. But these same authors then recognize the need for government to pass laws to implement the stakeholder concept and make it operable in society.

> To be sure, it remains to implement in law the sanctions, rules, and precedents that support the stakeholder conception of the corporation . . . Yet over time, statutory and common law are almost certainly capable of achieving arrangements that encourage a broader, stakeholder conception of management—one which eschews single-minded subservience to shareowners' interests—while at the same time restraining the moral hazard of self-serving managers.[16]

Thus the implementation of stakeholder principles depends upon government, as it is the only entity that has the legitimacy to speak for society as a whole and can thus change the way corporations are governed and managed. The implementation of such principles and the continued operation of a stakeholder system of management are not going to happen voluntarily, and the implied premise that stakeholder theory will eventually evolve into a full-blown operative system because of its inherent inevitability is illusory.

STAKEHOLDER THEORY AND INDIVIDUALISM

Many definitions of stakeholder theory assume that stakeholders are iso-latable, individual entities that are identifiable by management, and that their interests should be taken into account in the decision-making process. Each stakeholder has individual interests that must be acknowledged by the manager in arriving at a responsible and effective decision. This assumption stems from the same individualistic conception that undergirds capitalism and is based on the view that the individual is the basic building block of a society or community, and such collectivities are nothing more than the individuals of which they are comprised. In this philosophical view, individuals as well as institutions are isolatable units that have well-defined boundaries, can be considered as separate from their surrounding environment, and are not an integral part of the community or society in which they function.

The problem that individualism poses for stakeholder theory is noted in an article by Andrew Wicks et al., where recognition is given to the role that individualism has played in the development of stakeholder theory. The authors talk about the celebration of the individual and the respect for personal freedom that characterize the post-Enlightenment West, particularly the U.S. with its image of the pioneer. They then go on to describe the problem of individualism and how it is embedded in definitions of stakeholder theory.

> One of the assumptions embedded in this world view is that the "self" is fundamentally isolatable from other selves and from its larger context. Persons exist as discrete beings who are captured independent of the relationships they have with others. While language, community, and relationships all affect the self, they are seen as external to and bounded off from the individual who is both autonomous from and ontologically prior to these elements of context. The parallel in business is that the corporation is best seen as an autonomous agent, separate from its suppliers, consumers, external environment, etc. Here too, while the larger market forces and business environment have a large impact on a given firm, it is nonetheless the individual corporation which has prominence in discussions about strategy and preeminence in where we locate agency.[17]

The authors then go on to point out that as a result of this assumption, stakeholders are understood as people who are affected by the corporation but "not integral to is basic identity," a view "reflected in the understanding of stakeholders offered by a number of authors. These definitions shared the implicit premise that the basic identity of the firm is defined independent of, and separate from, its stakeholders. The macro level view of the world of business is seen as a collection of atoms, each of which is colliding with other atoms in a mechanistic process representative of the interactions and transactions of the various firms." [18]

In their effort to reinterpret some of the traditional ways of thinking housed in stakeholder theory, Wicks et al. turned to feminist views that focus on relationships as the vehicle for such a reinterpretation. They suggest some important shortcomings of earlier versions of stakeholder theory, principally that they rely too much on an "individualistic autonomous-masculinist mode of thought to make it intelligible which discounts many of the feminist insights . . . which can be utilized to better express the meaning and purposes of the corporation."[19]

They go on to argue that persons are fundamentally connected with each other in a web of relationships that are integral to any proper understanding of the self, and that any talk of autonomy or search for personal identity must be qualified and located within this more organic and relational sense of the world. "The stakeholder concept, understood in feminist terms," they state, "makes explicit how the boundaries of the self extend into areas far beyond what we can easily recognize and into areas clearly outside the corporation."[20] Internal/external distinctions fade into a sense of communal solidarity in which the corporate identity is seen within an entire network of stakeholders and in a broader social context.

The authors thus move away from a long-held understanding of the corporation, which, according to them, views the corporation as an autonomous entity confronting an external environment to be controlled; an entity that is structured in terms of strict hierarchies of power and authority and in which management activities are best expressed in terms of conflict and competition; one in which strategic management decisions result from an objective collection of facts via empirical investigation and a rationally detached decision-maker distanced from their leanings, biases, and emotion-laden perceptions.

Instead, they move toward an understanding of the corporation as a web of relations among stakeholders; a web that thrives on change and pluralism in establishing ongoing harmonious relations with its environment, one whose structure in contoured by radical decentralization and empowerment, one in which activities are best expressed in terms of communication, collective action, and reconciliation; and management decisions result from solidarity and communicatively shared understandings rooted in caring relationships. This is quite an ambitious agenda, and one has to wonder whether feminist theory alone can provide philosophical support for this kind of radical redefinition of the corporation and its responsibilities.

In a concluding statement, Wicks et al. point to the importance of philosophic underpinnings in rethinking the nature of the corporation. They ultimately argue that since nothing less than a redefinition of the corporation is needed, such a redefinition requires as well a redefinition of the self. And ultimately such a reconstructed self requires a reconstructed philosophic context within which to conceptually locate the corporation's relational nature. The move toward a relational understanding of managing stakeholders does not make competition irrelevant, but rather it becomes a secondary virtue in their view. A firm becomes competitive as an effect of successful collaboration and team work. Changing the priority of competition places it in a new worldview that excludes the old framework. This changes the "logical place" of competition in the relational network. Thus the concept of competition and other dimensions of corporate life are transformed by, and gain their importance from, the new relational network.[21] What remains is to provide solid philosophical support for this relational view of the corporation and its environment.

4   Public Policy

Both social responsibility and stakeholder theory were plagued by individualism that permeated their formulation and application. In social responsibility, business and society were considered to be separate entities and were not integral to each other's existence. In stakeholder theory, stakeholders were also considered to be separate entities and were not integral to the corporation's existence. In both theories, corporate management remained the locus of agency in that they decided what social issues were important and what stakeholder issues deserved consideration, making management accountability a problem in both approaches. Consequently, neither idea provided much of a challenge to the philosophical underpinnings of capitalism and business did not respond on anything like a large enough scale to make much of a difference in regard to either social or stakeholder issues.

What did make a difference was the development of social regulation by the federal government in the 1960s and 1970s, as new laws were passed and new agencies created to promote equal opportunity in the workplace, job safety, consumer protection, and environmental responsibility. These efforts were based on the notion of rights—that workers had a right to a safe workplace, consumers had a right to safe products and accurate and relevant information about the products they were buying, minorities and women had a right to be treated equally in the workplace, and everyone had a right to a clean environment. Even certain animals had a right to be protected from becoming extinct, as enshrined in the Endangered Species Act for example.

It was an emphasis on these rights that resulted in major changes in business behavior and advanced these causes in society, as human and civil rights began to take precedence over property rights. These laws and regulations interfered with the ability of business to make a profit and increase shareholder wealth. Business could no longer hire anybody they wanted but had to develop affirmative action programs to hire and promote more minorities and women. They could no longer dump toxic wastes in the cheapest possible manner but had to adhere to a set of regulations regarding appropriate and safe disposal of these wastes. They had to spend money to improve workplace safety and keep statistics on their performance in this regard. And business was forced in many cases to issue costly recalls when there was a possibility of an unsafe product.

The concept of community that was implied in social responsibility and stakeholder theory was not given a theoretical underpinning such that this idea could begin to take root in society and capture the imagination of people. Thus the effort to base responsibilities in this idea of community never took root either, and no means to make management accountable to the larger society or to stakeholders was ever devised. Nor was any means developed to measure corporate performance relative to society or stakeholders that took precedence over traditional accounting practices to shareholders. It was only when government got involved with social regulation that gave rights to various groups in society that business had to take its responsibilities in these areas seriously. Thus the responsibilities business had to respond to social and stakeholder issues stemmed from the rights people were given by the political and legal system.

SOCIAL REGULATION

The new wave of regulation that appeared in the 1960s and 1970s in response to the social values and concerns of society was a radical departure from the traditional type of industry regulation that had been in existence for some years. Industry regulation began with the passage of the Interstate Commerce Act in 1887, which, as the name suggests, focuses on particular industries. Social regulations, such as safety and health regulations, however, affect virtually all business organizations, not just a particular industry, and are thus much broader in scope. Regulations issued by the Interstate Commerce Commission (ICC) are limited to surface transportation companies, whereas safety and health regulations apply to every employer engaged in a business affecting commerce. Social regulation is issue-oriented rather than industry-oriented.

Furthermore, social regulation affects the conditions under which goods and services are produced and the physical characteristics of products that are manufactured, rather than focusing on markets, rates, and the obligation to serve. The Environmental Protection Agency (EPA), for example, sets limits on the amount of pollution a manufacturer may emit in the course of its operations. The Consumer Product Safety Commission (CPSC) sets minimum safety standards for products. The Occupational Safety and Health Administration (OSHA) regulates safety and health hazards in the workplace.

These agencies are concerned with noneconomic matters and sometimes pay little or no attention to an industry's basic mission of providing goods and services to the public. Their impetus comes from social considerations related to improving the quality of life for workers and consumers based on their rights as human beings rather than ownership of property. They often ignore the effects of their regulations on such economic matters as productivity, growth, employment, and inflation.

Social regulation often means that the government becomes involved with very detailed facets of the production process, interfering with the traditional prerogatives of business management. For example, OSHA sometimes specifies precise engineering controls that business must adopt to protect workers from harm. The CPSC mandates specific product characteristics it believes will protect consumers from injury. The Federal Trade Commission (FTC) deals with specific advertising content, in some cases involving misleading or false advertising. These activities involve the government in many more details of business management than industry regulation.

One reason often used to support social regulation is related to the nature of the modern workplace and marketplace. It is often argued that when goods and technology are complex and their effects largely unknown, consumers are incapable of making intelligent judgments on their own regarding the safety of products, and workers may not know the risks they face on various jobs or may not be able to acquire the necessary information regarding exposure to harmful substances. Expert judgment is needed in these areas to protect consumers and workers from unnecessary risks that they cannot assess for themselves.

Another reason for this type of regulation is the existence of externalities when the actions of a company have a harmful effect on third parties. The cost of external diseconomies, such as air and water pollution, cannot be voluntarily assumed by companies unless a government agency exists to set and enforce standards equally across all companies in an industry. Voluntary assumption by some companies would place them at a competitive disadvantage; thus regulation is needed to make all companies meet the same standard, leaving them in the same competitive position.

Little doubt exists that regulation was a growth industry during the 1970s, and the leading product was the new areas of social regulation. During the 1960s and 1970s, Congress enacted over 100 laws regulating business activity. Many new agencies such as OSHA, the EPA, the CPSC, and the Equal Employment Opportunity Commission (EEOC) were created to implement this legislation. These new agencies, as well as existing agencies, issued thousands of new rules and procedural requirements. Overall regulatory expenditures in 1980 were more than four times the 1970 level, while staff had increased by 74 percent. These laws and regulations addressed the major social problems of the day in a way that social responsibility and stakeholder management could not hope to approach. They gave new rights to workers and consumers that challenged the traditional prerogatives of management as well as the rights of property owners to use their property in their own self-interest. Management and property owners now had to take the public interest into account as specified in these laws and regulations.

THE CREATION OF NEW RIGHTS

The Occupational Safety and Health Act was passed in 1970 by a bipartisan Congress "to assure as far as possible every working man and woman in the Nation safe and healthful working conditions and to preserve our human resources."[1] This law gave workers a general right to a safe and healthful workplace and gave OSHA the mandate to develop mandatory safety and health standards and enforce them effectively. The law also gave OSHA other responsibilities, such as maintaining a reporting and record-keeping system to monitor job-related injuries and illnesses. Business, of course, had a responsibility to meet these standards and comply with the regulations issued by the agency. The law also enumerated more specific rights and responsibilities for both employees and employers.

During the 1960s and 1970s, Congress passed more consumer protection legislation than at any time in its history to address various problems in the marketplace. This legislation was based on the notion of rights that consumers possessed, which, it was believed, were not adequately protected by the marketplace. These laws gave additional responsibilities to existing agencies, such as the Federal Trade Commission (FTC) and the Food and Drug Administration (FDA), and created new agencies, such as the CPSC and the National Highway Traffic Safety Administration (NHTSA). The CPSC was given the responsibility to develop and enforce uniform safety standards for all products under its jurisdiction, ban consumer products deemed to be hazardous, and initiate and monitor recall of hazardous products. The responsibilities of NHTSA included setting and enforcing mandatory average fuel economy standards for new motor vehicles, regulating the safety performance of new and used motor vehicles and their equipment, and investigating auto safety defects and requiring manufacturers to remedy these defects.

Former president John F. Kennedy listed four rights of consumers that he believed needed protection. These included the right to safety, the right to a choice, the right to know, and the right to be heard. If business could not protect these rights, legislation would be necessary.

The Right to Safety: The consumer has a right to be protected from dangerous products that might cause injury or illness and from the thoughtless actions of other consumers.

The Right to a Choice: The consumer has the right to be able to select products from a range of alternatives offered by competing firms.

The Right to Know: The consumer must have access to readily available, relevant, and accurate information to use in making purchase decisions.

The Right to be Heard: The consumer must be able to find someone who will respond to legitimate complaints about abuses taking place in the market and products that do not meet expectations.

This idea of a consumer bill of rights caught on in other areas over the years as organizations formulated such rights in relation to specific areas of concern. For example, an organization called Digital Consumer proposed a Consumer Technology Bill of Rights to deal with what they believed was an erosion of the rights of consumers to use digital content that was becoming more available. The California Department of Consumer Affairs proposed a Bill of Rights for consumers of certain types of telephone services within the state. And in January 2000, Fannie Mae announced a "Mortgage Consumer Bill of Rights" to help advance consumer protections for more home buyers in America.

Business responded to these rights and regulations by giving increasing attention to quality control systems to eliminate defective products, and to product design to eliminate hazards by using design safety concepts. It also paid more attention to warnings about potential dangers in the way consumers used products. Part of this concern was motivated by changes in thinking about product liability, as corporations were forced to bear more of the costs associated with unsafe and defective products, because it was believed they could take greater steps to promote safety in the products they sell in the marketplace. Thus consumers also had more right to sue manufacturers under a doctrine of strict liability, where business organizations were strictly liable for damages if a product proved to be defective and injured consumers.

The Civil Rights Act of 1964 forbade discrimination in employment by an employer, employment agency, or labor union on the basis of race, color, sex, religion, or national origin in any term, condition, or privilege of employment. The law forbade discrimination in hiring and firing practices, wages, fringe benefits, classifying, referring, assigning or promoting employees, extending or assigning facilities, training, retraining, apprenticeships, and other employment practices. Thus employees were given the right to be treated equally with regard to all employment practices of private employees. The law created the EEOC to implement the act and gave it responsibilities to issue guidelines on employment discrimination, investigate charges of discrimination, and settle cases where discrimination exists through conciliation, or if necessary, litigation.

Other laws were passed that targeted specific groups or problems, such as the Pregnancy Discrimination Act of 1978, which prohibited disparate treatment of pregnant women for all employment-related purposes; the Equal Pay Act of 1963, which prohibited discrimination because of sex in the payment of wages, including overtime, for equal work on jobs that require equal skill, effort and responsibility, and that are performed under similar working conditions; the Age Discrimination in Employment Act, forbidding discrimination against people between the ages of 40 and 65 in hiring, firing, and promotion or other aspects of employment; and the Americans with Disabilities Act, passed in 1990, which bars employment discrimination against people with physical or mental disabilities.

Thus workers in general and specific groups in particular were given rights to equal treatment in the workplace and could sue to pursue these rights if necessary. Cases were brought against many corporations and usually resulted in some kind of settlement for the people bringing the lawsuit. Business adopted many programs to respond to these rights and avoid costly lawsuits. Many of these programs were some type of affirmative action programs, in which positive steps were taken to hire more minorities and women and promote them into better paying positions—in other words, to give them preferential treatment in hiring and promotion decisions. These programs proved to be controversial from the beginning, and the Supreme Court has had to weigh in on several occasions with an opinion on what kinds of programs, if any, were acceptable.

Finally, rights were created in the environmental area, as many laws were passed to deal with air and water pollution, toxic substances, hazardous waste disposal, and pesticide usage. The EPA was created in 1970 to implement these laws by establishing and enforcing standards and monitoring pollution in the environment. Other agencies such as the FDA, the Department of Agriculture, and the Interior Department are also involved in environmental problems. Business organizations can be sued for noncompliance with regulations issued by the EPA, and the agency itself has been sued by environmental organizations for not adequately enforcing its own regulations.

These areas of workplace safety, consumer protection, equal employment, and the environment constitute the main areas of social problems where new rights were created to address these problems. It was not because of the social responsibilities of business or stakeholder management that business responded on a large enough scale to make a difference in addressing these problems. It was by creating rights through public policy that business was given new responsibilities that derived from these rights. And as law-abiding citizens they had to implement new programs and procedures to respond to these rights. Thus it was through the public policy process that these problems began to be addressed and the responsibilities of corporate America were expanded to include the social dimension of their impacts on society.

PUBLIC POLICY

These rights were created through the public policy process, which made them into legal rights that could be enforced by government agencies or by individuals and groups that could sue corporations for noncompliance. The term "public policy process" refers to all the various ways in which public policy is made in our country. Public policy can be made through legislation passed by Congress, regulations issued by government agencies, executive orders issued by the president, or decisions handed down by the

Supreme Court. The process of making public policy begins in the society as problems and issues are defined.

The public policy agenda is that collection of topics and issues with respect to which public policy may be formulated. There are many problems and concerns that various people and groups in society would like to see some action on, but only those that are important enough to receive serious attention from policymakers comprise the public policy agenda. Such an agenda does not exist in concrete form but is found in the collective judgment of society, actions and concerns of interest groups, legislation introduced into Congress, cases being considered by the Supreme Court, and similar activities. The manner in which problems in our society get on the public policy agenda is complex and involves many different kinds of political participation.

Resources necessary to address certain problems on the public policy agenda are allocated through a political process in which values emerge relative to common objectives and courses of action. The function of a political process is to organize individual effort to achieve some kind of social goal or objective that individuals or groups find difficult, if not impossible, to achieve by themselves. Suppose some people in a community want to build a road, which nobody in the community can or would want to build by themselves. To get the road built, enough people in the community have to agree they want a road and contribute the necessary resources to getting it built. Even after this decision is made, these people are going to have different ideas as to what kind of road should be built, where it should be located, and other related matters. These differences have to be resolved through the political process in order for the road to be constructed.

The task of a political system is to adjudicate such conflicts by (1) establishing rules of the game for participants in the system, (2) arranging compromises and balancing the interests of the various participants, (3) enacting compromises in the form of public policy measures, and (4) enforcing these public policies.[2] The outcome of a political process depends on how much power and influence people have, how skillful they are at compromising and negotiating, and the variety and strength of the interests involved in making the decision. Decisions can be made by majority rule, by building a consensus, or by exercising raw power and coercing other members of a group to agree on a given course of action.

The reason public policy decisions have to be made through a political process is the nature of the goods and services that are provided through the public policy process. These goods and services can appropriately be referred to as public goods and services, as distinguished from the private goods and services exchanged in the market system. Public goods and services are provided to meet the needs of people as expressed through a political system which deals with things that are held in common, such as clean air and water, and the ideal of equal opportunity for all participants in the workplace.

These things held in common are indivisible in the sense that they cannot be divided into individual units to be purchased by people according to their individual preferences. For all practical purposes, for example, one cannot buy a piece of clean air to carry around and breathe wherever one goes. Nor can one buy a share of national defense over which one would have control. This indivisibility gives these goods and services their public character, because if people are to have public goods and services at all, they must enjoy roughly the same amount.[3] No one owns these goods and services individually; they are collectively owned in a sense or held in common and private property rights do not apply. Thus there is nothing to be exchanged on the market and the values people have in regard to these goods and services and decisions about these goods and services cannot be made through an exchange process.

There is also something of a perverse incentive system in regard to public goods and services. If one person were concerned about clean air such that he or she paid extra money to have pollution control equipment installed on their car, this action would make no difference in the quality of the air he or she lived in and he or she would be getting nothing for their money. If, on the other hand, enough people did make this decision to have an impact on air quality, one would be motivated to be a "free rider" and buy a car without pollution control equipment and enjoy cleaner air without paying a cent for its provision.

Because of these characteristics of human behavior and the nature of public goods and services, the market system will not work to provide public goods and services for a society that wants them. When goods and services are indivisible among large numbers of people, individual consumers' actions as expressed in the market will not lead to the provision of these goods and services.[4] Society must register its desire for public goods and services through a political process because the bilateral exchanges facilitated by the market are insufficiently inclusive.[5] Only through the political process can compromises be reached that will resolve the conflicts that are inevitable in relation to public goods and services.

Value conflicts are more pronounced in the public policy process because of the existence of diverse value systems. There is no underlying value system into which other values can be translated; no common denominator by which to assess trade-offs and make decisions about resource allocation to attain some common economic objective, such as improving one's financial situation or increasing the nation's gross national product. What is the overall objective, for example, of clean air and water, equal opportunity, occupational safety and health and similar public goods and services? One could say that all these goods and services are meant to improve the quality of life for all members of society. But if this is the objective, what kind of common value measure underlies all these goods and services so that benefits of specific programs can be assessed in relation to costs and trade-offs analyzed in relation to this common objective of improving the quality of life?

The costs of pollution control equipment can be determined in economic terms. The benefits this equipment provides should be positive in improving health by reducing the amount of harmful pollutants people have to breathe and making the air look and smell better. The difficulty lies in translating these benefits into economic terms so that a direct comparison with costs can be made. What is the price tag for the lives saved by avoiding future diseases that may be caused by certain pollutants? What is the value of reducing the probability that children will be born with abnormalities because of toxic substances in the environment? What is the value of preserving one's hearing because money has been spent to reduce the noise emitted by machinery in the workplace? What is the appropriate value of being able to see across the Grand Canyon and enjoy whatever benefits this view provides?[6]

The difficulty of expressing all these intangibles in economic terms so that people's individual preferences can be matched should be apparent. When people make individual choices about private goods and services offered on the market, diverse value systems present no problems. They are forced to translate these diverse values into economic terms and make choices accordingly. But making choices about public goods and services is another matter. There seems to be no way to force a translation of diversity into a common value system that is acceptable, realistic, and appropriate. Thus the political process seems to be a reasonable way to respond to the diversity of people's values to make a decision about a common course of action. Values emerge for particular public goods and services from the interactions of the millions of people who participate in the political process.

The average person participates in the political process by voting for a representative of his or her choice, contributing money to a campaign, writing elected public officials on particular issues, and similar actions. Joining large social movements, such as the civil rights movement, is another way for the average person to exercise political influence. Widespread support for issues has an effect on the voting of elected public officials. People can join public interest groups or support them with contributions and fulfill a political role in this fashion. Most citizens, however, are probably content to simply elect others to engage in the business of governing the country and go about their daily tasks with a minimum of political participation.

The vote is the ultimate power that citizens have in a democratic system and gives them a degree of sovereignty over the public policy process. A public official can be voted out of office if he or she does not perform as the majority of citizens in his or her constituency would like. A major problem with such sovereignty, however, is the reputation that the average citizen has with regard to participation in the political system. Voter turnouts are low in many elections, and most of those who do vote probably know little about the candidates and the issues that are at stake in the election. Most people are not interested in public issues much of the time, particularly those that do not affect them directly.

Taking such an interest means spending time on political concerns that might be more profitably devoted to family or leisure activities. Most citizens do not derive primary satisfactions from political participation, and unlike the marketplace, they do not have to participate to fulfill their basic needs and wants. The cost of participation in public affairs seems greater than the return. People who do not participate thus sacrifice their sovereignty and power to the minority in society who do have a strong interest in political life and choose to actively participate in the formulation of public policy for the society as a whole.[7]

Through the public policy process, the self-interest of all the participants is aggregated into a collective whole that represents the public interest.[8] Something of a supply and demand process occurs here in that if enough citizens demand something, at least in a democratic society, the system will eventually respond. But the decisions about resource allocation are visible in that certain people in the public policy process, elected public officials and government bureaucrats, for example, can be held accountable for these decisions if they are not acceptable. The concept of the invisible hand is thus appropriate for a market system but not for the public policy process.

Many, if not most, managers see the government as intruding on what are essentially private decisions made in the interests of promoting economic efficiency. Government intrusion in any form is seen as interfering in the workings of the free market system and is best kept to a minimum. Managers think they are operating in something called the private sector that is judged by an efficient use of resources, while government operates in the public sector that operates on different criteria for measuring success.

The free market system, however, does not exist in a vacuum. It is instead embedded in a social system that can exercise control over corporate activities. The free market cannot stand alone, and no society can organize all of its activities according to free market principles. While our society makes many decisions through the market, it also makes many decisions through the public policy process. Society as a whole decides what to do with certain issues that are more public than private in nature.

When it comes to thinking about public policy and its role in society, different levels of abstraction are often confounded. Public policy is not to be equated with government, even though government formulates and implements most public policies in our society. However, public policy must be considered at the same level as the market and must not be saddled with all the ideological baggage that is involved in discussing the role of government in our society. Government is an institution at the same level as business, while public policy and the market are at a different level of abstraction.

One important issue at this level is which problems can best be addressed by the market and which by the public policy process. This is a different question than asking whether business or government is the best institution to deal with a particular problem. When the market does not work in dealing with certain problems the society deems important, adjustments to corporate behavior must be made through some other process that is different from the market. These changes are simply implicit in the nature of corporations as social entities that are subject to change along with the society of which they are a part. In other words, corporations do not stand apart from society; they are embedded in society and subject to its changing values.

Over the past several decades, public policy has become an ever more important determinant of corporate behavior, as market outcomes have been increasingly altered through the public policy process. What happens in the public policy process has become more and more important to corporations and they have become more active in politics through lobbying, campaign contributions, and other activities of this sort. Most corporate social behavior is the result of responding to government regulations of one sort or another. These changes are making it increasingly clear that business functions in both the market system and public policy process, and both processes are necessary to encompass the broad range of decisions a society needs to make about the corporation and its role in society.

As stated so well by Lee Preston and James Post, public policy is, along with the market mechanism, the source of guidelines and criteria for managerial behavior. The public policy process is the means by which society as a whole articulates its goals and objectives and directs and stimulates individuals and organizations to contribute to and cooperate with them. Appropriate guidelines for managerial behavior are to be found in the larger society, not in the personal vision of a few individuals or in the special interest of groups. Thus a business organization should analyze and evaluate pressures and stimuli coming from public policy in the same way it analyzes market experience and opportunity.[9]

PROBLEMS WITH SOCIAL REGULATION

The issues that receive attention in the public policy process and the shape of policies with respect to these issues reflect the values of society at large. And if those values stem from an individualistic conception of rights, then clashes between rights will inevitability occur. This began to happen when the Reagan administration came into office in 1980, promising to get government off the backs of business organizations, stating that government was the problem and not the solution. Social regulations were costing business too much money, adversely affecting productivity and resulting in the closing of plants that could not remain economically viable while meeting government standards. The Reagan administration came into office promising to cut back or at least slow the growth of this regulatory onslaught.

Immediately upon taking office, this administration froze dozens of regulations that were promulgated during the final days and hours of the previous administration. It also ordered a halt to the issuing of any new regulatory rules for at least sixty days. Soon thereafter, the president formed a Presidential Task Force on Regulatory Relief, chaired by the vice-president. The major purposes of this task force were to review new proposals by regulatory agencies in the executive branch, assess regulations already in effect, and oversee the development of legislative proposals as appropriate. Thus the backlash against social regulation was engaged.

A month after his inauguration, President Reagan issued an executive order that required agencies in the executive branch over which he had control to prepare a "regulatory impact analysis" for each major rule being considered. This analysis involved preparing an accurate assessment of the potential benefits and costs of each major regulatory proposal. In addition, the executive order required that the agencies choose regulatory goals and set priorities to maximize the benefits to society, and choose the most cost-efficient means among legally available options for securing the goals to be attained.

The president also staffed major regulatory agencies such as the EPA, OSHA, FTC, and NHTSA with individuals who shared his commitment to reduce the regulatory burden on business. Budgets were cut in some of the agencies, there was a slowdown in enforcement activities, and staffing was reduced. This administration thus adopted a strategy of working through the bureaucracy itself to effect change, a strategy that came to be called the "purse strings" approach to regulatory reform.

During the first four years of the Reagan administration, there was a real slowdown in both spending and staffing of regulatory agencies. But in the second term, social regulation resumed a growth pattern, leading some to conclude that the "purse strings" approach to regulatory reform revealed more continuity than change.[10] The Reagan administration abandoned its attempt to bring about major changes in federal regulatory policies as political pressures, lawsuits, and bureaucratic resistance caught up with administrative efforts to slow down and cut back on the regulatory apparatus.[11]

The Presidential Task Force on Regulatory Relief was disbanded in 1983, claiming to have effected savings of over $150 billion over the ensuing decade through administrative and legislative changes. About $110 billion of these savings was supposed to come from modification or rescission of unnecessary existing regulations, and the other $40 billion was supposed to be generated by the removal of interest rate ceilings.[12] However, there was some skepticism about these claims, as some believed that they represented savings from deregulatory actions taken by previous administrations as well as from the repeal of regulations that had been proposed but not adopted. It was also stated that the abolition of this task force represented the de facto abandonment of the Reagan administration's commitment to reduce government controls over corporate social conduct.[13]

Regulation continued to grow under the first Bush administration, as the number of pages in the Federal Register, where new regulations are published, grew to 67,716, compared with 53,376 in the last year of the Reagan administration. The number of federal employees devoted to issuing and enforcing regulations rose to 124, 994, surpassing the previous record of 121,706 under the Carter administration. The administrative costs of running regulatory agencies increased 18 percent during the Bush years. Several new laws were enacted that were largely responsible for these increases: the Clean Air Act Amendments of 1990, the Americans with Disabilities Act of 1990, the Civil Rights Act of 1991, and the Nutrition Labeling and Education Act of 1990.[14]

Both the administrative costs of federal regulation and staffing reached an all-time high at the end of the Clinton years. Spending for the 54 regulatory agencies was budgeted to reach $19.8 billion in 2001, and staffing was forecasted to grow to 132,000, a 2 percent increase from the previous year. During the entire Clinton presidency, spending grew by more than 22 percent, while the number of people needed to run the agencies increased by 5 percent. In 2001, only four agencies were scheduled to decrease regulatory spending, 41 agencies had increased budgets, and nine remained the same. Of all the costs related to regulatory activities, fully 79 percent were for social regulation.[15]

Between 2000 and 2005, the costs of administering federal agencies increased another 37.8 percent, and staffing, after a 1.6 percent decline in 2001, increased by 60,000 people during this period. The establishment of the Transportation Security Agency (TSA) in 2003 caused the regulatory workforce to jump 31 percent because of hiring a large staff of airport screening agents. This was by far the largest annual increase in the country's history. Even so, during this period the cost of administering social regulations increased 41.5 percent, while those involved in economic regulation grew only 20.1 percent. Those outlays devoted to social regulation were about five times larger than those devoted to economic regulation.[16]

The major concern with social regulation over the years has been the costs that it imposes on business organizations. These costs are largely hidden from public view, as the only visible costs of regulation are the costs of running the agencies themselves, which show up in the federal budget. But these so-called administrative costs are only the tip of the iceberg. The bulk of the costs that regulation involves are compliance costs, the costs of developing and implementing affirmative action programs, the costs of installing pollution control equipment, the costs of installing safety devices on machinery, and other compliance measures.

Studies began to be developed to estimate these compliance costs. The earliest such study was completed at the Center for the Study of American Business, a research center directed by Murray L. Weidenbaum, former chairman of the Council of Economic Advisors under the Reagan admin-istration. This study showed that compliance costs were $62.9 billion in 1976 and were expected to rise in 1979 to $102.7 billion.[17] A subsequent study by Robert Hahn and John Hird of the American Enterprise Institute estimated the cost of regulation to be between $123 and $154 billion in 1988, while a study completed by Thomas Hopkins at the Rochester Insti-tute of Technology figured the annual cost of federal regulation in 1990 to be between $395 and $510 billion, or between $4,100 and $5,400 per household.[18]

These regulatory costs are substantial and resulted in higher prices for consumers, lower wages for employees, and, of course, reduced dividends and stock appreciation for shareholders. But it must be pointed out that one person's costs are another's benefits. While the costs of social regulation were largely borne by business organizations and passed on to consumers, employees, and shareholders, the benefits were diffused throughout soci-ety, as minorities and women benefited from affirmative action programs, workers benefited from safer workplaces, consumers benefited from safer products, and society as a whole benefited from cleaner air and water, and proper disposal of toxic wastes.

The continued growth of social regulation, in spite of numerous efforts at regulatory reform largely directed at halting and even reversing this growth, led some to advocate new strategies. Murray Weidenbaum, for example, recognized that the regulatory reform effort of the past two decades seemed to have run its course. He advocated a new strategy that focused greater attention on the basic regulatory statutes initially passed by Congress, reducing their shortcomings to eliminate the barriers to agencies doing regulatory analysis, as well reducing the discretion they often exer-cise in going beyond what Congress intended. Each congressional commit-tee that is considering legislation should be required to present estimates of the likely benefits and costs of regulatory actions that would be necessary to implement this legislation. He also recommended that Congress estab-lish an independent Congressional Office of Regulatory Analysis staffed with experienced apolitical analysts to perform this task.[19]

An even more effective way to stop social regulation in its tracks is the transformation of the judiciary that is taking place. The entire structure of government's ability to regulate business and other institutions in society is changing. This change is the result of both changes in personnel and the judicial philosophy dominating our courts. In a book entitled *Radicals In Robes*, by Cass R. Sunstein, this change is spelled out in great detail. The author claims that since the election of Ronald Reagan, high-level Republi-cans in the White House and Senate have been able radically to transform the federal judiciary from one with a tendency towards left-wing activism towards one tending towards right-wing activism.[20]

The agenda of this judiciary includes the following: (1) to reduce the power of the federal government including Congress itself, (2) to scale back the rights of those accused of crime, (3) to strike down affirmative action programs, (4) to eliminate campaign finance laws, (5) to diminish privacy rights, above all the right to abortion, (6) to invigorate the Constitution's Takings clause in order to insulate property rights from democratic control, (7) to forbid Congress from allowing citizens to bring suit to enforce environmental regulations, and (8) to protect commercial interests, including commercial advertisers, from government regulation.[21]

People supporting this agenda believe that the American Constitution has been in exile at least since the 1930s, when the New Deal of Franklin Roosevelt took effect. Before 1932, the national government had sharply limited power, and the system of constitutional rights was radically different from what we see in effect today. With the Great Depression and the New Deal, the Supreme Court abandoned its commitment to the Constitution as it was originally written. Thus the real Constitution, sometimes called the Constitution in Exile, must be restored, and affirmative action programs, campaign finance regulation, and environmental regulations, among other things, must be struck down. The Constitution means what it meant when it was ratified, and we must return to that interpretation even if it results in a radical change in our institutions and in certain rights Americans have come to take for granted.[22]

Thus constitutional questions become historical ones, and it must be read to fit with the original understanding of the founding fathers according to this philosophy. If it was not originally understood to ban sex discrimination or racial segregation, protect privacy, or protect the environment at the expense of property rights, then judges have no authority to depart from this original understanding.[23] From this view comes the idea of strict construction, that judges should not legislate from the bench but should follow strict guidelines laid down in the Constitution. They should not impose their own values and preferences when making judicial decisions.

While there are many problems with this philosophy, Sunstein argues that those who adhere to some kind of original understanding of the Constitution, what he calls fundamentalists, offer an unmistakable partisan vision of the Constitution that fits with the extreme right wing of the Republican Party. Their view of the Constitution casts serious doubts on affirmative action programs, gun control laws, restrictions on commercial advertising, environmental regulations, campaign finance reform, and laws that permit citizens to sue to enforce federal laws. It questions the existence of many federal agencies, such as the Environmental Protection Agency. It questions a right to privacy and allows the federal government to discriminate on the basis of race. And it imposes sharp limits on Congress's power to regulate interstate commerce and enforce the guarantees of the Fourteenth Amendment.[24]

Over the past two decades, Sunstein claims, such fundamentalism has had a large influence on the Supreme Court, as the Rehnquist Court invalidated about three dozen congressional enactments from 1985 to

2005, a record of activism unparalleled in the nation's history.[25] But the fundamentalists want a lot more, and they may get it with the Supreme Court appointments of the Bush administration. If judges Roberts and Alito share this philosophy, as the evidence suggests, then the Supreme Court is only one judge away from having this philosophy dominate the court's thinking and decisions. This would mean a radical change in the ability of government to formulate and implement public policy to regulate business in the public interest and change the balance of power relative to property rights.[26]

The underlying issue with respect to social regulation is one of rights—civil and human rights versus property rights. Whose rights should take priority—the rights of workers to a safe workplace, the rights of minorities and women to be treated equally, the rights of consumers to safer products, the rights of all citizens to a clean environment, or the rights of shareholders to the highest return on their investment? Social regulations cost money and they affect the property rights of shareholders, as the corporation can no longer be operated solely in their interests. Social issues have to be taken into account, and the corporation can either comply with these regulations or be taken to court and sued for noncompliance.

> All democracies have championed the freedom to participate in government, and most have also sought to enshrine in law certain individual rights which seek to secure for individuals some inalienable areas of freedom of action and thought. Progress has, in part, been defined in the liberal tradition as the gradual extension of these individual freedoms and rights. The central problem for liberal democracy, however, is that one person's right to freedom of action may clash with another person's right not to be harmed . . . But in our increasingly interconnected and congested world, many people argue that surprisingly few actions by individuals are without important consequences for others. The crucial debate has centered around what role democratic government should have in trying to ensure greater harmony of interests between members of society, and what role government should have in forging the best social and environmental outcome for society as a whole.[27]

When rights are seen as stemming from an individualistic conception of the self, such clashes are inevitable. While the concept of public policy does contain some notion of community, as does social responsibility and stakeholder theory, it, like them, is undermined by an individualistic approach, where public policy represents nothing more than the aggregation of citizen preferences for public goods and services as expressed through the political process. This is the same way a market system works as it aggregates individual preferences for private goods and services.

This view is reinforced by the notion of rights that inhere in individuals and are part and parcel of their nature. Thus public policy reflects these ideas of individualism and rights that are part of the society at large, and the process ends up being in irreconcilable conflict over which rights take priority as individuals and groups battle each other in pursuing their interests. What would help is a new framework for understanding these tensions that exist within society, one that undercuts the notions of isolatable individuals with absolute rights in favor of inherently social persons that are an integral part of a larger community.

5 Ethics

In addition to the emphasis on individualism and rights, capitalism was also supported by an ethical system that helped to form a capitalistic culture based upon a set of values that required certain behavioral traits of its adherents. Economic systems do not develop in a vacuum but emerge in a social and moral context that facilitates and supports their development. Culture and its institutions mutually affect each other. Business institutions, which are the dominant economic force in our society, affect the culture, and as the culture adjusts to changing conditions, this adjustment affects the direction of and ongoing development of economic activity. As these dynamics have worked themselves out over time, the changes taking place can be viewed in terms of successive conceptual shifts among moral frames in which capitalism and market activity have been placed. Through this process, the market system has gradually gained its independent stature and dominating force in society.

The social context for the emergence of capitalism was provided by the Protestant Reformation and the resultant social upheaval it produced in leading to the breakup of medieval society. Feudalism proved to have inadequate answers to the social and economic problems created by the growth of towns, the expansion of trade, the development of technology, and the growth of banks and other large-scale enterprises. Economic forces had to be given their own course free from the domination of the church. Eventually, a new economic order emerged, which we now call capitalism, with new power centers and new sources of wealth.

> Leading the rebellion were the merchants, traders, shopkeepers, bankers, and independent professionals of the social middle class (collectively referred to as "the bourgeoisie"), who felt most resentful of the older feudal order. These people resented the degree to which the church had set limits on their own economic activities. For example, the church often set a "fair price," a "fair profit," and a "fair wage," in ways that impeded the creation of a free market. The traders and shopkeepers did not want the larger society to limit the profits they could make or to demand that they be responsible for the well-being of their workers.[1]

A new moral context was provided by the Protestant Ethic that informed the development of capitalistic systems and provided a legitimacy for their existence. In this sense, ethics became part of the capitalistic system itself in offering a moral justification for the pursuit of wealth and the distribution of income that resulted from economic activity within this system. The Protestant Ethic, as it was called, had both behavioral implications regarding the conduct of people who were within the system, and moral implications in providing legitimacy for the system and infusing its adherents with moral purpose.

THE PROTESTANT ETHIC

Max Weber provided us with the first comprehensive study of the significance of the Protestant Ethic.[2] In his book *The Protestant Ethic and the Spirit of Capitalism*, he sought to provide an explanatory model based upon religious beliefs for the growth of capitalistic activity in the sixteenth and seventeenth centuries. Weber's thesis was based on certain sociological phenomena that he observed in Post-Reformation Europe, especially in England and the Low Countries, which became the center of capitalistic development. As a sociologist, he observed that the trading classes of the bourgeoisie were found chiefly in the ranks of Protestantism and argued that the proportion of leading industrialists, traders, financiers, and technical experts was greater among Protestants than Catholics. Business leaders and owners of capital, as well as the higher grades of skilled labor and the technically and commercially trained personnel of modern enterprise were overwhelmingly Protestant. These classes in the sixteenth and seventeenth centuries, said Weber, were mainly found not merely among the Protestants in general, but among the Protestants of Calvinistic or Calvinistically allied churches, the Huguenots of France, the Dutch traders, and the Puritans of England.[3]

Weber attempted to explain these differences by looking into the intrinsic character of these Calvinistic beliefs and establishing a relationship between these beliefs and the capitalistic mentality of which the Calvinistic bourgeoisie were the leading exponents. The religious element was of primary importance in his explanation and provided a source for the values that influenced the behavior of those people who understood the potential of a newly emerging economic order and were able to benefit from this new order. Weber was not claiming, however, that religion was the only factor in the rise of capitalism, as other factors were involved in the development of capitalism. He was simply isolating those elements in the development of capitalism that he believed could not be explained by other factors but only by an appeal to religious beliefs and attitudes.[4]

> . . . It is a fact that the Protestants (especially certain branches of the movement to be fully discussed later) both as ruling classes and as

ruled, both as majority and as minority, have shown a special tendency to develop economic rationalism which cannot be observed to the same extent among Catholics either in one situation or the other. Thus the principle explanation of this difference must be sought in the permanent intrinsic character of their religious beliefs, and not only in their temporary external historical-political situations.[5]

What Weber did in his thesis was to develop an idealization of the kind of ethical imperatives that are a part of this Calvinistic belief system and show how they are logically related to rational economic behavior that is conducive to the development of capitalism. His investigations showed how the religious ideals and values of Calvinism entered in a very real way into the development of capitalism and markets to offer an alternative to the Marxist view of historical causality, which placed its emphasis on material conditions alone through its materialistic interpretation of history. Weber did not deny the importance of material conditions, such as technology, physical resources, or geographical location, and other such factors, but he wanted to show how religious ideals and values also play a part in shaping history.[6]

These religious beliefs, which Weber called the Protestant Ethic, produced a certain type of personality with a high motivation to achieve success in worldly terms by accumulating wealth and working diligently to create more wealth. This ethic contained two major elements: (1) an emphasis on the importance of a person's calling, which involved a primary responsibility to do one's best at whatever worldly station to which one was assigned by God rather than to seek religious meaning in withdrawing from the world, and (2) the rationalization of all of life by Calvin's notion of predestination, through which work became a means of dispersing religious doubt by demonstrating membership in the elect to oneself and others.[7]

The self-discipline and moral sense of duty and calling that were at the heart of this ethic were vital, according to Weber, to the kind of rational economic behavior that capitalism demanded (calculation, punctuality, productivity). The Protestant Ethic thus contributed to the Spirit of Capitalism, a spirit that was supportive of individual human enterprise and accumulation of wealth necessary for the development of capitalism. Within this climate, people were motivated to behave in a manner that proved conducive to rapid economic growth of the capitalistic variety and shared values that were consistent with this kind of development.[8]

Within this ethical system, work was understood to be something good in itself and was neither a curse nor something fit only for slaves. Rather work itself, which in the period before the Reformation was by and large considered to be a morally neutral activity at best, was given a clear moral sanction. Every person's work was of equal value in the eyes of God and contributed to the creation of more and more economic wealth in society. Former president Nixon stated it best when he said on some occasion that emptying bedpans was every bit as important as his job as president of the United States.

This ethic thus motivated one to work hard to be productive and accumulate wealth. But this wealth was not to be pursued for its own sake or enjoyed in lavish consumption, because the world existed to serve the glorification of God and for that purpose alone. The more one had, the greater was the obligation to be an obedient steward and hold these possessions undiminished for the glory of God by increasing them through relentless effort. The accumulation of material wealth was as sure a way as was available of disposing of the fear of damnation. One was not to rest on his or her laurels or enjoy the fruits of his or her own labor. Whatever wealth one was able to accumulate must be reinvested to accumulate more wealth in order to please God and as a further manifestation of one's own election.

> The upshot of it all, was that for the first time in history the two capital producing prescriptions, maximization of production and minimization of consumption, became components of the same ethical matrix. As different from medieval or communist culture these norms were not reserved for or restricted to specific individuals or groups. Everyone hypothetically belonged to that universe from which the deity had drawn the salvation sample, without disclosing its size or composition. The sampling universe had no known restriction of biological or social background, aptitude, or occupational specialization. Nobody could opt out from the sampling process, indeed, everyone had to act as if indeed he had been selected. For the mortal sin was to mock the deity by contradicting through his behavior God's primeval sampling decision. Everybody not only could but had to presume potential sainthood and correspondingly optimize his performance both as producer and consumer. The more his performance excelled relative to his reference group's, the higher the probability that indeed he had been selected. The ethic then pressured equally towards effective production and efficient consumption, which, while sustaining maximum productivity also maximizes savings and potential investment capital.[9]

Not only did the ethic thus stress physical work on the part of every person, but also whatever money one had was also to be put to work in making more money. A worldly asceticism was at the heart of this ethic, which gave a religious sanction for the acquisition and rational use of wealth to create more wealth. This new understanding of acquisitiveness and the pursuit of wealth became something of a moral imperative, as what formerly had been regarded as a personal inclination and choice had now become something of a moral duty.

The Protestant Ethic was an ingenious social and moral invention that offered a moral sanction to behavior that was of crucial importance in the early stages of capitalism. It emphasized both the human and capital sources of productivity and growth, by focusing on hard work and the aspect of the calling, but also advocating that the money people earned should also be put to work in earning more money. Inequality was thus morally justified if the money earned on capital was reinvested in further capital accumulation, which would benefit society as a whole by increasing production and creating more economic wealth.

The Protestant Ethic proved to be consistent with the need for accumulation of capital that is necessary during the early stages of industrial development. Money was saved and reinvested to build up a capital base. Consumption was curtailed in the interests of creating capital wealth. People dedicated themselves to hard work at often disagreeable tasks and accepted the rationalization of life that capitalism required. Such attitudes and activities represented a major shift away from the behavior and attitudes that informed medieval agrarian society.

The Protestant Ethic served to pattern behavior, and for its adherents it helped to make sense of the new industrial order, where people had to learn new roles and occupations. The pursuit of gain was legitimized and made something of a moral duty. People were to work diligently at their ordained tasks and accumulate wealth for the glory of God and as an indication of their own salvation. The Protestant Ethic was something of a road map that provided a guide for behavior in the midst of a terribly confused and disorganized cultural system. It gave meaning to people's lives in the form of a religious and moral symbol system in a rapidly changing society and enabled its adherents to act purposively within the emerging economic system. It provided a moral foundation for productive activity and legitimized the pursuit of profit and accumulation of wealth on the part of those who worked hard and invested their money wisely.

While the Protestant Ethic contained a moral limit on consumption in the interests of generating more economic wealth and building up a capital base to increase production for the entire society, it also made production of wealth an end in itself by not providing a moral purpose for production that was rooted in concrete human existence. It was tied to religious justifications that were abstractions from human existence and allowed for exploitation of both humans and nature in the interests of increasing production. Natural law in which the state confines itself to the protection of individual rights in the context of an emphatic respect for the free market became sanctioned, along with a utilitarian ethics, which imposed only one moral demand on the new industrialists, that is, to strive for the greatest possible quantity of utilities for themselves and, so it was thought, for their fellow men.[10]

During the enlightenment, nature came to connote not divine ordinance, but human appetites, and natural rights were invoked by the individualism of the time as a reason self-interest should be given free play. The conception that the church possessed of its own authority an independent standard of social values, which it could apply to the practical affairs of the economic world, grew weaker.[11] Economic life came to be grounded in a naturalistic conception of society in which the world of human affairs is regarded as self-contained and in need of no supernaturalistic explanation.

It was precisely in the spiritual climate provided by deism, which looked upon the social and economic life of man as a cosmos controlled by natural laws and completely accessible to human analysis, that the science of economics could gradually emerge. The character of this science of course presupposed a primarily mechanistic view of the world. The timepiece manufactured by the clockmaker could, so to speak, now be opened up by man, and the wheelwork inside could be analyzed as carefully as possible.[12]

This ethic was of particular importance in American society as capitalism developed and economic wealth was created. The country needed investment capital to expand industry and build railroads and canals to link the country together. People worked hard and saved their money to be invested in this expansion and share in the growth of the economy. The opportunities in this country seemed limitless and resources were considered to be infinite. One could become as wealthy as one wanted by taking advantage of these opportunities and pursuing the American dream. But this dream was never realized; it was always in the future and was thus something that continued to provide motivation and purpose.

Until recently, the Protestant work ethic stood as one of the most important underpinnings of American culture. According to the myth of capitalist enterprise, thrift and industry held the key to material success and spiritual fulfillment. America's reputation as a land of opportunity rested on its claim that the destruction of hereditary obstacles to advancement had created conditions in which social mobility depended on individual initiative alone. The self-made man, archetypical embodiment of the American dream, owed his advancement to habits of industry, sobriety, moderation, self-discipline, and avoidance of debt. He lived for the future, shunning self-indulgence in favor of patient, painstaking accumulation; and so long as the collective prospect looked on whole so bright, he found in the deferral of gratification not only his principal gratification, but an abundant source of profits. In an expanding economy, the value of investments could be expected to multiply with time, as the spokesman for self-help, for all their celebration of work as its own reward, seldom neglected to point out.[13]

The notion of the Protestant Ethic eventually became secularized in American society and stripped of its religious trappings. Secularization refers to the process of de-emphasizing the religious elements of any particular notion or concept and increasingly referring to worldly or temporal elements as distinguished from the spiritual or eternal realm. Thus a secular view of life or of any particular matter is based on the premise that religion or religious considerations should be ignored or purposely excluded. The Protestant Ethic thus became known as simply the work ethic and is now almost exclusively discussed in secular terms, with very little reference made to its religious origins except in certain scholarly and religious circles.

However, its basic assumptions about the importance of work and investment remained much the same and continued to inform American society. Embedded in the notion of the Protestant Ethic is the moral imperative both for the maximization of production and for the minimization of consumption. This ethic thus pressured equally towards effective production and efficient consumption, which also maximized savings and potential investment capital. But of even deeper significance is the fact that while the Protestant Ethic contained a moral limit on consumption in the interests of generating more economic wealth and building up a capital base to increase production, production of this wealth became an end in itself as the ethic became secularized.

Production was no longer part and parcel of a social process; its purpose was no longer part of the ongoing enrichment of human existence. While it was initially tied to religious doctrine, it was an abstraction from human experience and allowed for exploitation of both humans and nature in the interests of increasing production. As these religious ties were loosened and as the Protestant Ethic gave way to the more general work ethic, even its religious justification lost its moorings. Production became a self-justifying end in itself. And, intertwined with the notion of production as an end in itself, came the view of the "economic system" as having a life of its own guided by economic principles and the single-mindedness of the "profit motive."

CONSUMPTION

For many years, the Protestant Ethic was one of the most forceful shapers of American culture, but in the 1970s people began to take note of a gradual conceptual shift in values. One topic of interest and concern that appeared frequently in both popular and professional literature during this time was the weakening or disappearance of the Protestant Ethic from American culture. There was a good deal of evidence to suggest that the traditional values regarding work and the acquisition of wealth as expressed in the Protestant Ethic were changing in some fashion. Many articles indicated that young adults in particular had little interest in the grinding routine of the assembly line or in automated clerical tasks. They were turning away, it was suggested, from their parents' dedication to work for the sake of success and were more concerned about finding meaningful work, something that was satisfying and personally rewarding in terms other than money.

Young people were seeking to change existing industrial arrangements to allow these intangible goals to be pursued.[14]

Changes in values were already noted as early as 1957 by Clyde Kluckhohn, who did an extensive survey of the then available professional literature to determine if there had been any discernible shifts in American values during the past generation. As a result of this survey, he discovered that one value change that could be supported by empirical data was a decline of the Protestant Ethic as the core of the dominant middle-class value system.[15] Kluckhohn cited numerous studies to support this conclusion.

> The most generally agreed upon, the best documented, and the most pervasive value shift is what Whyte has called "the decline of the Protestant Ethic." This a central theme of Whyte's book. It is a clear-cut finding of the Schneider-Dornbusch study of inspirational religious literature. It is noted by essentially all the serious publications on recent value changes and on the values of the younger generation.[16]

Related to this fundamental shift are a number of others mentioned by Kluckhohn, which have the Protestant Ethic as their central point of reference. These shifts are interconnected and mutually reinforcing and are a result of the weakening of the Protestant Ethic, but may also, in turn, contribute to this weakening. There has been a rise in value upon "being" or "being and becoming" as opposed to "doing," according to many studies cited by Kluckhohn. Another such shift is the trend towards "present time" in contrast to "future time" value orientation, which means that the notion of deferred gratification was changing.[17]

Lastly, there was a trend towards an increase of aesthetic and recreational values as good in themselves, a development of "values which the Puritan Ethic never placed upon recreation (except as a means to the end of more effective work), pleasure, leisure, and aesthetic and expressive activities. Americans were enjoying themselves more and with less guilt than ever before. Moreover, there was a remarkable diversification and broadening of the base of leisure-time activities within the population."[18]

The next comprehensive discussion relative to the weakening of the Protestant Ethic in contemporary American society was written in 1976 by Daniel Bell, who argued that the Protestant Ethic has been replaced by hedonism in contemporary society—the idea of pleasure as a way of life. During the 1950s, according to Bell, the American culture had become primarily hedonistic, concerned with fun, play, display, and pleasure. The culture was no longer concerned with how to work and achieve but with how to spend and enjoy.[19]

> In the early development of capitalism, the unrestrained economic impulse was held in check by Puritan restraint and the Protestant Ethic. One worked because of one's calling, or to fulfill the covenant of the

community. But the Protestant Ethic was undermined not by modernism but by capitalism itself. The greatest single engine in the destruction of the Protestant Ethic was the invention of the installment plan, or instant credit. Previously one had to save in order to buy. But with credit cards one could indulge in instant gratification. The system was transformed by mass production and mass consumption, by the creation of new wants and new means of gratifying those wants.[20]

Thus the cultural if not moral justification of capitalism had become hedonism. This cultural transformation was brought about by (1) demographic change that resulted in the growth of urban centers and shift in political weight, (2) the emergence of a consumption society with its emphasis on spending and material possessions rather than thrift and frugality, and (3) a technological revolution, which through the automobile, motion picture, and radio broke down rural isolation and fused the country into a common culture and a national society.[21]

Bell argued that this abandonment of the Protestant Ethic left capitalism with no moral or transcendental ethic, and produced an extraordinary contradiction within the social structure of American society. The business corporation requires people who work hard, are dedicated to a career, and accept delayed gratification, all traditional Protestant Ethic virtues. Yet in its products and advertisements, the corporation promotes pleasure, instant joy, relaxing, and letting go, all hedonistic virtues. In Bell's words, "one is to be straight by day and a swinger by night."[22] Capitalism thus continued to demand a Protestant Ethic in the area of production but needed to stimulate a demand for pleasure and play in the area of consumption.[23]

Perhaps the crowning blow to the Protestant Ethic was noted by Daniel Yankelovich, who stated that traditionally Americans had been a thrifty and productive people adhering to the major tenants of the Protestant Ethic, and in the process helped to create an abundant and expanding economy.[24] But in the two decades prior to the publication of his book, he argued that Americans loosened their attachment to the ethic of self-denial and deferred gratification and were committed in one way or another to the search for self-fulfillment. Yankelovich presents evidence from polls and life histories to describe this search and support his assertion that about 80 percent of contemporary adults are involved in this search to varying degrees.[25] The old ethic of self-denial that was giving way to a search for self-fulfillment is described by Yankelovich in terms of a change in the giving-getting compact.

> The old giving/getting compact might be paraphrased this way: I give hard work, loyalty, and steadfastness. I swallow my frustrations and suppress my impulse to do what I would enjoy, and do what is expected of me instead. I do not put myself first; I put the needs of others ahead of my own. I give a lot, but what I get in return is worth it. I receive an

ever-growing standard of living, and a family life with a devoted spouse and decent kids. Our children will take care of us in our old age if we really need it, and thank goodness will not. I have a nice home, a good job, the respect of my friends and neighbors; a sense of accomplishment at having made something of my life. Last but not least, as an American I am proud to be a citizen of the finest country in the world.[26]

This compact provided support for the goals of America in the post-World-War-II period. Most Americans pursued material well-being, and self-denial and sacrifice to attain a rising standard of living made sense. But doubts about these rules set in as more and more people questioned whether these rules were worth the bother.[27] The search for self-fulfillment did not reject materialistic values, but it broadened them to embrace a wider spectrum of human experience. This search accepted social pluralism as the norm and included a new freedom to choose one's lifestyle. The search for self-fulfillment involved a search for intangibles such as creativity, autonomy, pleasure, participation, community, adventure, vitality, and stimulation. It involved satisfaction of both the body and the spirit, the addition of the joy of living to the efficiency of a technological society.[28]

Finally, Christopher Lasch argues that a new ethic of self-preservation had taken hold in American society. The work ethic had been gradually transformed into an ethic of personal survival.[29] The Puritans believed that a godly man worked diligently at his calling not so much in order to accumulate personal wealth as to add to the wealth of the community.[30] The pursuit of self-interest was changing from the accumulation of wealth to a search for pleasure and psychic survival. The cult of consumption, with its emphasis on immediate gratification, created the narcissistic man of modern society. Such a culture lives for the present and does not save for the future because it believes there may not be a future to worry about.[31]

This alleged weakening of the Protestant Ethic, with its inherent restriction on consumption, is consistent with behavioral changes in American society. Prior to World War II, people by and large were savings-oriented and lived by the ethic of deferred gratification. They would not buy houses with large mortgages and run up huge credit card balances, as these options were not available to many people. Rather, they would save their money until they could buy things outright. Gratification of their desires was deferred until they could afford to satisfy them and then, and only then, was it appropriate to buy things to enjoy. In other words, people lived within their immediate means and did not borrow for purposes of increased consumption.

After the war, this ethic changed into one of instant gratification, as a consumer society was created where people were encouraged to satisfy their desires now rather than wait until they had the money in hand. Buying on credit was encouraged and long-term mortgages became the order of the day with respect to housing. Why defer gratification when one could buy things immediately and pay for them in the future? Companies helped to create this kind of society by making credit easy to obtain through the use of credit cards and by using more sophisticated forms of advertising to increase demand for their products.

These were the days when the throwaway society was created and obsolence was built into products so that people would have to buy newer products sooner than planned. Packaging was improved so that products looked more attractive and could be purchased more easily. This meant the amount of stuff to be disposed of increased dramatically, as products that had outlived their usefulness had to be discarded along with all the packaging materials that were used to encase products. Eventually the country began to experience problems with waste disposal, which resulted in regulations of one sort or another to assure this waste material was disposed of properly and safely.

The United States became a society where consumption was emphasized and money was made available so people could buy on credit and pay their debts sometime in the future. Television fed this change with sitcoms that portrayed the typical American family as one that lived in a nice house in the suburbs, with two cars and all the latest kitchen appliances and electronic gear in the rest of the house. Advertising on television also became more sophisticated to stimulate demand for products. Companies fed this consumption binge with a proliferation of products that appealed to every taste that could be imagined, which encouraged people to go into debt to enjoy the pleasures these products could bring immediately rather than in some future time period.

Government contributed to the development of this culture with the notion of entitlements and the development of programs based on the idea that people in American society were entitled to certain amenities whether or not they earned them in the traditional sense. Social security was provided to assure that people could retire with a certain level of income. Welfare programs were established to provide a minimum level of goods and services to those who were not working. Medicare and Medicaid programs provided medical care to older people and those in poverty. All of these entitlement programs came at great cost and involved the government itself going into greater and greater debt to pay for them.

Perhaps the development of the atomic bomb also had an impact on generations growing up after World War II, because the future has never been as certain since that time, as we have had to live with the knowledge that humans have the ability to destroy the planet. Thus one might as well live as well as one possibly can now rather than defer gratification for some future time that may not be there. Changes in religion and the increasing secularization of society at that time may also have weakened belief in an afterlife, and more people came to hold the belief that you only go around once in life and might as well enjoy it to the fullest extent possible.

There were many factors behind this change in behavior and no one factor in particular was responsible for this change. They all helped to create a new approach to consumption, where instant gratification became a cultural trait, in contrast to earlier times when saving for the future was emphasized. The implications of this change were profound for lifestyles and habits of people, as society became more wealthy and prosperous. Many people lived more interesting lives and had more diversity available to them as never before. They traveled more miles, wore more and different clothes, drove more expensive and sophisticated cars, and in general enjoyed rising standards of living that involved consumption of the latest products.

Thus the Protestant Ethic failed to provide a moral framework for production and consumption activities as it apparently did during the early stages of industrial development. In the midst of affluence and advanced technology that made possible a high level of consumption, it did not enable many people to act purposively in keeping the system going and in enjoying the benefits of technology. It has not provided the kind of information necessary to deal adequately with the present cultural and economic situation nor did it provide a means of effectively responding to environmental problems. It became more and more irrelevant to the economic system as it emerged and changed to deal with new concerns.

In a consumer society, the emphasis on production has remained strong as the secularized work ethic continued, but the restraints on consumption provided by the Protestant Ethic have given way to an ever-increasing demand for products that can produce pleasure and self-gratification. In a consumer culture, consumption activities have become separated from whatever moral limits and justifications the Protestant Ethic provided. The purposes and meanings provided by this moral matrix are no longer relevant to a consumer culture, which emphasizes instant gratification and increased consumption. Now not only production but also consumption has become an end in itself. Both production and consumption are now divorced from any broader or larger moral purpose beyond the production and consumption of more goods and services themselves. Moreover, the assumed external relation of business and the natural environment, which had remained somewhat innocuous until recent years, began to take on ominous dimensions as increased production and consumption resulted in more waste that needs to be disposed of, more pollution that harms human health and the environment, and uses more resources, all to support a growing consumer culture that has become worldwide.

The demise of the Protestant Ethic left capitalism without a comprehensive ethical or moral system to provide legitimacy for the accumulation of wealth and root capitalism in a larger moral purpose beyond itself. The system became self-justifying and any ethical concerns had to adapt themselves to the requirements of the economic system. Perhaps this was inevitable, as during the Reformation the authority of the medieval Catholic Church was broken and the unity of civilization it symbolized was destroyed, setting secular forces loose to develop free from the Church's overpowering domination. Economic forces in particular were set free to develop without being hampered by the notions of "just wage" or "just price" that were of concern to medieval religion. Wages and prices were set by the laws of supply and demand, rather than some moral principles stemming from religion, and the capitalistic system came to operate according to its own "scientific" principles born out of an enlightenment philosophy. While the Protestant Ethic may have played a role in the development of capitalism, it had to shape itself to the capitalistic organization of production.

> As a result of the Reformation the relations previously existing between the Church and State had been almost exactly reversed. In the Middle Ages the Church had been, at least in theory, the ultimate authority on questions of public and private morality, while the latter was the police officer which enforced its decrees. In the sixteenth century, the Church became the ecclesiastical department of the State, and religion was used to lend a moral sanction to secular social policy . . . Religion has been converted from the keystone which holds the edifice together into one department within it, and the idea of a rule of right is replaced by economic expediency as the arbiter of policy and the criterion of conduct.[32]

C. E. Ayres makes the same point: "as industry and thrift came to be recognized as Christian virtues, inevitably the Christian conscience adjusted itself to the rewards of industry and thrift—to the accumulation of capital."[33] The fact of the matter is that people began to find capitalistic society much more exciting and full of promise than the status quo the Church was trying to maintain. The world for many people became a more interesting place in which to live, and worldly activity came to be valued for its own sake and not merely as preparation for an afterlife of some kind. Production and consumption eventually became ends in themselves and religion could not dominate these activities or provide any meaningful moral purpose for the system.

BUSINESS ETHICS

This doesn't mean that ethics and morals were of no concern to business organizations. These concerns were formalized in a new field of study that developed in the 1970s in response to the growing scandals in business that resulted in a demise of the public's perception of business activities. The answer was to provide ethics education for business students and provide ethics training for practitioners. Thus schools of business and management began to develop courses in business ethics, and professional organizations developed to help people already in business deal with ethics issues. The hope was to sensitize students and business practitioners to ethical issues and provide them with analytical tools to think their way through these issues to arrive at a decision that was ethically justified. These efforts grew throughout the last years of the twentieth century to comprise something of an ethics industry.

The usual approach to ethical theory in these efforts was to present either in cursory form or sometimes in greater detail the theory of utilitarianism based on the writings of Jeremy Bentham and John Stuart Mill, as representative of a more general class of what was called teleological ethics, and Kantian ethical theory, related to the categorical imperative, as representative of the deontological approach to ethical decision-making. Certain notions of justice were also usually considered, such as the egalitarianism of John Rawls and the opposing libertarianism of Robert Nozick. A discussion of rights was also usually included and sometimes a variation of virtue theory.

This approach to ethical theory leaves one with a kind of ethical smorgasbord in which one can choose from various theories that are supposed to shed some light on the ethical problems under consideration and lead to a justifiable decision. But students and practitioners were never told exactly how to decide which theory to apply in a given situation, what guidelines to use in applying these different theories, what criteria to determine which theory is best for a given situation, and what to do if the application of different theories resulted in totally different courses of action. The authors of the leading textbooks in business ethics seemed to recognize this problem, but did not know how to deal with it in a satisfactory fashion. For example, after presenting the theories of consequentialism, deontology, and what they called human nature ethics—what could be seen as a variation of virtue ethics—Tom Donaldson and Patricia Werhane state:

> Indeed, these three methods of moral reasoning are sufficiently broad that each is applicable to the full range of problems confronting human moral experience. The question of which method, if any, is superior to the others must be *left for another time*. The intention of this essay is not to substitute for a thorough study of traditional ethical theories—something for which there is no substitute—but to introduce the reader to basic modes of ethical reasoning that will help analyze the ethical problems in business that arise in the remainder of the book.[34]

Another author states the problem in the following manner:

> Our morality, therefore, contains three main kinds of moral considerations, each of which emphasizes certain morally important aspects of our behavior, but no one of which captures all the factors that must be taken into account in making moral judgments. Utilitarian standards

consider only the aggregate social welfare but ignore the individual and how that welfare is distributed. Moral rights consider the individual but discount both aggregate well-being and distributive considerations. Standards of justice consider distributive issues but they ignore aggregate social welfare and the individual as such. These three kinds of moral considerations do not seem to be reducible to each other yet all three seem to be necessary parts of our morality. That is, there are some moral problems for which utilitarian considerations are decisive, while for other problems the decisive considerations are either the rights of individual or the justice of the distributions involved . . . We have at this time no comprehensive moral theory capable of determining precisely when utilitarian considerations become "sufficiently large" to outweigh narrow infringements on a conflicting right or standard of justice, or when considerations of justice become "important enough" to outweigh infringements on conflicting rights. Moral philosophers have been unable to agree on any absolute rules for making such judgments. There are, however, a number of rough criteria that can guide us in these matters . . . But these criteria remain rough and intuitive. *They lie at the edges of the light that ethics can shed on moral reasoning.* [35]

These statements seem to be making a virtue of a necessity and beg the questions posed earlier. In none of these theories can there be guidance in deciding when to use a particular theory, for each theory is self-enclosed or absolute. No principle or rule can provide any guidance for the moral reasoning that underlies the choice among the various principles or rules. What, then, determines the decision as to which theory is appropriate in a given situation? The basis for this choice, which now becomes the heart of moral reasoning, the very foundation for moral decision-making, remains mysterious and outside the realm of philosophical illumination.

The litany of conflicting theories and principles, each of which was initially meant as a universal approach to ethical problems, gives conflicting signals to people in positions of responsibility in business or other organizations. Shifting between utilitarianism and the categorical imperative or between theories of justice and rights involves at best an unreflective or shallow commitment to ethics and a moral point of view. These theories cannot be applied or ignored at will as the situation may seem to dictate because each of them involves commitment to the philosophical framework on which it is based, and these frameworks are often in conflict. The philosophical framework on which Kant's deontological ethics is based is radically different from the philosophical framework on which utilitarianism is based. To be a Kantian at one time and a Benthamite at another is to shift philosophical frameworks at will. This shifting has been called, quite aptly, "metaphysical musical chairs." [36]

What we are really dealing with in all these instances is moral pluralism, which is the view that no single moral principle or overarching theory of what is right can be appropriately applied in all ethically problematic situations. There is no one unifying principle from which lesser principles can be derived. Different moral theories are possible depending upon which values or principles are included. According to moral pluralism, none of these theories provides guidance in deciding when to use a particular theory, for each theory is self-enclosed or absolute; no principle or rule can provide any guidance for the moral reasoning that underlies the choice among the various principles or rules of different theories.

Robbin Derry and Ronald Green conclude, after a broad study of the field of business ethics, that there is "a persistent unwillingness to grapple with the tensions between theories of ethical decision making, and this hampers an understanding of ethical decision making."[37] A deeper, unifying level must be reached to explain why and how we reconstruct rules and traditions and choose among various ethical principles in an ongoing process of dealing with change and novelty. An adequate moral pluralism, like any adequate moral theory, requires a solid philosophical grounding that emphasizes community and responsibility and over against individualism and rights.

Traditional ethical theory is shot through with individualism, as the longstanding nonrelational view of the self, the self as an isolatable building block of community, dominates the ethical tradition. The conflict between the individual and community is manifested in the different approaches of Bentham and Kant to ethical decision-making. The utilitarianism of Bentham assumes that the whole is no more than the sum of the parts; one adds up the cost and benefits of particular courses of action in whatever units are appropriate to arrive at a decision that will create the greatest amount of social welfare, however this is defined. Kant stresses the autonomy of the individual as over against aggregate social welfare and holds that certain principles are to be adhered to with no exceptions, regardless of the consequences. Rights are often used to protect the individual from being oppressed because of utilitarian considerations. Contemporary views of justice as diverse as that of Rawls and Nozick both presuppose an individual self that can be considered theoretically in isolation from, and prior to, a community.[38] Virtue ethics focuses on the individual and offers no understanding of the self as a creative agent that outstrips the inculcation of roles and habits of behavior in order to evaluate and reconstruct the very tradition that engendered these roles and habits.

What we are left with in business ethics is thus a litany of theories, no one of which provides a comprehensive ethic that can take the place of the Protestant Ethic in shaping the behavior of people in our society. Business ethics is largely "sold" on the basis of its contribution to the "bottom line," that good ethics is good business, that being ethical will somehow lead to greater profits for the organization, either in the positive sense of creating a more functional organization that can successfully compete in the marketplace, or in the negative sense of avoiding lawsuits that stem from unethical behavior. Ethics is subservient to economics, and it is economic considerations that are paramount in management decision-making. The behavior of people is largely shaped by economic considerations and business ethics has to shape itself to be consistent with this dominant value system.

Business ethics has not been able to effect major change in the way managers view their responsibilities. The bottom line is still the bottom line, and when push comes to shove, ethics takes a back seat to the profitability of the corporation. This was amply demonstrated during the scandals involving Enron, WorldCom, Tyco, HealthSouth, and other corporations. The common denominator in many of these situations was the never-ending drive to increase the company's stock valuation. So many entities, including shareholders, creditors, and employees, have their fortunes bound up with an ever-upward valuation, which became the overriding consideration as ethics went out the window. What seems to be necessary is a comprehensive ethic based on community and responsibility that might serve to mitigate the dominance of economic considerations.

Part II

A Theoretical Framework for New Directions in Capitalism

6 The Social Self and Community
The Foundation of the Framework

The task in this chapter is to lay out an alternative view of selfhood that is not individualistic and that entails a conception of community that is part and parcel of the self rather than an aggregation of individuals.[1] This view will be difficult for people to understand since most of us are rooted in an individualistic view of persons and think of community as the sum of all the individuals who are involved in some kind of collective endeavor. In other words, the whole is merely the sum of the parts, and we usually break the whole down into parts that can be better understood and manipulated. This is the way science works, and this is the way we tend to think of organizations. If there is a problem with organizational life, we break it down into parts to find out what is wrong.

The problem with this approach is that we lose sight of the whole by focusing so much of our attention on the parts, and when we do think of the whole, we try and put the parts back together to create the whole, forgetting that the whole is already there and is, in fact, always present and does not have to be recreated. Developing an alternative view involves focusing on both parts and wholes, and discussing them in such a way that they are integral to each other. In other words, the parts do not exist apart from the whole and the whole does not exist without the parts. Neither self nor community are prior to each other but are bound up with each other, such that when one is present the other is present.

Rethinking capitalism involves rethinking the nature of selfhood that is involved in economic activities and the nature of the communities in which selves function. This is the basic problem addressed in this book—how to think about ourselves and community to overcome the individualistic notions that form the philosophical base of capitalism along with the idea of rights that are rooted in the individual rather than the community. Rethinking capitalism involves rethinking the nature of the corporation, and as Freeman has recognized, "Redescribing corporations means redescribing ourselves and our communities."[2] It is this task that will be attempted in this and the remaining chapters.

THE SOCIAL SELF

The most important question concerning the self is whether the self is an isolatable, discrete entity, or is it by its very nature part of a social context. The view of the individual as an isolatable entity is firmly rooted in traditional thinking and is in fact very much taken for granted in our everyday existence. The view that singular or discrete individuals exist and have no moral ties to any associations except those they choose to form for their own self-interested purposes was the philosophical basis for the French and American revolutions and is clearly embedded in John Locke's view of property rights as well as in other social contract theories. These presuppositions are also the basis for understanding the nature of capitalism as an agglomeration of individuals seeking their material self-interest in a competitive system that pits them against each other for the limited resources a society has at its disposal.

This accepted, unquestioned, presupposed view of the atomicity of the person or self is pinpointed by Charles Taylor as the common basis for positions as diverse as traditional individualistic or interest-group liberalism and traditional conservative laissez-faire economics.[3] Such an atomistic view, which sees the self as an atom separable and distinct from other atoms, pits the individual squarely against communitarian constraints, such as government regulations that attempt to codify the concerns of the society as a whole. Once the individual is taken as an isolatable unit, then the individual and community become pitted against each other in an ultimately irreconcilable tension.

The movement in American philosophy known as classical American pragmatism offers a unique and helpful framework for overcoming this tension and will be used in this chapter to develop a relational understanding of the self and community.[4] The pragmatic understanding of the nature of selfhood and the relation between the self and the other and the resulting dynamics of community rejects the long history of the individualistic self, which offers the choice between the collective whole at the expense of the individual or the individual at the expense of the collective whole. It offers a new way of understanding the self and community that is inherently social in nature.

According to this pragmatic view, to have a self is to have a particular type of ability, the ability to be aware of one's behavior as part of a social process of adjustment and to be aware of oneself as a social object, as an acting agent within the context of other acting agents. Not only can selves exist only in relation to other selves, but no absolute line can be drawn between our selfhood and the selfhood of others. Our own selves exist and are part of our experience only in so far as other persons exist and enter into our experience. The origins and foundations of the self are thus social or intersubjective rather than individualistic in nature. We do not grow up isolated from our surroundings but develop in a social context where we incorporate elements of that context into our own consciousness.

When cooperative action is necessary, as it is in any social context, human organisms take the perspective of the other in the development of their conduct; they have to be aware of the interests and concerns of others who are part of the cooperative entity. In incorporating the perspective, attitude, or viewpoint of the other, the developing self comes to take the perspective of others as a complex, interrelated whole. In this manner, the self comes to incorporate the standards and authority of the group, the organization or system of attitudes and responses that George Herbert Mead terms "the generalized other."[5] This is the passive dimension to the self, the dimension structured by role-taking in a social context, that aspect of the self that Mead refers to as the "me." This generalized other is not merely a collection of others, but an organization or structural relation of others, for the generalized other represents attitudes or perspectives that have been internalized by the self as it develops in a social context.

Mead uses the example of a baseball team as an example of a generalized other functioning in a group context. The person who plays a position on the team must understand the role of everyone else involved in the game, and these different roles must have a definite relationship to each other. Any one participant must assume the attitudes of the other players as an organized unity, and this organization controls the response of the individual participant. Each one of the participants' own acts is determined by "his being everyone else on the team," in so far as the organization of the various attitudes controls his own response. "The team is the generalized other in so far as it enters—as an organized process or social activity—into the experience of any one of the individual members of it."[6]

In sum, as selves grow and develop they incorporate or internalize the standards and attitudes of the groups that comprise their social context. People internalize these standards and attitudes from their families, churches, schools and other collective endeavors in which they find themselves. These attitudes and standards comprise the generalized other that has been formed over the years through an amalgam of the attitudes and standards of the people who comprise those collectives. This amalgam is more than just the sum of the parts—it is a unique creation of each collective entity that is concerned with its own survival and has to continue to perform a useful function in society. The group has an existence that is not separate from the individuals that comprise the group, but that is in reality more than these individuals and has the ability to shape the behavior and attitudes of individuals who are its members.

The "me," then, represents the conformity of the self to the past, to the norms and practices of a society or a group. Yet in responding to the perspective of the other, each individual responds as a unique center of creative activity; there is a creative dimension to the self, which Mead refers to as the "I." The "I" represents the unique, creative dimension of the self that brings its novel reactions to present situations. By its very nature, the self incorporates both the conformity of the group perspective or group attitudes and the creativity of its unique individual perspective.

Thus the tensions between tradition and change, conformity and individuality, conservative forces and liberating forces, emerge as two dynami-
cally interacting poles or dimensions that form the very nature of selfhood.[7]
Freedom does not lie in opposition to the restrictions provided by norms and
authority, but in a self-direction, which requires the proper dynamic interaction of these two dimensions within the self.[8] Because of this dynamic
interaction constitutive of the very nature of selfhood, the perspective of
the novel, "liberating" dimension always opens onto a common, "conserv-
ing" perspective.

This dynamic interrelationship provides one with the ability to think of
oneself in terms of the group to which one belongs and lay upon oneself
the responsibilities that belong to the members of that group. This interrelationship also bestows the ability to admonish oneself as others would
and to recognize what are one's responsibilities as well as one's rights as a
member of the group.[9] But these responsibilities and rights have themselves
resulted not just from the internalization of the perspective of the generalized other, but from the effect on this perspective by one's own creative
input. Not only is one's creative individuality not enslaved by or determined
by the generalized other, but the generalized other has itself been formed in
part from one's own past creative actions.

COMMUNITY

The unique individual both reflects and reacts to the common or group perspective in his or her own unique manner. Moreover, this novelty in turn
changes the group attitude or perspective. This new perspective emerges
because of its relation to dominant institutions, traditions, and patterns
of life that conditioned its emergence, and this perspective gains its significance in light of the way it changes the common perspective. The dynamic
of community is found in this continual interplay involving adjustment of
attitudes, aspirations, and factual perceptions between the common perspective as the condition for the novel perspective and novel perspective as
it conditions the common perspective.[10]

To ask if a new perspective is a product of an individual of a community, to ask which comes first, the individual or the community perspective, is an irrelevant question. The creativity of the individual can
be contrasted with the conformity represented by the common perspective, but not with community. True community occurs in the interplay
between the individual and the generalized other, between the "I" and
the "me," and this takes place through ongoing communication in which
each adjusts to or accommodates the other. The ongoing adjustment or
accommodation between these two dimensions is essential for community. The individual and the generalized other exist only within the context of community, and without the individual and the generalized other

there is no community. But without the ongoing interaction of adjustment or accommodations, which is the very essence of community, there is no individual or generalized other. They are an integral part of each other.

This adjustment is neither assimilation of one perspective by another nor the fusion of perspectives into an indistinguishable oneness; the adjustment can best be understood as an "accommodation" in which each individual creatively affects and is affected by the other through an accepted means of adjudication. Thus a community is constituted by, and develops in terms of, the ongoing communicative adjustment between the activity of the novel individual perspective and the common group perspective, and each of these two interacting dimensions constitutive of community gains its meaning, significance, and enrichment through this process of accommodation or adjustment. Thus a free society, like a free individual, requires both the influencing power of authority as embodied in its institutions and traditions, and the innovative power of creativity as expressed in individual actions. In John Dewey's terms:

> No amount of aggregated collective action of itself constitutes a community . . . To learn to be human is to develop through the give-and-take of communication an effective sense of being an individually distinctive member of a community; one who under-stands and appreciates its beliefs, desires, and methods, and who contributes to a further conversion of organic powers into human resources and values. But this transition is never finished.[11]

The intelligence that transforms societies and institutions, then, is itself influenced by these institutions. In this sense, even individual intelligence is social intelligence. And social intelligence, as the historically grounded intelligence operative within a community and embodied in its institutions, although not merely an aggregate of individual intelligence but rather a qualitatively unique and unified whole, is nonetheless not something separable from individual intelligence.

There is an intimate functional reciprocity between individual and social intelligence, a reciprocity based on the continual process of adjustment. Although the generalized other indeed represents social meanings and social norms, social development is possible only through the dynamic interrelation of the unique, creative individual and the generalized other. William James expresses this interrelation in his observation that the influence of a great man modifies a community in an entirely original and peculiar way, while the community in turn remodels him.[12]

Novelty within society is initiated by individuals, but such initiation can occur only because individuals are continuous with others and with the historically situated social institutions of which they are a part. Part of the life process is the ongoing adjustment between the old and the new, the stability of conformity and the novelty of creativity. The interrelation of continuity and novelty, stressed by virtually all the classical pragmatists, provides the conceptual tools for understanding how the uniqueness of the individual and the norms and standards of community are two interrelated factors in an ongoing exchange, neither of which can exist apart from the other. Because of the inseparable interaction of these two dimensions, goals for "the whole" cannot be pursued by ignoring consequences for the individuals affected, nor can individual goals be adequately pursued apart from the vision of the functioning of the whole entity.

The development of the ability both to create and to respond constructively to the creation of novel perspectives as well as to incorporate the perspective of the other, not as something totally alien but as something sympathetically understood, is what growth of the self entails. Such growth incorporates an ever more encompassing sympathetic understanding of varied and diverse interests. This leads to tolerance of other people's perspectives, which are seen as an enlargement of the self rather than a sacrifice of one's own position. Thus to enrich, deepen and expand the community is at once to enrich, deepen and expand each person involved in ongoing community interactions.

CONFLICT RESOLUTION

Problematic situations that arise in any and every community can be resolved through the use of social intelligence in a way that enlarges and reconstructs the situation and the selves involved, providing at once a greater degree of authentic self-expression and a greater degree of social participation. In cases where incompatibility of perspectives arises, the problematic situation must be reconstructed based on the problem situation and the history within which it has emerged. This reconstruction cannot be imposed by eliciting the standards of a past that most often does not contain a way to resolve the problem. Such reconstruction must be accomplished by calling on a more fundamental and creative level of activity.

The relation of individual selves to the generalized other requires the openness of perspectives rather than a mind closed to new ways of looking at things. The adjustment of perspectives that is necessary to reach agreement on a problem does not involve an imposition of some perspective or standards from "on high" but rather a deepening to a more fundamental level of human rapport. This deepening process involves an openness for breaking through seeming incompatibilities and situations that, on the surface at least, seem impossible to resolve. This process allows us to grasp different contexts, to take the perspective of "the other," and to participate in genuine dialogue with other people.

Characterizations of a community usually include the notion of a common goal that the community is trying to attain. The ultimate "goal" of this open-ended, dynamic process, however, is enriching growth or development, not final completion. This in turn indicates that differences between people should not be eradicated because these differences provide the necessary materials by which a society can continue to grow and develop. As Dewey stresses, growth by its very nature involves the resolution of conflict.[13] A true community that incorporates different perspectives is far from immune to conflict, but such clashes provide the material for ongoing development as these different perspectives are adjusted and accommodated by the community.

What needs to be cultivated in the community is the motivation, sensitivity, and imaginative vision needed to change irreconcilable factionalism into a growing pluralistic community. The ability to tolerate radically diverse ways of life or of making sense of things is not to be found from above by imposing one's own perspective upon such diversity, but rather from beneath, by penetrating though such differences. Different ways of making sense of the world emerge in any community, but these differences emerge from the essential characteristics of beings that are fundamentally alike that are confronting a common reality in an ongoing process of change. The diversity of responses to cope with this reality represents a strength rather than a weakness of community and is to be celebrated rather than negated.

Such a deepening does not negate the use of intelligent inquiry; rather the deepening opens it up and frees it from the rigidities and abstractions of the past and focuses it on the dynamics of human existence. This deepening may change conflict into an increased diversity or it may lead to an emerging consensus that one of the conflicting positions is unworkable. In this way over the course of time, incompatible perspectives are not proved right or wrong but are resolved by the weight of argument as reasons and justifications are worked out in the ongoing course of inquiry. If such adjustments do not emerge, then community has broken down and what remains is sheer factionalism.

This approach does not destroy reason, but it brings reason down to earth, so to speak. What it does destroy is the belief that reason has an absolute hold on truth and values in the abstract, that scientific objectivity is the privileged domain of rationality or that the revealed truth of religious belief is absolute in some sense. Reason brought down to earth is concrete, imaginative, and deepened to operate with possibilities that have been liberated from the confines and rigidities of abstract rules and procedural steps or the confines of inculcated tradition, whether a scientific or a religious tradition.

When a community is operating within a common system of meaning and values on any one issue, then investigation of an issue will tend toward convergence. The manner of adjustment between a new perspective as a novel interpretation of the facts and the perspective of the generalized other as the previously accepted interpretation is resolved by verification of the factual evidence and a gradual acceptance of a new interpretation that makes better sense of the facts than the old interpretation. However, when a novel viewpoint brings with it a novel set of meanings and values by which to delineate facts, the process of adjustment that constitutes the dynamics of sociality within a community is not so easily accomplished.

In this case, there is no longer a question of testing varying interpretations of the facts; there are now different perceptions of what facts are available. There are now not only different interpretations to account for the facts, but there are also different facts to consider. In other words, people do not just see things differently, they see different things. Discussions to bring about an adjustment of perspectives must then stem from a generalized stance of agreement concerning what standards are to be applied in making decisions among incommensurable frameworks. Such standards may be difficult to elucidate, but because these standards are implicitly operative in the process of adjustment among divergent meaning systems, they can be elicited for clarification through reflective focus on what is operative in the process of adjustment.

Nonetheless, novel perspectives may at times emerge that are "incommensurable" not only with another way of delineating experience through the determination of what kind of facts exist in the world, but which also incorporate standards and criteria related to the selection of problems that are important to be resolved that are "incommensurable" with those of another perspective. There are not only different facts, but also different methods, standards, and criteria for determining which system of facts should be accepted. In a sense, these divergent perspectives have carved out divergent worlds, the most fundamental sense of incommensurability that can be experienced. These different worlds encompass not just differing facts, but differing goals, differing problems of importance, differing criteria for resolving differences, and hence differing organs for bringing about a process of adjustment.

Such incommensurable perspectives are in a sense structuring different worlds, as for example the gulf that exists between the religious and scientific worldviews. But they cannot be closed to rational discussion for possibilities of socializing adjustment within a given community. Diverse perspectives for delineating facts must work, for better or worse, in measuring up to the standards and criteria by which the community judges them and in solving the problems that the community decides are important. Diverse perspectives that incorporate diverse standards, criteria, and problems can be discussed in terms of the ability of these perspectives to address the problems we experience as organisms embedded in a universe in which we must learn to flourish. Such workability is reflectively incorporated in differing traditions and rituals and the emergence of differing problems that need resolution. Such diverse articulations stem from a vague, elusive, but real sense of workability embedded in the primal drive of every organism to interact successfully with its environment.

In the ongoing process of socializing adjustment, some arguments gain validity while others go by the wayside. Though none of these arguments are ultimately proved right or wrong, we eventually discard some and move on in yielding to the force of others. Such a process is based on rational discussion guided by the inescapable criteria of workability. Although abstract articulations of workability itself can be diverse and at times seem incommensurable, the primal sense of workability serves as the ineffable but inescapable and inexhaustible wellspring of vitality from which a community moves forward through rational and open discussion, leaving behind reasons and arguments that have become lifeless.

The relation of the individual and the generalized other in the process of socializing adjustment within a community requires the openness of perspectives. No community need be constricted by closed horizons, either in terms of the possibilities of penetrating to more fundamental levels of community or to wider breadth of community. Expansion in breadth is at once expansion in depth. As two communities recognize their openness in coming to understand the perspective of the other, there is a socializing adjustment founded on a deeper and broader community. Such a socializing adjustment involves neither assimilation of perspectives, one to the other, nor fusion of each into an indistinguishable oneness, but an accommodation in which each creatively affects and is affected by the other.

In coming to understand the pluralism and the dynamic of socializing adjustment constitutive of this kind of community, one can at the same time come to recognize the enrichment to be gained by understanding the perspective of the other. But just as important is to recognize the enrichment to be gained by understanding what is implicitly operative in one's own perspective. The pragmatic framework described here offers the foundation for a perspectival pluralism, rather than the drive towards unanimity in final knowledge.

Some may object that the novelty and diversity in this kind of perspectival pluralism lead to the view that true progress in knowledge is impossible, that there is no progress in this kind of process but only difference. However, knowledge as cumulative and knowledge as changing do not lie in opposition to each other, but rather knowledge as changing is also knowledge as cumulative, for any novel perspective emerges from a cumulative process or history of socializing adjustment, which yields enrichment of intelligibility of both the old and new perspectives. Furthermore, to the extent that any perspective is reflective of its own contextual conditions, the perspective advances, for in such reflection it becomes conscious of its openness onto a deeper community and the possibilities contained therein.

7 The Capitalist System

What are the implications of this view of the self and community for the capitalistic system, which, it was earlier argued, is founded on individualism and rights, primarily property rights that are believed to inhere in the individual? The social self as described in the last chapter is not the individualistic self of traditional capitalism that encourages the pursuit of self-interest in a competitive environment and views rights as being individualistic in nature. The social self is not an isolatable entity but is an integral part of a community, such that it cannot be separated from the community in which it grows and develops, nor can the community be considered apart from the selves of which it is constituted. The self and community are an integral part of each other. What does this view mean for capitalism and a revised understanding of the capitalistic system?

CAPITALISM AS A SOCIAL SYSTEM

First of all, capitalism as an economic system seems to have won the day as far as organization of economic activity is concerned. It has proven to be more productive in providing goods and services to consumers and providing a way for people to pursue economic goals with greater freedom than alternatives such as socialism. Given its success, capitalism, or some variation thereof, has come to be the primary way people in countries around the world organize themselves to provide for their material needs and comfort. The institutions of capitalism, in which many people spend a majority of their lives, give people a sense of identity and belonging in addition to providing them with the means to earn an income. These institutions provide the context in which much of their social life takes place and the setting for many of their social interactions.

When capitalistic societies came into existence, they replaced the traditional social systems that had been in place that had served to prescribe roles and activities for people and provide meaning for their everyday existence. Economic activity had always been subordinated to the social system and was merely a part of a larger social reality in which economic activities were embedded. But capitalism took over, so to speak, and became a social system in and of itself, and other aspects of social life became subordinated to the duties and roles that are part of the capitalistic system. Societies organized themselves according to capitalistic principles, and the roles of producer, consumer, investor, worker, and the like became the primary roles in society.[1]

Capitalism thus eventually turned human and social relations around and altered the relationship of humans with nature. Whereas in earlier times economic relations were embedded in and secondary to their broader social context, capitalism actually embedded social relations into the economic system as social relations became defined by economic relations. Society and social relations were subordinated to the "laws" of the market. The evolution of capitalism occurred through the transformation of nature, humans, and capital, the so-called factors of production, into fictitious economic commodities that can be bought and sold on the market. Such a fictionalizing of fundamentally social entities into economic elements ushered in a period of production of economic goods and services never before experienced. But it also resulted in massive social dislocation and created problems that needed to be addressed. Once the market is separated from the fabric of society, social protectionism is a natural response to help people cope with economic disruptions.

The capitalistic system eventually became rooted in science, in keeping with the rise of science in general. Economics is a social science and as a scientific discipline provides a scientific explanation of how the system works to produce goods and services to meet consumer preferences and provide employment and income to workers. Macro-economics describes the working of the economy as a whole and is concerned with the growth and stability of the overall economy, while micro-economics is concerned with the behavior of the firm in a competitive environment. Economics treats the self as an economic entity that is solely concerned with its economic well-being and thinks of community in terms of the economic wealth that can be generated by capitalistic society. Other aspects of the self and community are not considered to be part of the system and are abstracted out of consideration. In recent decades, economics has become a highly mathematized discipline and has no need for any moral considerations related to the distribution of wealth in our society or to the adverse effects of economic growth.[2]

Economics as a scientific discipline prescribes the role of business in a capitalistic society and provides a justification for its existence. Business is solely an economic institution, whose purpose is to create more and more economic wealth. This purpose is able to be quantified and measured by the ability of a business organization to generate profits and increase the price of its shares traded on the stock exchanges. The success of society as a whole is measured by an increase or decrease in gross national product, or gross domestic product as it is sometimes called. Our fascination with and belief in quantification is reflected in these measures of success. When things go wrong as indicated by these measures, we have confidence that we can manipulate things in the economy, such as interest rates, or change certain aspects of corporate behavior to make things right.

The economy, however, cannot be so neatly separated from or absorb the rest of society. The economic system is fully woven into the fabric of society as only one dimension, inseparable from other dimensions of the sociocultural matrix in which we act out our day-to-day existence. The economic dimension is but one aspect of our existence, and the economic system, far from being a reality engulfing the social aspect, is the result of giving a supposedly independent status to a discriminable dimension of our total existence, an existence that is inherently social in nature. The economic system ultimately cannot even stand on its own conceptually, and to isolate it for purposes of analysis and manipulation severs it from the very context that makes it intelligible as a discriminable and moral force in society.

Thus a redefinition of the self as social and inseparably tied to community is necessary to reconceptualize capitalism as a social system that has social impacts on the self and community that need to be taken into account. Capitalism is not simply an organization of fictionalized commodities that can be bought and sold on the market; it is an organization of real people who are trying to make a life for themselves and their families and find meaning and fulfillment in the society in which they find themselves. These people and the institutions in which they work cannot be mathematized and plugged into abstract formulas that focus only on the economic aspects of their existence, thus dehumanizing them in the process.

WEALTH

The capitalistic system is better at creating economic wealth than other systems, but what is economic wealth and how is it created? Economic wealth is supposedly created when resources that have no economic value in themselves are combined in such a way that goods and services are produced that are of value to the society. Most natural resources, for example, have no utility or economic value in their natural state. They have to be mined or harvested, in most cases, and processed through several stages in order to be made into something useful that can be sold in the marketplace. Similarly, land in its natural state usually has no economic value in and of itself, but must be plowed so that crops can be planted and eventually processed into food products, or reshaped so that it can be used for a housing development or for some commercial project.

When these resources are then made into useful products that can be sold in the marketplace, the economic wealth of the nation is increased. If companies have done things right in the sense of producing something people want to buy because it is useful to them, and has done so efficiently so that people can afford to buy the things that are produced, they are rewarded with profits, which represent companies' share of the wealth that has been created. These profits are used to support the operations of the corporation and are paid out as dividends to shareholders, who have risked their money by investing in the stock of the corporation.

Wealth is generally considered to be a neutral entity as far as morality is concerned. It is thought of as an economic concept that has no moral implications. However, wealth does not exist in a vacuum but exists in a particular social context. How that wealth was created and how it is distributed has all sorts of moral implications. Was it created by an honest effort, where employees were paid reasonable wages and salaries and consumers were provided with a product that was safe to use as directed? Or was it produced by exploiting employees and producing a product that harmed people? Did managers take an unreasonable share of that wealth to put in their own pockets, or was it shared fairly with employees and shareholders? Were the resources extracted from nature in a way that preserved the environment or was the natural environment seriously degraded in the process? These are all moral questions that can have serious consequences for the society at large.

Economic wealth is an elusive concept and something of a fiction. Several trillions of dollars disappeared from the American economy during the first years of the twenty-first century, as all the major stock exchanges plummeted from their highs reached only a year earlier. Nasdaq was once over the 5000 level but plunged below the 2000 level as high-tech and dot.com stocks took a beating. The Dow went below the 12,000 level and stayed there for many months. A company such as Cisco Systems, which in March 2000 had the largest market capitalization of any company in the country, larger even than General Electric or Microsoft, saw its stock, which at one time had been close to $90 a share, plunge to less than $20 a share. What happened to all this wealth? Where did it go? Can such wealth ever be created again?

A major reason for this loss was the end of the high-tech revolution, in particular the dot.com companies that had been created to revolutionize retailing. Many of these companies, such as E-Toys, which had one of the best web sites in the business, did not make it and went out of business. Others, such as Amazon.com, struggled through this period and continued as viable companies. There was talk during the dot.com frenzy that economic realities such as profits were no longer relevant, as many of these companies continued to increase in wealth as measured by their stock prices, regardless of whether they made any profits. But economic realities eventually set in, and profits again became relevant.

Apparently many of the assumptions behind the dot.com revolution failed to materialize, and many of these companies, despite the initial euphoria, did not produce something that was useful to enough people in society to make them viable entities. People were not going to sit at home at their computers and do all their shopping. What may have been forgotten is the social nature of shopping, that people like to go to malls, even though it may be inconvenient, and do their shopping in a social context. Thus the large retailers like Wal-Mart and Sears were not put out of business by the dot.com companies. The economic wealth that the latter companies generated through an increase in stock prices was fictional and based on speculation that these companies were eventually going to be profitable entities that would continue in existence. But this did not prove to be true, and the wealth they generated disappeared as fast as it was created.

Thus economic wealth has a fictional quality; it is an abstraction that represents something, but that something is elusive. Are the routers and other equipment Cisco Systems produces any less important to the future development of the internet than they were before its stock price plunged and it became worth a great deal less in economic terms? What is the real worth of a company like General Motors or General Electric? Who gets to decide what any company listed on the stock exchange is worth?

The real worth of these companies, one could argue, lies in the goods and services they produce and whether these goods and services enhance the lives of people such that they are willing to buy them in the marketplace. But people change their minds about what is of value to them, and sometimes this change can take place quite rapidly. The point is that wealth is more or less whatever the community says it is; wealth is not completely objective in nature. What something is worth does not reside in the product itself, nor does it lie in an individual consumer, but emerges from the interaction of millions of people who participate in the marketplace. Value is an emergent property that represents the judgments of millions of people who express their preferences through marketplace transactions. It is a community or common product rather than an individualistic and objective quality.

Value, then, is not something subjective housed either as a content of mind or in any other sense within the organism, but neither is it something "there" in an independently ordered universe. When we interact with objects in our natural or cultural environment, this interaction gives rise to qualities such as alluring or repugnant, fulfilling or stultifying, appealing or unappealing, and so forth. These qualities are real emergent properties that arise in the context of our interactions with our natural and cultural environments. These qualities are immediately experienced and are irreducible to other qualities and are as real in their emergence as the processes within which they emerge. Our value judgments make claims about the importance of promoting or not promoting the production of these qualities.

Values change, however, as our experience within nature and culture undergoes continual change. Some aspects of this experience are relatively stable, other aspects are unstable. Values can become problematic in certain situations. Humans have a strong desire to hold onto some values as a permanent basis of security in an uncertain world, and it is all too easy to focus on certain value aspects of experience and then falsely project them into an absolute, unchanging reality. Modern science challenges this view of values as absolute and claims that values are whatever an individual thinks or feels is valuable. Value is merely subjective and relative in this view and a highly individualistic affair, no more than a subjective feeling or matter of opinion.

However, as emergent properties, values are neither subjective nor objective, neither absolute nor relative; they are emergent in the ongoing course of experience. The experience of value is both shared and unique. Values are not experienced by the individual in isolation from a community nor are they to be put in conflict with or in opposition to community values. Yet community values are not merely the sum of individual values nor are individual values merely a reflection of community values. Instead, value in its emergence with everyday experience is a dimension of social experience. The adjustment between the shared and unique features of value gives rise to new dimensions of social change, brings creative solutions to the resolution of conflicting and changing value claims, and restructures the behavior and practices and institutionalized ways of behaving.

Thus the price of a stock represents the judgments of all the people who participate in the stock exchange as to the continued viability of a particular company. The price of a product represents the values of all the people who make a judgment about the usefulness of that product to themselves. This is the genius of market systems, as they allow for much more information to be exchanged and thus can come up with some level of wealth that represents the judgment of the community as a whole. Socialistic systems that did not allow this kind of information to be processed had trouble coming up with values that were workable such that the system could perform efficiently. This inefficiency eventually led to their downfall.

The invisible hand of Adam Smith, then, is not all that invisible. The interactions of millions of people in the marketplace give rise to values as to how much a company is worth or how much a given product is worth to consumers as a whole. These values represent wealth, economic wealth that we are able to quantify and count, which gives it a certain objective status. But this status is illusory; wealth is constantly changing as people's values change relative to what is important in their lives. This value dimension of human experience is what is most important, and it is what companies try to tap into with their products and marketing programs that try to create new values and new experiences that are valuable to consumers.

Economic wealth, then, is a community product. But communities are interested in much more than just economic wealth, as the people in those communities live out their lives in multiple contexts, with the economic system being one of their concerns. The community is also concerned about the state of its human resources, the health and educational level of its population, among other things. It is also concerned about the state of its culture and whether there are enough cultural activities for its people to enjoy. Society is also concerned about the state of the environment, its natural capital if you will, and whether this is being depleted or degraded significantly so that the long-term prospects of the community will be seriously affected. These are all aspects of a community's wealth, if you will, and notions about wealth need to be expanded beyond just economic wealth to take in more contexts and embrace the fullness and richness of human existence in its entirety.

GROWTH

Consistent with viewing capitalism as solely an economic system is the focus on economic growth or wealth creation as the be-all and end-all of society. Economic growth, measured in terms of production and consumption, is a moral end in itself, a self-justifying process that has a life of its own. Capitalistic societies have to keep growing economically; they have to keep producing more and more goods and services to keep going. People have to be encouraged to keep working at producing things and persuaded to keep buying the things they are producing. Capitalism is a never-ending cycle of production and consumption that has no end and keeps using up natural and human resources in a quest for continued economic growth. In a sense, capitalism has no reason for existing other than to continue the production of goods and services for consumption. As Adam Smith said, the wealth of nations consists of the goods and services they can produce for their citizens.

But if we view the economy as being embedded in a larger social system of which economics is only a part, it is legitimate to ask what larger purpose all this production and consumption serves. Supposedly it is to make people's lives better in some sense, but in many cases the focus on economic growth seems to be an intrusion into the search for meaningfulness and enrichment of life, which consists of multiple dimensions and is embedded in multiple environments. Yet people in capitalistic societies spend the majority of their lives in just the economic dimension, playing out their roles as producers with jobs in capitalistic institutions and as consumers in the marketplace, which is filled with ever more goods and services that promise an elusive fulfillment.

Viewing capitalism as a social system involves an understanding of growth that can provide direction for our productive and consumption activities in a manner that nourishes the desire of humans for a full and rich existence, the infusion of experience with meaningfulness and self-development and for the flourishing of the multiple environments in which they are embedded. This entails a radical rethinking that roots economic growth in a moral vision of human existence that provides production and consumption activities with moral direction rooted in the goal of the enhancement of human existence in all its richness and complexity. Economic growth is not an end in itself nor is it an unmitigated good in itself, but should be seen and evaluated in the total social context in which humans exist and how it enhances the life of the community.

With the pragmatic understanding of self and community, growth cannot be understood in terms of mere accumulation or mere increase of anything. Rather, growth involves the ongoing enhancement of experience to bring about the integration and expansion of the social contexts with which selfhood is intertwined. Growth is a process by which humans achieve fuller, richer, more inclusive, and more complex interactions with the multiple environments in which they are relationally embedded. To speak of economic development as enhancing the quality of life, while destroying the environments within which humans achieve ongoing growth, shows the abstract and nonrelational understanding of the self incorporated in the concept of economic development.

From the pragmatic perspective, economic growth is an abstraction from the complexity of a situation, and when economic growth stifles rather than furthers growth of the self and community, this indicates that economic growth is an abstraction that has become distortive of the fullness of the reality in which it is embedded. It is a fallacy to think that an abstract and quantified view of economics has an ontological independence from the qualitatively rich, value-laden reality from which the abstraction of a quantified economic system developed. This abstraction removes the economy from its moral purpose and makes it into a mechanistic reality that operates according to its own laws without any larger moral purpose. However, the moral purpose of the economic system is embedded in its nature as a dimension of ongoing growth of the self and community.

Alan Durning has written a book entitled *How Much Is Enough?*, in which he argues for the creation of what he calls the culture of permanence—a society that lives within its means as far as usage of resources is concerned and that seeks fulfillment in a web of friendship, family, and meaningful work. Yet he recognizes the difficulty of transforming consumption-oriented societies into sustainable ones and the problem that the material cravings of developing societies pose for resource usage. Reducing the consumption levels of consumer-oriented societies and tempering material aspirations elsewhere bucks the trend of centuries. Yet, according to Durning, it may be the only option if we are to live in a sustainable manner.[3]

Other questions have been posed, asking, "How good are goods?," implying that economic goods are not an unmitigated blessing.[4] These questions can only be answered in specific contexts, however, because goods and services are only as good as their contributions to the enrichment of human existence, and this always occurs in specific situations. Economic wealth can enslave people, as they spend more and more time worrying about their investments and have more and more goods to worry about, or wealth can offer further opportunities for ongoing growth. Too often, increased consumption serves as a desperate substitute for meaning and purpose, but such consumption can also offer possibilities for enhanced attunement to the esthetic-moral richness of human existence.

Too often in the contemporary world, the economy is pitted against the environment; we have to choose between continued economic growth at the expense of the environment, or we have to choose to enhance and pre-serve the environment at the expense of economic growth. This choice is an artificially created alternative, however, which distorts the very nature of the richness of the reality that both the environment and the economy ulti-mately serve. The protection of the environment and economic growth are inextricably joined through their dependency on the esthetic-moral nature of growth, as involving the ongoing integration and expansion of multiple contexts in their full qualitative richness. Human development is connected with its ecological as well as its economic context. The deepening and expansion of perspective to include ever-widening horizons must extend beyond the economic to the natural world, with which we are inseparably intertwined.

If a holistic approach to growth is taken, the collision course between the economy and the environment could be undercut. Reduction of consump-tion in industrial societies can have severe repercussions. Since about two-thirds of gross national product or its equivalent in developed countries consists of consumer purchases, any severe reduction of consumer expendi-tures would have serious implications for employment, income, investment and everything else tied to economic growth. Lower consumption could be destructive to advanced industrial societies. Yet if consumption is not reduced, ecological forces may eventually dismantle advanced societies in ways we can't control and that would be even more destructive.[5]

What seems to be necessary to deal with these kinds of problems is a new moral consciousness that can guide production and consumption in ways that allow for the ongoing development of human existence in its entirety. Economic and environmental policies must constantly be evaluated in terms of their contribution to this goal. If this change in moral consciousness can be brought about, consumers in industrial societies may begin to curtail the use of those things that are ecologically destructive and instead cultivate the deeper nonmaterial sources of fulfillment, which writers like Durning claim are the main psychological determinants of happiness, such as family, social relationships, meaningful work, and leisure. In this way, economic growth could be directed toward furthering the development of pathways that accommodate the ongoing enrichment of these human needs.

To accomplish this goal, there must be a reversal of the long, gradual evolution of the severing of the economy from its moral foundation, which led to the establishment of production and consumption as ends in them-selves and to an acquisitive society that sees growth as the accumulation of more and more economic wealth. These destructive abstractions must be returned to the moral ground of growth of the self and community, which ultimately gives them meaning and vitality. What is needed is a new moral milieu, a new moral/cultural consciousness that undercuts the chasm between the economy and the environment as well as other contexts in which humans live and work out a meaningful existence.

RIGHTS

As stated in a previous chapter, capitalism is based on an understanding of humans that is individualistic in nature, and rights theories focus on abstract, individualistic humans with rights that join together by entering into contracts that bind them through external ties, contracts that require they give up certain absolute rights. Thus any kind of community or society is always in some sense an infringement on these rights that are rooted in the individual and a conflict between individual rights and community interests is inevitable. This view is pervasive in the literature about rights, as chronicled by Alan Gewirth in his work on the interrelation between rights and community.

> In one of the main modes of interpretation, to focus on rights in moral and political philosophy entails giving consideration to individuals conceived as atomic entities existing independent of social ties, while to focus instead on community is to regard persons as having inherent affective social relations to one another . . . According to these views, rights presuppose competition and conflict, since rights are intended as guarantees that self-seeking individuals will not be trampled in their adversarial relations with one another. Community, on the other hand, connotes the absence of such conflicts; it signifies common interests and cooperation, mutual sympathy and fellow-feeling. As a result, it is charged that the rights doctrine atomizes society and alienates persons from one another. But when persons maintain the ties of community that make for social harmony, there is no need for rights . . . The claiming of rights, then, is egoistic and antithetical to morality and community.[6]

Gewirth does point out that a more affirmative relation between rights and community has been offered by some scholars, but he doubts that they interpret "community" in the extensively cooperative, mutualistic sense that undercuts the asserted opposition between community and rights. Indeed, the author sketches the way in which the relations between rights and community developed by these scholars does not imply community in any important sense at all.[7] Thus there is a need to reconceptualize the notion of rights so that they are not in opposition to community and do not result in conflict between the individual and community.

The pragmatic reconceptualization of rights theory offers a new approach to rights and the social contracts in which they are usually rooted, a reconceptualization in which rights and community are not only compatible but also inextricably interwoven. From the pragmatic perspective, it can be said that what is more "natural" to humans is not absolute individual rights but contractual rights. However, this does not mean simply that individuals are born into societies that have been already formed, at least in theory, through a social contract involving the original participants. Nor does this view mean that rights are merely the result of government legislation or contractual agreements. Finally, it does not mean that abstract principles can be substituted for caring attunement to concrete situations and the individuals involved.

Rather, what the pragmatic view of rights intends to point out is that the "natural" state of being human is to be relationally tied to others and that apart from the dynamics of community there can be no individual rights, since individuals emerge within and develop in the context of community. Thus in the very having of rights, one has community obligations. These are two sides of the same coin. There can be no absolute individual rights because the need for adjustment between novelty and constraint is built into the internal structure of the self in the form of the I-me dynamics. The self consists of a creative ongoing interpretive interplay between the individual and social perspective.

Freedom of the self, then, lies in the proper relation between these two dimensions, and as stressed earlier, does not lie in opposition to the restrictions of norms and authority, but in a self-direction that requires the proper dynamic interaction of these two dimensions of the self. Freedom does not lie in being unaffected by others, but in the way one uses one's incorporation of the "other" in novel decisions and actions. As Mead states, this dynamic interrelationship provides one with "the ability to talk to oneself in terms of the community to which one belongs and lay upon oneself the responsibilities that belong to the community; the ability to admonish oneself as others would, and to recognize what are one's duties as well as one's rights."[8]

Given the dynamics of the self in pragmatic philosophy, these responsibilities have resulted not just from the internalization of the attitudes of the generalized other but from the effect on these attitudes by the past responses of one's own creative input. Not only is one's creative individuality not enslaved by or determined by the generalized other, but the generalized other has been formed in part from one's own creative acts. This generalized other, as stressed previously, is neither an absolute other nor an abstract other, but the other as part and parcel of the dynamics of selfhood and the community life in which the self is enmeshed.

Individual rights are thus also social rights; rights are inherently relational. There are no purely individual rights, but there are rights relations, and all rights relations involve both entitlement and obligation. Ongoing community adjustments, then, must be understood not as pitting the individual armed with rights against the common other that limits rights, but rather as community attempts to find the proper balance between the relational poles of entitlements and obligations, neither of which can function without the other.

A free society, like a free individual, requires this balance. In this way, the good of the whole is not the good of the commons or group other over against the individual. The good of the whole is the proper relation between the individual and the common other, because the whole is community and community encompasses the individual and the common other. If rights are understood as an individual possession upon which society infringes, pitting one individual against another or pitting the individual against the group, then rights will lead to self-interested factionalism and adversarial relationships rather than communal cooperation. As Dewey notes, "the principle of authority" must not be understood as "purely restrictive power" but as providing direction.[9]

The pragmatic position holds that humans are born into implicit contractual arrangements and grounds autonomy, solidarity, and fairness in the communal nature of human existence. Moreover, pragmatism recognizes the growth of each person as both a means for community development and as the end or goal of community development. Each human is neither a means to something else nor an end in itself, but is both contributor and recipient in a reciprocal relationship. Means are contributions to wholes or ends in which they are ingredients, and every ending is at once a new beginning of new possibilities to be fulfilled. There is no separation of means and ends. Everything has both relational and immediate qualities, instrumental and consummatory properties. The moral worth of the flourishing of the individual is inseparable from the moral worth of the flourishing of the human community.

One of the key insights of social contract/rights theory is its voluntary nature. Thomas Donaldson, in an insightful overview of various social contract theories and their basic differences, points out that "amid the various versions of the social contract theory a common strand exists: an emphasis on the *consent* of the parties."[10] Although humans are born into implicit contractual arrangements, acceptance of contracts is nonetheless voluntary within the pragmatic framework; the type of reciprocal relationships that the developing self incorporates is not imposed from without but internalized by the free, creative activity of the "I" that enters into the self-structuring of the "me" and the restructuring of the generalized other. Stated differently, the nature of the self requires internalization of the perspective of the other. Obligations resulting from rule-driven abstract conceptions of external claims are very different from caring attuned relationships based on the internalization of the perspective of the other.[11] One cannot internalize any right without internalizing a corresponding obligation, for what is being internalized is inherently relational.

Thus while one cannot escape the relational nature of human existence and the rights relation that is part of its dynamics, one can escape particular rights relations, including those into which one is born. Particular rights relations must be morally evaluated and will carry different moral weight depending on the role of these relations in providing enriching growth of community and the selves involved in community dynamics. Since the natural state of human existence is community existence, then the "natural rights" of the human should include the ability to participate in community. The natural rights of community existence, then, would seem to demand the right both to individual autonomy and of participation in the development of social authority. And this right of each individual is inextricably tied to the obligation of each individual to provide this right for all members of the community. The demand for freedom is the demand to move from narrow restrictive rights to those that allow for ongoing growth.

According to the pragmatic position, then, the relational nature of rights emerges within the reciprocal relation of rights and obligations inherent in community dynamics. Natural rights are natural precisely because they allow us to participate in the relational dynamics constitutive of the nature of human existence. It is the dimensions of freedom and constraint, rights and obligations, self and other, all embedded in the nature of the self and community alike, which give rise to the situational and relational nature of rights. Rather than pit one individual against another or the individual against the group, rights and their corresponding obligations can actually help tie communities together and enable them to reach the necessary compromises that contribute to ongoing community growth.

What does this view of rights mean for property rights, which, as mentioned in an earlier chapter, help to form the philosophical basis of modern capitalism? According to the theory of John Locke, when natural objects are taken out of a state of nature and mixed with human labor, those objects become the property of the individual. While things in a state of nature belong to everyone in common, when they are made useful the person or persons who mixed their labor with them have a natural right to possess them as their own. Government exists to protect this natural right to property and cannot take this property away without consent from the appropriate individuals involved.

However, property does not exist in a vacuum; it exists in a social and cultural context. It is the community as a whole, whether explicitly or implicitly, that decides that the best way to organize the commons to promote growth of the community is to allow individuals to have control over certain aspects of the commons and use it in the way they see fit within certain limitations. The commons is prior to the individual and can be organized in whatever way the community decides. Some cultures have no notion of property rights, and what we would call stealing is called borrowing in this cultural context. In market societies, allowing individuals to have control over some aspect of the commons seems to be the best way to promote the efficient use of nature's resources and better the lot of the community as a whole.

Individuals have to pay property taxes to support functions, like public education, that the community deems important. Since pollution and noise do not respect property boundaries, these have to be regulated by the community in the interests of those who are adversely affected. The community can take property for public purposes, like roads and the like, as long as the owner is fairly compensated. In a democratic society, the state cannot act arbitrarily and take property without fair compensation and without giving individuals a chance to have a voice in these decisions. These notions change over time, as currently municipalities can condemn property to use for purposes that were not foreseen even a few years ago, such as allowing higher-priced dwellings or commercial interests to use it, which will bring in more revenue to the municipality. The Supreme Court narrowly upheld this practice, which is a new interpretation of the "takings clause" of the constitution.

Thus the right to property is not a natural right; it is a right that arises in a community context and reflects the values of that community. It is believed that if individuals have control over property they will use it more efficiently than some kind of social ownership, and this increased efficiency will benefit the community as a whole. The abolishment of private property in socialistic systems did not lead to greater efficiency and did not benefit the community, but seemed to benefit only those who were in control of the bureaucracy that made decisions about the use of property. It was not an efficient system nor did it promote distributive justice in the allocation of the goods and services the system did produce. These systems by and large collapsed, as people became less interested in ideology and more interested in their material betterment.

Thus wealth, growth, and rights are reinterpreted from a pragmatic perspective to correspond with a social view of the self and community, where capitalism is seen as a social system to enhance the multiple dimensions of human existence. It is not just an economic system that focuses on the creation of economic wealth, the enhancement of economic growth, and the promotion of individual's right to use property in his or her own interests with no obligation to the community. Capitalism is much more than this and can be viewed as a system that enhances the efficient use of resources available to the community to enrich the total existence of the community in which individuals are embedded. Viewing capitalism in this manner means the multiple environments in which humans exist must be enhanced rather than exploited in the interests of promoting a narrow focus only on economic growth and wealth creation.

8 The Market System

The view of the self and community described earlier also has implications for the way we think about the market system and what functions it performs in society. While many may think that capitalism and the market can be used interchangeably in that they are basically the same thing, this is not necessarily the case. Capitalism refers to a system where capital, namely the means of production, the factories, shops and everything else necessary for the production and distribution of goods and services, are privately owned. Financial capital necessary for the financing of capitalistic enterprises is also provided through private means rather than by the government or some other public body. As such the capitalists, the owners of the means of production, stand to reap the bulk of the rewards that the system can generate.

The market, on the other hand, refers to a system through which decisions are made about what goods and services to produce, in what quantities they are to be produced, and what prices can be charged and other decisions of this nature. In a market system, these decisions are made by millions of individuals who participate in one way or another in the market, either as consumers, producers, investors, or other such roles that are critical to the operation of a market system. In a planned economy, these decisions are made by some government bureaucracy, but in a market system they are made by individuals. The market then coordinates these individual decisions into a collective demand schedule of some sort that guides corporate activities and in this sense acts as a planning mechanism to guide corporate behavior.

This distinction raises some interesting questions. For example, can one have a capitalistic system without a market system, i.e., private ownership of the means of production coupled with some kind of planning system, or a market system without a capitalistic system, i.e., social ownership of the means of production coupled with a traditional market system? Or are the capitalistic and market systems inextricably intertwined? This is something of a philosophical question, as history offers us no clear examples. But it does provide us with some evidence that may be useful in answering these questions.

The former Soviet Union abolished private property consistent with Marxist theory and also instituted a planning system to formally answer the critical economic questions of what to produce and so forth. The system ultimately proved to be unworkable, as it was both corrupt and inefficient and was incapable of being reformed, and, with a little push from the outside, it collapsed under its own weight. It was believed that there was a rational way to determine what to produce and in what quantities, and assign prices accordingly, and that this could be done by a government bureaucracy. But there is no way to make these decisions according to some rational calculus; they are value questions that cannot be determined by some rational, mathematical system.

In Yugoslavia immediately after WWII, a different system was implemented that many believe was a truer manifestation of communism than was the Soviet Union's system. Social ownership of the means of production was again instituted, but instead of a government bureaucracy making economic decisions, individual factories were under the control of a Worker's Council, consisting of elected representatives from all areas of the enterprise. These elected representatives were given training in economics, finance, marketing, and other areas of the business if they needed it, so they could make more intelligent decisions. However, these factories functioned in a market system rather than a planned economy, and what happened over time is that management took control of many of these enterprises despite their democratic structure. This became necessary because the Worker's Council proved to be too slow in making decisions, and a strong management emerged in many of these situations that could make quick decisions to take advantage of market opportunities. This experience raises another interesting question, namely, is the important element here not who actually owns the capital resources but rather who controls them? This question will be discussed in the chapter on corporate governance. In this chapter, we want to look at how a market system actually functions as a social mechanism.

THE FUNCTIONING OF A MARKET SYSTEM

At the heart of a market system is an *exchange* process, where goods and services are traded between the parties to a particular transaction. In a situation where bartering is involved and money is not used, goods and services are exchanged directly for other goods and services. When money is involved, it serves as an intermediate store of value, in that goods and services are sold for money and this same money can then be used to purchase other goods and services immediately or at some time in the future. Money has little or no value in and of itself but is valued for what it represents and for what it can purchase. The use of money greatly facilitates exchange over a barter type of economy and greatly increases the possible number of exchange transactions.

Thus in the market all kinds of exchanges between people and institutions are continually taking place. People exchange their labor for wages or salaries and in turn exchange this money for goods and services that are available on the market. Investors exchange money for new stock or bond issues in a corporation, which exchanges this money for purchases of raw materials or new plants and equipment. Farmers exchange their produce for money, which may be used to buy new farm machinery or seed for the next planting.

Decisions as to whether to exchange one thing for another are made by individuals and institutions acting in their own self-interest and based on what they think the entities being exchanged are worth to themselves. People decide whether the item they are considering is of sufficient value to them to warrant the sacrifice of something they already have, like money, that is also of value to them. Exchanges will not normally occur unless there is an increase in value for both parties to the exchange. The exchange process is usually a positive sum game, as both parties to the exchange believe themselves to be better off as a result.

Based on these individual market decisions, resources are allocated according to individual preferences for one kind of merchandise over another, one job over another, the stock of one corporation over another, and so forth across the entire range of choices the market offers. The value of particular goods and services emerges from these decisions and resources are allocated for the production of these goods and services according to these decisions. Enough people have to demand a particular good or service in order for it to be produced on a large enough scale so that it is affordable.

However, people are not just expressing their individual preferences through the exchange process, as the market is more than just the sum of these preferences. People are also creating a way of life for themselves through their choices on the market; they are expressing who they are and who they want to become. They are in some sense creating a future that they find attractive and believe the goods and services they choose to purchase on the market can contribute to this future. Thus there is a community aspect to these choices, as they are synthesized by the market, as participation in the exchange process creates a certain kind of community where people have to conform to certain rules for the market to work but also change what the market offers them through their individual decisions.

The nature of the goods and services exchanged on the market are *private* in the sense that they can be purchased and used by individuals or persons or institutions for their own purposes. They become the private property of the persons or institutions that attain them and are of such a nature that they do not have to be shared with anyone else. The goods and services exchanged in the market are thus divisible into individual units and can be totally consumed and enjoyed by the people or institutions who obtain the property rights to them.

Thus one can buy a house, car, or a piece of furniture, and these items become one's property to use and enjoy for one's own purposes. People can also contract for or purchase certain services and expect these services to be provided. The legal system supports property rights and enables persons and institutions to enforce these rights if necessary to protect their property from unwanted encroachment by others. This social and legal arrangement provides a degree of security regarding property and forces individuals and institutions to respect the property rights of others. Thus property rights can be assigned to the goods and services exchanged in the market because of their divisibility into individual units that can be privately owned and consumed.

Whatever value emerges from the exchange of goods and services in the market has to be expressed in common economic units or a *common economic value system* for exchange to take place. The worth of an individual's labor, the worth of a particular product or service, and the worth of a share of stock has to be expressed in economic terms, dollars and cents in our society, pounds in another. This is not to suggest that the fundamental value of everything is economic in nature. One person may value a particular automobile because of the status it confers, another may value a particular work of art because of the aesthetic pleasure it provides. However, for exchange to occur where money is involved, these other values must be translated into the economic units of value that are operative in that society.

An economic value system thus serves as a common denominator in that the worth of everything exchanged on the market can be expressed in a common unit of exchange. This facilitates exchanges and makes it possible for individuals to assess the worth of a good or service to them more easily than if such a common denominator were not present. People can make an informal benefit-cost analysis when making a decision in the marketplace by comparing the benefits a good or service will provide with the costs involved in acquiring the good or service. People enter a store, for example, with money they have earned or will earn and can assess the price of things they are interested in buying by comparing the benefits these goods will provide them with the real costs (the effort involved in earning the money to buy them) of attaining them. Because both sides of this benefit-cost equation are expressed in the same units, this assessment can be made rather easily.

This common value system allows a society to allocate its resources according to the collective preferences of its members. The diverse values that emerge in the exchange process are aggregated through the market system into a collective demand schedule facing corporations. If a particular product is not valued very highly by many people, aggregate demand for that product will not be very high and its price will have to be low for it to be sold if it can be sold at all. Thus not many resources will be used for its production, and it may eventually disappear from the market altogether.

Depending on general economic conditions, if a particular job is valued very highly by society and if the people who can perform that job are scarce relative to demand, the wage or salary paid to perform the job will have to be high to attract people to it. Resources are thus allocated according to the values of society as they emerge through the exchange process. Resources will go where the price, wage or salary, or return on investment is highest, all other things being equal, and are thus allocated where they can be combined to produce the greatest economic wealth for society compared with other alternatives.

In a market economy, people are free to buy and use property, to choose their occupation, and to strive for economic gain as they wish, subject to limitations that may be necessary to protect the rights of others to do the same thing. Society may also place limitations on the use of property and choice of occupation because of moral standards or other reasons considered important enough to override market forces. The selling of drugs, for example, is illegal in this country even though a huge market for them exists. The same is true of other uses of property for purposes that are not seen as contributing to the welfare of society.

The pursuit of *self-interest* is assumed to be a universal principle of human behavior that is a more powerful motivator than the pursuit of other interests. The pursuit of one's own interests is believed to elicit far more energy and creativity than would the pursuit of someone else's interests or the interest of the state, especially under coercive conditions. Not only is it difficult to ascertain the interests of others, it is often difficult to find a way to sustain a high level of motivation if much of the effort one expends benefits others.

The determination of what is in one's interest is not provided by government in a market economy but by each individual participating in the exchange process. If the self-interest of an individual were defined by someone else, the concept would lose all meaning. Self-interest is an individual concept in one sense, yet within a market system the definition of self-interest is not entirely individualistic in nature nor is it completely arbitrary depending on the whims of each individual. The existence of a common underlying economic value system gives the definition of self-interest a certain economic rationality.

If one is engaged in the market system, economic rationality dictates that self-interest take a certain form that involves maximization of one's return on his or her investment. Corporations are expected to maximize profits, investors to maximize their return in the stock market, and sellers of labor to obtain the most advantageous terms for themselves. Consumers are expected to maximize satisfaction to themselves through their purchases of goods and services in the marketplace. If people were to do otherwise, it would not lead to the maximization of wealth for the society as a whole. Thus self-interest is tied to community interest, as the community as a whole has an interest in using its scarce resources wisely and obtaining the maximum benefit it can from their usage. Society does not want to waste its resources by using them inefficiently, nor do the individuals who make up that society. Thus in the final analysis these interests are a social product rather than individualistic in nature.

Resources are allocated by an *"invisible hand"* according to Adam Smith, which is something of a mythological concept. But the point of this metaphor is that government should not be making decisions for society about what goods and services get produced and in what quantities and allocate resources accordingly. These decisions are made by individuals who participate in the marketplace and express their preferences based on self-interest. These preferences are aggregated by the market and, if strong enough relative to particular goods and services, elicit a response from the productive mechanism of society to supply the goods and services desired.

The invisible hand consists of the forces of supply and demand that result from the aggregation of individual decisions by producers and consumers in the marketplace. Resources are allocated to their most productive use as defined by these decisions collectively. From these decisions, values emerge relative to the worth of particular goods and services that are available on the marketplace. Society as a whole benefits from this kind of resource allocation, as the pursuit of self-interest without outside interference is believed to result in the greatest good for the greatest number. Thus from an ethical perspective, the system is given something of a utilitarian justification.

The most important role in a market system is arguably the role of consumer, because consumers are supposed to be sovereign over the system. What such *consumer sovereignty* means is that consumers through their choices guide the productive apparatus of society and collectively decide what kind of goods and services get produced and in what quantities. When enough demand exists for a product, resources will be allocated for its production. If there is not enough demand, the product will not be produced and resources will go elsewhere.

Consumer sovereignty is not to be confused with consumer choice. In any society, consumers have a choice to purchase or not purchase the products that are available in the marketplace. Consumer choice exists in a totally planned economy. Consumer sovereignty, however, implies that the array of goods and services with which consumers are confronted is also a function of their decisions and not the decisions of a central planning authority. Consumers are ultimately sovereign over the entire system.

Some would argue that consumer sovereignty in today's marketplace is a fiction and that consumers are manipulated by advertising, packaging, promotional campaigns, and other sales techniques to buy a particular product. Sometimes this manipulation is said to be so subtle that the consumer is unaware of the factors influencing his or her decision. Thus the demand function itself, so it is maintained, has come under the control of corporations and consumer sovereignty is a myth. Producers are sovereign over the entire system and consumers are manipulated to respond to the producer's decisions about what to produce.[1]

Although these views may hold some truth, they do not tell the whole story. It is hard to believe that consumers are totally manipulated by these techniques such that their decision-making power is taken over by corporations. It would seem that consumers must still make choices among competing products, and the producers selling these products are each trying to manipulate the consumer. In the final analysis, the individual consumer remains responsible for his or her decision and undoubtedly many factors other than the particular sales techniques used by a producer influence the purchase decision. In the absence of a central authority to make production decisions for society, it is safe to assume that some degree of consumer sovereignty exists. As long as competing products or acceptable substitutes exist, some products may not sell well enough to justify continued production. Thus they disappear from the marketplace, not because producers desire to remove them, but because consumers have decided not to buy them in sufficient quantities.

The reason products disappear when they do not sell is that there is no profit to be made. Profits are the lifeblood of a business organization, and without sufficient profits a business organization normally cannot survive. Profits are a reward to the business organization for the risks that have been taken in bringing a good or service to the market. If the management of a business organization guesses wrong and produces something people do not want and cannot be persuaded to buy, the market is a stern taskmaster, as no rewards will be received for this effort.

Profits are also a reward for combining resources efficiently to be able to meet or beat the competition in producing a product for which there is a demand. Some companies may be able to pay lower wages or employ a more efficient technology or have some other competitive advantage. Thus a lower price can be charged and high-cost producers are driven from the market. This effort is rewarded with increased profits, as society benefits from having its resources used more efficiently.

The *profit motive* is thus an important component of a market system. Producers are motivated to bring goods and services to the market in the hopes of reaping a profit for the organization. But making a profit is not necessarily what a business is all about. Profits are like breathing is to an organism. Breathing is necessary for the organism to continue in existence, but the organism does not exist solely to breathe. Thus profits are necessary but not sufficient in terms of justification for an organization's existence. If a business organization has done something that benefits society, profits will follow, all other things being equal. If a manager focuses solely on making a profit and loses sight of the larger purpose of his or her organization, which is to enrich the community in which the organization is embedded, this can be a problem for both the organization and society.

COMPETITION

Competition is obviously an important component of the market system and essential to its functioning, but the nature of competition deserves a section in its own right. In a market system, companies compete with each other, products compete with other products, and people compete for the jobs that are available. Competition keeps people on their toes, so to speak, as they need to be concerned about gaining a position they do not have or about losing the position they do have to a better competitor. Competition is also seen as something of a regulatory device that puts constraints on individual egos and prevents any one business organization from attaining a monopoly position, which would give it undue power in the market system. Such a monopoly would give a company the ability to set its prices and output based on general economic conditions rather than market forces, and would result in an inefficient allocation of resources. The company in such a position would have a strong tendency to sit on its laurels, so to speak, and not strive to introduce new and better products into the marketplace.

The ideal form of competition is pure competition, where the industry is not concentrated, where there are insignificant barriers to entry, and where no product differentiation exists. In this kind of competition, the individual firm has no other choice but to meet the competition, since buyers and sellers are so small that they have no influence over the market, thus ensuring that the forces of supply and demand alone determine market outcomes. In this kind of situation, competition will cause resources to be allocated in the most efficient manner, thus minimizing the cost of products and benefiting the consumer.

Markets are not perfectly competitive, however, as there are many problems with competition in the real world that have to be dealt with in order to keep the system going and make it function to the benefit of society as a whole. In practice, unregulated markets tend toward concentration, as competition in any industry is never perfectly balanced. If the object of firms is to win out over competitors, the natural expectation is that eventually one or a few firms will come to dominate the industries in which they compete because they were better competitors or were lucky enough to be in the right place at the right time with the right products. Thus most industries in today's economy are oligopolistic, containing a few large firms, which recognize the impact of their actions on rivals and therefore on the market as a whole.

Modern large corporations are not simply passive responders to the impersonal forces of supply and demand over which they have no control. These large firms do have some degree of economic power and some influence over the marketplace. They have some ability to control markets by the reduction of competition through merging with other firms in the industry to attain a larger market share and thus come to dominate the industry. Markets may also fail if the dominant firms in an industry are allowed to engage in collusive actions to maintain prices or interfere with the workings of supply and demand and the price mechanism in some other fashion. For these reasons, the society saw fit to establish antitrust laws to deal with these problems.

The purpose of these antitrust laws is to limit the economic power of large corporations that can control markets by reducing competition through concentration. The role of these laws is to maintain something called a "workable competition" on the theory that resources are allocated more efficiently and prices are lower in a competitive system than one dominated by large corporations. Workable competition refers to a system where there is reasonably free entry into most markets, no more than moderate concentration, and an ample number of buyers and sellers in most markets. The government tries to accomplish this goal by enforcing policies that deal with the conduct of corporations and the structure of the industries in which they function.

The competitive process is not a natural process that maintains itself indefinitely through the forces of supply and demand. It is not some mechanistic process that automatically holds the economic power of corporations in check through forces that are beyond the control of any economic actor. Managers do not necessarily like competition and do everything they can to drive competitors out of business. This is the name of the game, and it seems obvious that some corporations are going to be more successful than others and attain an ever-increasing market share that gives them more power to dictate the terms of the trade. Competition is something society strives to maintain because it is a commonly held value that the society views as essential for the enhancement of its welfare. The realization of this value is an achievement of society, not a naturally given fact embedded in a certain kind of economic system.

Perhaps some examples will help to make this point more effectively. Standard Oil Company was one of the first companies to feel the effect of antitrust laws. The petroleum industry that emerged after the Civil War was characterized by numerous small firms competing vigorously in an "anything goes" atmosphere. The result was a wildly fluctuating market where there were perennial imbalances between supply and demand. These imbalances caused both producers and refiners to seek ways of stabilizing their positions to reduce waste in the production and distribution process. However, voluntary efforts at cooperation, such as informal agreements, fell apart under the pressure of competition. It took a John D. Rockefeller to successfully analyze and manipulate this situation in order to gain control of the whole industry and mitigate competitive pressures.[2]

With the collapse of the National Refiners Association in 1872, which was created to control price and production in the oil industry, Rockefeller and his associates decided to bring a large part of the oil industry directly under their control. The trusteeship device allowed them to set up separate operating companies in several states with a central legal entity to direct the entire combination. The Standard Oil Trust Agreement of 1882 established such a trust to be the sole and central holding agency for all the securities of 41 participating investors in 40 named companies. This agreement vested the original nine trustees (a third of them were to be elected annually) with centralized administrative control over the operating companies, including the buying, transportation, storing, refining, and marketing of petroleum.[3]

Standard Oil grew into a multimillion-dollar integrated industrial enterprise, dominating its industry for many years. Standard Oil was the first enterprise to take this route and become a modern industrial business corporation by creating a structure that allowed administrative centralization over a vast empire.[4] Eventually, however, the federal government found Standard Oil guilty of violating Sections I and II of the Sherman Antitrust Act of 1890, which had been passed by a Congress concerned about the use of the trust device to create huge industrial empires controlled by one or a few persons.

It was believed that competition was disappearing as a regulator of business behavior, as more and more combinations were taking place in several industries, and that the country needed a law that gave the government power to break up those combinations that were especially onerous in order to protect the public and preserve a competitive system. Standard Oil was found guilty of creating a conspiracy to restrain trade and of attempting to monopolize an entire industry. The trust was ordered to be dissolved into several separate companies.[5]

A more recent case involved Microsoft Corporation, which was founded by Bill Gates in 1975 and became one of the most powerful companies in the world. Its most successful product is its Windows Operating System, which at one time held about 90 percent of the operating system market. It was this dominance and the way it was used that brought the company into conflict with the antitrust authorities. The government became concerned that Microsoft was using its Windows monopoly to dominate other markets and that the company had to be reined in, lest it gain a chokehold on further software developments. The underlying problem was Microsoft's ongoing practice of rolling new features into its operating systems, a process that made each new version of Windows better and more powerful.[6] Because computer users are essentially locked into Windows, it was easy for the company to get them to use its other software even if competitors made better products. This practice was called "bundling" and was said to dampen competition, reduce choices for consumers, and retard innovation in the industry.

The government pressed hard for a breakup of the company, similar to what had happened with Standard Oil, but the agreement eventually reached was not so drastic and not the bellwether case many had hoped for. The settlement did not do much in providing directions regarding the way in which antitrust law will be applied to so-called new economy companies. Under terms of the agreement, Microsoft had to give computer makers more freedom to choose software made by other companies and to share more technical information about Windows with rivals so they could design programs to run on the operating system. Other provisions were aimed at preventing Microsoft from retaliating against PC makers that did not favor the company's products.[7]

The agreement did not, however, prevent Microsoft from using its monopoly position to expand into new lines of business by bundling more application programs into Windows. Nor did the agreement force Microsoft to turn over its source code to competitors.[8] Since Microsoft still had a monopoly with its operating system, it could extend this monopoly power into other areas and effectively shut out competition for this business. Since there has been no direct impact on consumers because of this practice, in that prices for its operating system do not seem to be unreasonable, questions were raised about the impact on innovation that may result from this practice. There are certainly benefits in having one operating system that is the standard of the industry, but the power that this dominance gives to a company can be abused. The line between what constitutes abuse and what is honest and fair competition is constantly shifting and needs to be examined on a case-by-case basis.

Another feature of competition is that competitive behavior tends to sink to the lowest common denominator in an unregulated market system. If the object is to win in terms of market share or profits or some other economic indicator, there is always likely to be one or more competitors that will engage in predatory or questionable practices in an effort to emerge as the sole victor. If these practices allow the perpetrator to succeed, they will have to be engaged in by all competitors if they are to stay in business and remain competitive. If these practices continue long enough, they may eventually destroy the competitive system.

Perhaps a comparison with professional football would be useful in understanding this problem. If there were no rules and no one to enforce them on the field, some teams would most likely do anything they could to win games. They would hold defensive linemen to keep them from getting to the quarterback, defensive linemen would try to hit the quarterback long after the play was dead and hope to injure them, defensive backs would interfere with wide receivers any way they could to prevent them from catching the football, and other such practices. If these tactics resulted in winning football games, other teams would have to engage in the same behavior to stay competitive, even if they found some of these tactics offensive. The game would then degenerate into a free-for-all that nobody would want to watch. Thus there are rules to keep the game "honest" and referees and line judges to enforce them. The rules are changed from time to time to plug loopholes that develop as the game changes and to keep the game interesting for customers.

A good example of this process at work in the business world comes from the late 1980s, when consumers were inundated with a good deal of hype about oat bran, all-bran cereals, lite foods, and other foods that had certain characteristics that were supposedly going to make people healthier. Reputable companies such as General Mills and Kellogg's jumped on the bandwagon and made exaggerated claims about what their product would do to lower cholesterol levels and reduce the risk of heart attacks. Other companies advertised their products as having half the calories of previous servings by reducing their product to half its previous size, thus deceiving consumers in the process. Consumers were legitimately confused about all these health claims and had no way to determine the truth of these advertisements.[9]

The anything-goes era regarding health advertising began in 1987, when the Food and Drug Administration, under pressure from industry and the Reagan administration, abandoned a 90-year-old rule barring all health assertions from food advertisements. Manufacturers were then free to start making claims about what their products would do to prevent disease and promote health. Prior to this change, the FDA held that any product that claimed it could prevent or treat diseases had to be considered a drug and be subjected to the high levels of scientific proof needed to declare a drug safe and effective. As a result of this change, 40 percent of new products and a third of the $3.6 billion worth of food advertising in 1989 trumpeted such messages. Manufacturers proclaimed the disease-preventing qualities of items as diverse as fruit juice, breakfast cereal, and margarine.[10]

Finally, under pressure from consumer groups and government agencies, the government issued new food labeling rules in late 1992 that would carry out the 1990 Nutrition Labeling and Education Act passed by Congress. The rules took effect in 1994 and required all processed foods to show calories, total fat, saturated fat, cholesterol, sodium, carbohydrates, and protein in the context of a daily diet of 2,000 calories and 65 grams of fat. Serving sizes were also made uniform and designations such as "low-fat," "high-fiber," and "light" were based on federally imposed definitions.[11] The intent of the rules was to force food manufacturers to disclose what is in their products in a uniform manner, so that shoppers could make valid comparisons between competing products.

To deal with these situations, the government thus passes laws that deal with corporate conduct, and the structure of the industries in which they do business, as was done in the Standard Oil situation. These laws promote fair competition, by making certain forms of what are considered to be anticompetitive practices illegal, and by institutionalizing a concern with the structure of certain industries by giving the government the power to file suit against monopolies, such as Microsoft, if necessary and to block mergers that would reduce competition. Certain practices, such as price fixing and tying arrangements, would eventually destroy the system if allowed to continue and destroy trust in the fairness of competition. Monopoly power gives a corporation the potential to abuse that power to maintain its dominant position, and society does not trust this kind of power to be used in society's best interest.

A system of checks and balances is necessary to keep the free market functioning effectively, just as such a system is necessary to keep a democracy functioning effectively. The business community itself has a common interest in keeping the competitive system going. No matter how strongly various members of this community may object to specific legislative and regulatory requirements and decisions by the courts, they all hold the common value of maintaining a competitive system and doing what is necessary to keep the game going. They have no interest in letting the game degenerate into a free-for-all where anything goes and the system eventually is destroyed. Determining what is necessary to keep the competitive system going is an ongoing enterprise involving the entire society.

MARKET DEFICIENCIES

There are certain goods and services, however, where the market does not work, so that decisions about these goods and services have to be made in some other manner. These are called public goods and services and are of a different nature than the goods and services traded on the market as described earlier. One example of a public good that is often mentioned is national defense, something that is provided by government for all its citizens that cannot be provided by the citizens themselves. National defense is not something that can be purchased on the market, as it is not divisible into individual units that can then be exchanged on the market. People cannot buy their own little piece of national defense, if they want it, and use it for their own purposes. The government decides what amount of money to pay for this good or service and then taxes its citizens to pay for it, and thus everyone is provided roughly the same amount of national defense.

Pollution is generally considered to be an externality in the economics literature, defined as either a beneficial or detrimental (pollution is detrimental) effect on third parties, like a homeowner who lives close to a polluting factory, who is not involved in the transactions between the principals (customer and producer) who caused the pollution because of their activities in the marketplace. Yet the results of pollution control, such as clean air and water, are more appropriately called public goods, as they are entities with beneficial characteristics for human health that are widely shared in different amounts by the citizens of a society.

Again, clear air is not divisible, and for all practical purposes one cannot buy a certain amount of clean air on the marketplace to enjoy privately. If a society deems clean air important enough to spend some money for its provision, government has to pass laws establishing standards relative to how much of a certain pollutant is legally allowable and then enforce those laws through some enforcement mechanism. Government decides how much clean air to provide for all its citizens, and each citizen then enjoys roughly the same amount, depending on how close he or she may live to a freeway or an electric utility or factory that pollutes the air to the extent legally allowed. Citizens pay for this clean air through either increased taxes or increased prices for products that reflect the additional expenses producers have to pay to comply with pollution standards.

Water is a bit different in this respect, particularly drinking water. There is a huge market for bottled water, and there are many millions of dollars in profit involved in providing this product for consumers. Individual consumers in advanced countries can decide whether they want to incur this additional expense to provide themselves with safe drinking water or whether they will rely on tap water from municipal water systems. Thus drinking water is a private good that can be purchased on the market. But for most other uses, water is provided by local governments, and standards have again been developed to assure that water is clean enough to drink and use safely. Most people do not put in their own filtration systems to clean the water they use for themselves but depend on government to provide this public good for most purposes.

Something like equal opportunity might be called a social value that is consistent with free enterprise philosophy. The most efficient combination of resources should result if those with the best abilities and talents get the best economic opportunities. Society is better off because people will end up in positions where their talents will be utilized to the fullest and those who are unfit for these positions will have to find jobs elsewhere. The principle of equal opportunity ensures that the best performers in society, no matter where they were born, what they believe, or what race and sex they happen to be, have a chance to rise to the top based on their proven ability to use society's resources efficiently and effectively, to do things society wants done and is willing to reward commensurately.

People with superior abilities will thus be able to get the better paying positions in society and are morally justified in receiving a greater share of the rewards society offers, if they use their abilities to the fullest in benefiting society as a whole. People should be free to compete for these positions on the basis of merit and be free to go as far as their abilities, interests, and ambition will take them. Equal opportunity means that everyone in our society should be able to compete honestly and fairly on the basis of merit, referring to the performance of that individual in some capacity.

Considerations such as race, sex, religion, creed, or national origin are not supposed to be a factor, as the rewards are supposed to go to those who perform the best and compete most effectively. Thus the removal of these discriminatory barriers to employment and promotion is a good thing for society, and policies designed to promote equal opportunity produce a public good that benefits society. People cannot necessarily purchase this good themselves in the marketplace, and so government passes laws and regulations that mandate companies treat people equally when it comes to workplace decisions and take steps to eliminate discriminatory policies and practices that may pervade the workplace.

Thus the concept of public goods and services is an all-inclusive concept that refers to various entities that cannot be provided through the market. This broader usage also includes the maintenance of competition, mentioned previously, as this competition is a public good that assures an efficient combination of resources to meet consumer demands. These public goods and services have to be provided by means that are external to the market itself, and decisions about what public goods and services to produce and in what quantities are made through some other process, most likely through government, which decides on the basis of political considerations what to do in this regard and how much money to spend for their provision.

In some cases, the market may be able to be used for some of these determinations. A good example is the cap and trade system that is being advocated for control of carbon dioxide emissions, which are said to be the major culprit in global warming or climate change.[12] If the climate can be stabilized, at least to some extent, this again is a good thing because climate change on the scale forecast will result in major expenses for societies all around the world, as they cope with rising sea levels, drought conditions for much of the world, the collapse of some industries dependent on a stable climate, and other effects that have been predicted. Again, this is not a public good that can be bought and sold on the market in an ordinary manner, as climate change is not divisible into private property. But the market can be used for some of the decisions that have to be made about global warming.

Taking a look at the cap and trade system that was implemented several years ago to control sulfur dioxide emissions will help in understanding how the market is used in this regard. Sulfur dioxide was believed to be the major culprit in causing acid rain, which became a problem in many parts of the country. Before the 1970 Clean Air Act, sulfur dioxide emissions in the United States were increasing dramatically and were traceable to the burning of fossil fuels in power plants and factories. By 1986, annual sulfur dioxide emissions had declined by 21 percent, but even more reductions were needed to solve the problem.[13]

The 1990 Clean Air Act contained provisions for large reductions in emissions of sulfur dioxide. By the year 2000, sulfur dioxide emissions were to be reduced nationwide by 10 million tons below 1980 levels, a 40 percent decrease. These reductions were to be obtained through a program of emission allowances, where each utility could "trade and bank" its allowable emissions. Power plants covered by the program were to be issued allowances that are each worth one ton of sulfur dioxide released from smokestacks during a specified year. To obtain reduction in sulfur dioxide pollution, these allowances were to be set below the current level of sulfur dioxide releases. Plants could release only as much sulfur dioxide as they had allowances to cover. If a plant expected to release more sulfur dioxide than it had in allowances, it had to buy allowances from plants that reduced their releases below their number of allowances and therefore had them to sell or trade. These allowances were to be bought and sold nationwide, with stiff penalties for plants that released more pollutants than their allowances covered.[14]

The first trade under the program took place in 1992 when Wisconsin Power & Light agreed to sell pollution credits to the Tennessee Valley Authority and the Duquesne Light Company of Pittsburgh.[15] The Chicago Board of Trade began offering futures contracts on sulfur dioxide credits in 1993 and hoped to become the pollution clearinghouse for the nation, but a vibrant off-exchange pollution rights market also developed.[16]

In its 2003 progress report, the EPA reported that in that year there were 10.6 million tons of sulfur dioxide emissions, which represented a 38 percent reduction from 1980 levels. The program was thus on target to reach its goal of 8.95 million tons by 2010. The electric power industry had achieved nearly 100 percent compliance with the requirements of the program, as only one unit had emissions exceeding the sulfur dioxide allowances that it held. The report also indicated that, over the last decade, sulfur dioxide and sulfate levels were down more than 40 and 30 percent respectively in the eastern part of the country and that there were signs of recovery in acidified lakes and streams in the Adirondacks, the northern Appalachian Plateau, and the upper Midwest. These signs included lower concentrations of sulfates, nitrates, and improvement in acid-neutralizing capacity.[17]

This cap and trade program allows sources to select their own compliance strategy rather than having this dictated by the federal government with a command and control approach. They can use coal containing less sulfur, wash the coal, or use devices called scrubbers to chemically remove pollutants from the gases leaving smokestacks. They can also use a cleaner-burning fuel like natural gas or reassign some of their energy production from dirtier units to cleaner ones. Sources may also reduce their electricity generation by adopting conservation or efficiency measures or switch to alternative energy sources such as wind power or solar energy.

It is important to note, however, what the market does and does not do in these situations. The market does not make the decision to reduce emissions of sulfur dioxide or carbon dioxide. These decisions are made by the government; they are public policy decisions that are made by a public body accountable to the citizens. The government also decides what level or standard to set regarding the overall amount of these pollutants that are allowable in a certain time frame. Thus the government makes the decisions about what to produce and the quantities involved, e.g., how free the air should be of these pollutants, based on the best scientific evidence relative to the objectives of reducing acid rain to deal with the destruction it was causing and slowing climate change to manageable levels. The government creates a market for pollution credits that it issues, and the market is only used to promote a more cost-efficient way to reduce these pollutants, by allowing greater freedom for companies to develop their own way of meeting the standards.

In the examples mentioned so far, the dividing line between public and private goods and services seems clear enough, as in general these public goods and services cannot be bought and sold on the market and private property rights do not apply. In other cases, however, the line is not so clear and whether a particular good or service is public or private is debatable. The provision of electricity is a case in point. In an article appearing in the *Denver Post*, Marjorie Kelly and Richard Rosen criticize the nation's attempt to deregulate electricity, calling it a misguided experiment that has left consumers in many states paying electricity bills that are as much as 100 percent higher than was true in the immediate past.[18]

The main culprit, they claim, is the Federal Energy Regulatory Commission (FERC), which has been steadily undermining the consumer-friendly electricity regulatory framework for nearly two decades. As a result, in 2006 consumers in deregulated states paid 55 percent more for electric power that those in regulated states. Increased volatility hit some states hard, as in California, when in just one year the cost of power quadrupled from $7 billion to $28 billion. The cause was a runaway wholesale market for electricity. The FERC is supposed to see that electricity prices are "just and reasonable," but in stripping authority from state utility commissions and handing electricity price-setting over to markets, it eliminated any and all means of protecting consumers. Four states filed suit against the FERC, claiming that the switch to market-based pricing was illegal in that the agency violated its own mandate to protect consumers.[19]

Perhaps the most interesting comment in the article, however, is the following: "What we must remember is that public services like electricity are not commodities but public goods, necessities of life essential to the well-being of all, and thus must be subject to public oversight and not left to markets."[20] Is this the case, is electricity a public good or service? What are people buying when they purchase electricity? On the one hand, it could be argued that people are buying a service provided by utilities, and electricity is not a good at all. When people hook into the local grid, they are purchasing the right to a service. On the other hand, the product provided is able to be measured, so is what people are really purchasing the current that flows into their dwelling, which is billed to them on a monthly basis?

Besides this complication, consumers cannot shop around among competing providers to find the lowest rate; they have to take whatever is charged by the local utility company. There is no market setting the price, as far as consumers are concerned, and there is no competition at the retail level that keeps prices under control. Does this mean, then, that we have to have public service commissions at the state level to see that these prices are "just and reasonable"? Is this the only way to protect consumers? While the government does not provide electricity and actually own the utilities, should it have the authority to regulate prices in the "public interest" on the supposition that, even though electricity is provided by private utilities, it is a public good or service and prices need to be determined by some public body acting in the "public interest" rather than by the market?

Health care is another case, as it has become privatized in recent years. The result has been one of the most costly health care systems in the world, with 45 million people uninsured and 16 million or so underinsured. When a severe health problem hits these people, they are wiped out economically. Is the problem that health care is a public good or service and that all people in this country have a right to some level of health care, regardless of their economic resources? Should we have a single-payer system that guarantees the best care at the lowest cost to all citizens? Should Medicare, for example, which many have argued is an efficient system, be extended to all citizens of the country? Do we want people running the health care system who are interested in making a profit rather than having the health of the populace foremost in their decisions?

There has been a trend to privatize more and more public services over the past several years on the assumption that these services can be provided more efficiently by the private sector. But the high cost of our health care system challenges this assumption. This privatization also extends into our national park system, where park employees have been eliminated in the interests of privatizing some of the services they provided. But do we want people in our national parks that are mainly interested in exploiting the parks to make a profit, rather than dedicated public servants like the park rangers who are interested in preserving the parks for present and future generations to enjoy? These are questions that need to be asked in the rush to privatization.

The market is not always the best means to provide these goods and services, particularly if they have some of the characteristics of public goods and services. It is always assumed that the market is more efficient than the government, despite evidence to the contrary. People do not necessarily take care of private property any better than do public servants paid by the government to look after public resources. We all know people who do not take care of their lawns or their cars and let their houses deteriorate. The efficient use of resources and their upkeep depend on many factors other than simply private property and the market. We need to get over this blind faith in the market and ask questions about the nature of the goods and services in question and whether these goods and services are better provided by the market or the public policy process. Community interests need be kept in mind rather than the single-minded pursuit of profits for private entities.

9   The Natural Environment

Nothing would seem to be more important at this juncture of human existence than the emergence of a new moral consciousness to guide the direction of production and consumption in ways that enhance the natural environment in which we are embedded. We are destroying our own habitat, but the human need to shape and develop nature to suit ourselves seems to be inexhaustible and is like a bulldozer that cannot be stopped. Sometimes it seems inevitable that we are going to build something on every square inch of the earth, exploit every last resource the earth can provide, and industrialize every last bit of wilderness. The human ego seems to have no bounds or limits, which creates a problem because the world we live in does have limits. Our refusal to live within those limits will surely lead to our demise unless something like an environmental ethic emerges to guide our behavior. This ethic must function as a comprehensive ethic based on our relation to and responsibilities for the natural environment. A continuing emphasis on only individualism and rights will not make this happen.

THE END OF NATURE

Several years ago, a very thoughtful book written by Bill McKibben, entitled *The End of Nature*, provided a new way of viewing nature that has profound implications for the way we think about our relationship to the natural environment.[1] By the "end of nature" the author did not mean that nature does not matter but that nature as we have known it in the past no longer exists. Human beings have conquered nature, as the entire natural world now bears the stamp of humanity and we have left our imprint on nature everywhere. We have made nature a creation of our own and have lost the "otherness" that once belonged to the natural world, as it is so affected by human activities that it is more and more becoming one of our own creations. Nature is no longer the autonomous entity in which we sought refuge from human activities and where we could find something that was beyond our control and feel humble in its presence.

What this view suggests is that the world has crossed a threshold with respect to the environment, where human activities can alter natural processes to a far greater extent than anyone could have imagined even a few decades ago. Nature has been subjugated and reconfigured according to human needs and desires, as science and technology have given us the ability to alter the natural environment to suit our values and objectives. We can reshape the landscape to make it suitable for a housing development, tear apart whole mountains for the ore or coal they contain, alter the course of rivers and the amount of water that flows through them, build huge indoor malls with a controlled climate, create cities with millions of people in the middle of a desert where most everything to sustain life has to be imported, and we are even altering the world's climate with our industrial activities.

This ability gives us a sense of power to manipulate the environment to serve human purposes better, but with it comes a sense of responsibility to deal with the environment in ways that do not destroy the very foundation of our existence. We simply cannot proceed as we have in the past to exploit nature and not worry about the environmental consequences of our activities. Nature can no longer take care of itself, and we have to take responsibility for our activities and their impact on nature. Thus far we are not doing a very good job in this regard. Daily news reports give ample evidence of collapsing fisheries, eroding soils, deteriorating rangelands, expanding deserts, disappearing wetlands, falling water tables, more destructive storms, melting glaciers, rising sea levels, and dying coral reefs. The world is said to be losing its biological diversity as plant and animal species are being destroyed by human encroachment on their habitats. Deforestation continues and shows no sign of slowing as demand mounts for wood and wood products. The earth continues to get hotter and more and more wildfires are one result. And the population keeps on growing and now stands at six billion and counting.

Taking responsibility for nature involves making conscious and responsible value judgments regarding the kind of planet we want. These value judgments include the answer to such questions as, how much species diversity should be maintained? How much of nature should be preserved and placed off-limits to industrial development? What natural resources do we wish to leave for our children? How much climate change is acceptable? Does population growth need to be limited in some fashion? Science can tell us something about the broad patterns of global transformation taking place, but value judgments about the pace and directions of those patterns have to be made through political and economic systems.

It is not a matter of saving planet Earth, as it is often put in the literature. The planet will be here for millions of years and will have some kind of a natural environment. The real question is whether that environment is such that it can continue to sustain human life and provide an enriching experience for human existence. Creating such an environment involves a new approach that emphasizes responsibility and community—taking responsibility for enhancing the environment to promote a human community that can thrive and experience continued enrichment of its existence. A continued emphasis on the right to use one's property in one's own individual interests will not get us where we need to go and will only continue down the path of self-destructiveness.

It seems that the consumer culture that has emerged over the past several decades cannot continue on its current path. Yet other countries are trying to emulate the United States and develop consumer cultures of their own, countries, like China and India, that have huge populations. The implications that economic growth in these countries has for continued pollution and resource usage is profound, making the need for some kind of ethic to direct these activities along sustainable pathways critical. Consumer culture is built on two critical assumptions: (1) that the world contains an inexhaustible supply of raw materials, and (2) that there are bottomless sinks in which to continue to dispose of waste material. Both of these assumptions have been questioned in the past several decades, causing many to take a look at the sustainability of consumer culture into the future. These concerns have profound implications for corporate activity that is based on the never-ending quest for profits through the promotion of consumption and an ever-increasing material standard of living throughout the world.

Concerns for the environment, as embodied in sustainable growth and other such concepts, provide ample evidence for the emergence of an environmental ethic. Many are beginning to recognize that nature provides an enriching experience in itself and that harming nature is ultimately destructive of the search for meaningfulness and self-fulfillment. Environmental concerns about pollution, climate change, resource usage, and the enjoyment of nature obviously run headlong into cultural values related to increased production and consumption and immediate gratification. Production, consumption, and continued economic growth, with their own self-justifying ends, seem on a collision path with a concern for the environment and the self-fulfillment it provides.

Questions are being asked as to whether advanced industrial societies like the United States are sustainable from an environmental point of view and whether they are just in relation to the rest of the world from a moral point of view. Questions are also being raised about the feasibility and morality of our society, hooked on an ever-increasing standard of living, which uses up more and more of the world's resources and causes more and more pollution of the environment. Do the United States and other advanced industrial societies need to cut back on consumption and share some of their largess with developing nations? Do developed societies need to save something for future generations if they take the concept of sustainability seriously?

These are moral questions related to intragenerational and intergenerational equity. They are critical questions that need to be raised as more and more nations around the world develop some form of market economies and promote economic growth as the way to modernize their societies. Does the earth have sufficient carrying capacity to sustain such economic growth for the ever-increasing population of the world? Is there a need for some new kind of ethic that would essentially function as the Protestant Ethic did, by providing moral limits on consumption and directing production into less environmentally harmful paths?

Alan Durning, writing in a book entitled *How Much Is Enough?*, which was mentioned in an earlier chapter, argues that our society must learn to live within its means by drawing on the interest provided by the earth's resources rather than its principle. He calls this a culture of permanence, which is based on the idea of sustainability. Yet it is not easy to transform consumption-oriented societies into sustainable ones, to say nothing about the material cravings of developing societies. These forces cause what he calls a conundrum.

> We may, therefore, be in a conundrum—a problem admitting of no satisfactory solution. Limiting the consumer life-style to those who have already attained it is not politically possible, morally defensible, or ecologically sufficient. And extending the life-style to all would simply hasten the ruin of the biosphere. The global environment cannot support billions of us living like American consumers, much less 5.5 billion people, or a future population of at least 8 billion. On the other hand, reducing the consumption levels of the consumer society, and tempering material aspirations elsewhere, though morally acceptable, is a quixotic proposal. It bucks the trend of centuries. Yet it may be the only option.[2]

For the past several decades, the overriding goal of people in western industrial societies has been buying more goods, acquiring more things, and increasing their stock of material wealth. These goals are now spreading to other countries, like China and India, with enormous populations. Companies have profited from this expansion of consumer culture by catering to their needs, bombarding them with advertising, and in general promoting a consumer society by creating a certain materialistic conception of the good life. Because of this trend, the world's peoples have consumed as many goods and services since 1950 as all previous generations put together. Since 1940, according to Durning, the United States alone has used up as large a share of the earth's mineral resources as did everyone before it combined.[3]

Reduction of consumption in industrial societies will have severe repercussions. Since about two-thirds of gross national product or its equivalent in developed countries consists of consumer purchases, it seem obvious that any significant reduction of consumer expenditures would have serious implications for employment, income, investment, and everything else tied into economic growth. Lowering consumption could be self-destructive to advanced industrial societies. Yet if such measures aren't taken, ecological forces may eventually dismantle advanced societies anyhow in ways that we can't control and that would be even more destructive.[4]

ENVIRONMENTAL ETHICS

What seems to be needed is the development of an environmental ethic as a comprehensive ethic that can place production and consumption activities in a moral context. An environmental ethic of some kind is the best candidate for a comprehensive ethic because of the persistence and pervasiveness of environmental problems. Such an ethic is necessary to guide the direction of production and consumption in a manner that nourishes the desire of humans for opportunities to live a meaningful life and for self-development that enriches their existence. This entails the growth and flourishing of the multiple environments in which they are embedded and that contribute to the fullness of human existence in all its richness and complexity. An answer to environmental problems is not to be found in a forced choice between artificially created alternatives, such as the conflict between economics and the environment. These alternatives distort the nature of the reality they must ultimately serve, that of enriching the life of humans in all the multiple dimensions in which they work out a meaningful and fulfilling life for themselves.

The theories that are part of business ethics, such as utilitarianism and the like, are not congenial to the needs of an environmental ethic because they have no philosophical structure to provide an inherent relatedness of the individual and the broader natural environment. For all of these positions, the source of ethical action lies either in the application of abstract rules to cases or in the inculcation of tradition. Neither approach incorporates the type of attunement to nature that is required for an environmental consciousness. They are by and large anthropocentric in nature and view the environment as something separate or external to humans. They reflect the individualism and dualism of the modern worldview, where the environment has merely instrumental value. Thus in the environmental literature one finds little application of these theories to the natural environment.

This problem has given rise to a separate area of ethics called environmental ethics, which has developed its own approaches and theories. One such approach is called *moral extensionism and eligibility*, which has to do with the extension of rights to the natural world. As mentioned in an earlier chapter, rights have been extended to blacks and other minorities in civil rights legislation, rights have been given to women under equal rights legislation, rights have been extended to workers regarding safety and health in the workplace, and rights have been provided to consumers for safe products and other aspects of the marketplace. The question is whether rights can also be extended to the natural world or at least some aspects of it and whether this approach can help deal with environmental problems in an effective manner. Where does the ethical cutoff fall with regard to moral eligibility? What aspects of nature can justifiably be brought into the moral realm in this manner?

Many philosophers extend such rights only to animals on the grounds that animals are sentient beings, in that they are able to suffer and feel pain. But more radical thinkers widen the circle to include all natural organisms, including plants. Still others see no reason to draw a moral boundary at the edge of organic life and argue for ethical consideration for rocks, soil, water, air, and biophysical processes that constitute ecosystems. Some are even led to the conclusion that the universe has rights superior to those of its most precocious life form.[5]

Peter Singer thinks that believing the effects of our actions on nonhuman animals have no moral significance is arbitrary and morally indefensible. He makes an analogy between the way we treat animals and the way we used to treat black slaves. The white slave owners limited their moral concern to the white race and did not regard the suffering of a black slave as having the same moral significance as the suffering of a white person. Thus the black could be treated inhumanly with no moral compulsion. This way of thinking is called racism, but we could just as well substitute the word speciesism with regard to the manner in which animals are treated. The logic of racism and the logic of speciesism are the same.[6]

Just as our concern about equal treatment of blacks through legislation and regulation moved us to a different level of moral consciousness, so will treating animals as beings who have interests and can suffer and therefore deserve moral consideration move us to a different level of moral consciousness. Moving to this level with regard to animals may involve stopping certain practices, such as using animals for testing purposes and subjecting them to slow and agonizing deaths. It may also involve stopping the practice of raising animals in crowded conditions solely for the purpose of human consumption. Decisions to avoid speciesism of this kind will be difficult, but no more difficult, thinks Singer, than it would have been for a white Southerner to go against the traditions of society and free his slaves.[7]

The creatures in Singer's moral community have to possess nervous systems of sufficient sophistication to feel pain, that is, they have to be sentient beings. Ethics ends at the boundary of sentience for Singer. A tree or a mountain or a rock being kicked does not feel anything and therefore does not possess any interests or rights. Since they cannot be harmed by human action they have no place in ethical discourse. There is nothing we can do that matters to them and thus they are not deserving of moral consideration.[8]

Other philosophers, such as Joel Fineberg, also limit their moral concerns to animals. Fineberg excluded plants from the rights community on the grounds that they had insufficient "cognitive equipment" to be aware of their wants, needs, and interests. He also denied rights to incurable "human vegetables," and using the same logic disqualified certain species from moral consideration. Protection of rare and endangered species became protection of humans to enjoy and benefit from them. Even less deserving of rights were mere things.[9] While many philosophers found these requirements too limiting, Singer and Fineberg did help to liberate moral philosophy from its fixation on human beings.

Scholars such as Christopher Stone pushed the boundaries of moral eligibility further to include other aspects of the natural world. Stone saw no logical or legal reason to draw any ethical boundaries whatsoever. Why should the moral community end with humans or even animals? While this idea may sound absurd to many people, so did the extension of certain rights to women and blacks at one point in our history. The extension of rights in this manner, according to Stone, would help environmentalists better protect the environment and also reflects the view that nature needs to be preserved for its own sake and not just for the interests of human beings.[10]

Stone's experience with the Mineral King case in the late 1960s stimulated him to write his landmark essay, which made a case for the extension of moral concern to the plant community. Mineral King was a beautiful valley in the Southern Sierras that was the subject of a proposal by Walt Disney Enterprises for the development of a massive ski resort. The Sierra Club saw itself as a long-time guardian of this region and tried to stop the development. But the U.S. Court of Appeals of California ruled that since the Club was not itself injured, it had no standing or legal reason to sue against the development. But something was going to be injured, Stone reasoned, and the courts should be receptive to its need for protection. Thus he argued in his essay that society should give legal rights to forests, oceans, rivers, and other natural objects in the environment, and indeed, to the natural environment as a whole.[11]

The attempt to extend rights in this manner represents an effort to build a wider moral community that includes all or parts of the natural world and overcome the anthropocentrism that separates humans from nature. But while moral extensionism and eligibility in environmental ethics attempt to bring animals and even other aspects of nature into the moral community by extending rights to them, these arguments are subject to strong theoretical attack. Rights are bestowed on animals and other aspects of nature by humans, thereby making the moral standing of nonhuman aspects of nature dependent on humans. Animals cannot pursue their own interests through the courts but need someone to take up their cause for them. While rights theory in environmental ethics thus tries to overcome traditional limitations on rights by extending them to animals and other aspects of nature, it is caught up in the theoretical web of anthropocentrism and atomic individualism that is found in the tradition of rights theory.

Partly as a result of problems with moral extensionism and eligibility, a *biocentric ethics* or *deep ecology* developed as an alternative approach to the environment. Kenneth Goodpaster argued that the extension of rights beyond certain limits is not necessarily the best way to deal with moral growth and social change with respect to the environment. The last thing we need, he states, is a liberation movement with respect to trees, animals, rivers, and other objects in nature. The mere enlargement of the class of morally considerable beings is an inadequate substitute for a genuine environmental ethic. The extension of rights to natural objects does not deal with deeper philosophical questions about human interests and environmental concerns. Moral consideration should be extended to systems as well as individuals. Societies need to be understood in an ecological context and it is this larger whole that is the bearer of value. An environmental ethic, while paying its respects to individualism and humanism, must break free of them and deal with the way the universe is operating.[12]

John Rodman protests the whole notion of extending human-type rights to nonhumans because this action categorizes them as "inferior human beings" and "legal incompetents" who need human guardianship. This was the same kind of mistake that some white liberals made in the 1960s with regard to blacks. Instead, we should respect animals and everything else in nature "for having their own existence, their own character and potentialities, their own forms of excellence, their own integrity, their own grandeur." Instead of giving nature rights or legal standing within the present political and economic order, Rodman urged environmentalists to become more radical and change the order. All forms of domestication must end along with the entire institutional framework associated with owning land and using it in one's own interests.[13]

J. Baird Callicott, an admirer of Aldo Leopold's land ethic, declared that the animal liberation movement was not even allied with environmental ethics as it emphasized the rights of individual organisms. The land ethic, on the other hand, was holistic and has as its highest objective the good of the community as a whole. The animal rights advocates simply added individual animals to the category of rights holders, whereas "ethical holism" calculated right and wrong in reference not to individuals but to the whole biotic community. The whole, in other words, carried more ethical weight than any of its component parts. Oceans and lakes, mountains, forests, and wetlands are assigned a greater value than individual animals that might happen to reside there.[14]

Thus deep ecology leads to a devaluation of individual life relative to the integrity, diversity, and continuation of the ecosystem as a whole. This perspective on environmental ethics created entirely new definitions of what liberty and justice mean on planet Earth and involved an evolution of ethics to be ever more inclusive. This approach recognized that there can be no individual welfare or liberty apart from the ecological matrix in which individual life exists. "A biocentric ethical philosophy could be interpreted as extending the esteem in which individual lives were traditionally held to the biophysical matrix that created and is sustaining those lives."[15]

This approach holds that some natural objects and ecosystems have intrinsic value and are morally considerable in their own right apart from human interests. Nature has value in and of itself apart from human interests. This ethic respects each life form and sees it as part of a larger whole. All life is sacred and we must not be careless about species that are irreplaceable. Particular individuals come and go, but nature continues indefinitely, and humans must come to understand their place in nature. Each life form is constrained to flourish in a larger community according to this view, and moral concern for the whole biological community is the only kind of environmental ethics that makes sense and preserves the integrity of the entire ecosystem.[16]

Nature itself is a source of values, it is argued, including the value we have as humans, since we are a part of nature. The concept of value, according to this position, includes far more than a simplistic human-interest satisfaction. Value is a multifaceted idea with structures that are rooted in natural sources.[17] Value is not just a human product. When humans recognize values outside themselves, this does not result in a dehumanizing of the self or a reversion to beastly levels of existence. On the contrary, it is argued, human consciousness is increased when we praise and respect the values found in the natural world and this recognition results in a further spiritualizing of humans.[18] Thus this school of thought holds that there are natural values that are intrinsic to the natural object itself apart from humans and their particular valuing activities. Values are found in nature as well as humans. Humans do not simply bestow value on nature, as nature also conveys value to humans.[19]

The world of nature is not to be defined in terms of commodities that are capable of producing wealth for humans, who manage them in their own interests. All things in the biosphere are believed to have an equal right to live and reach their own individual forms of self-realization. Instead of a hierarchical ordering of entities in descending order from God through humans to animals, plants, and rocks, where the lower creatures are under the higher ones and are ruled by them, nature is seen as a web of interactive and interdependent life that is ruled by its own natural processes. These processes must be understood if we are to work in harmony with nature and preserve the conditions for our own continued existence.[20]

Deep ecology thus accords nature ethical status that is at least equal to that of human beings. From the perspective of the ecosystem, the difference is between thinking that people have a right to a healthy ecosystem and thinking that the ecosystem itself possesses intrinsic or inherent value.[21] Deep ecologists argue for a biocentric perspective and a holistic environmental ethic regarding nature. Human beings are to step back into the natural community as a member and not the master. The philosophy of conservation for Holmes Ralston was comparable to arguing for better care for slaves on plantations. The whole system was unethical, not just how people operated within the system. In Ralston's view, nothing matters except the liberation of nature from the system of human dominance and exploitation. This process involves a reconstruction of the entire human relationship with the natural world.[22]

Both of these approaches are useful in understanding the relationship between humans and nature, but these approaches treat the environment differently and make different assumptions about the locus of moral consideration. Moral extensionism and eligibility use the vehicle of rights to extend moral concern to various aspects of nature, but these rights are bestowed by humans and are not intrinsic to nature itself. Deep ecology assumes nature already has intrinsic value that needs to be recognized by liberating nature from the system in which it is currently trapped, and in recognizing this intrinsic value of nature, the last remnants of anthropocentrism, still operative in moral extensionism and eligibility, is supposedly excised. Further, while moral extensionism and eligibility stress the individual to the exclusion of the whole, deep ecology subordinates the individual to the good of the whole.

The biological egalitarianism of deep ecology provides no means to make distinctions between which parts of nature to preserve and which to use for the promotion of human welfare. The debate over systems versus individuals is still rooted in atomic individualism, and deep ecology does not provide an adequate framework for understanding the relation of humans and nature in all its richness. Extending rights to animals and other parts of nature involves the same kinds of problems that human rights have, as mentioned in an earlier chapter. Each of these alternatives may provide a sense of moral concern for nature, but neither offers a useful framework for understanding the moral dimensions of business activity in relation to the natural environment.

A DIFFERENT APPROACH

An environmental ethic must be based on a philosophical system that considers humans and nature in a relational context.[23] Neither human activity in general nor human knowledge can be separated from the fact that humans are natural organisms embedded in and dependent upon a natural environment with which they are continuous. Human development is connected with its biological world and the self is not something that can be viewed apart from its rootedness in nature. The human being is located in nature and emerges from and opens onto the natural world in which humans function. We are not only part of a human community, but also part of a broader community that includes the natural environment, and we have a responsibility to and for that larger community.

The effort to reclaim community should include broadening our understanding of community to include the natural world on which humans radically depend. It will require an "anthropocosmic" world-view—an understanding of humans as embedded in the cosmic order—in place of the Enlightenment view of humans as being apart from nature. It will be deeply relational, with a web as the appropriate metaphor, so that humans understand profoundly their intimate connection to all of creation. An anthropocosmic worldview would affect the way we think about everything, from law to education to the way we build economies.[24]

Humans and their environment, organic and inorganic, take on an inherently relational aspect. To speak of organism and environment in isolation from each other is never true to the actual situation, for no organism can exist in isolation from an environment, and the environment is what it is in relation to an organism. What exists is an indivisible whole and it is only within such an interactional context that humans can function and develop. The relational nature of humans and the natural world undercuts the problematics of subjective experience set over against an alien objective universe.

Nature cannot be dehumanized nor can humans be denaturalized. Science treats nature objectively in the interests of manipulating nature to suit human interests, but in doing so it abstracts nature from the relational context in which humans exist and flourish. It treats nature as something external to humans that can be exploited for self-interested purposes. It treats nature in instrumental terms as existing only to serve human needs and interests. Religion takes humans out of nature with belief in the supernatural and, in doing so, too often abstracts humans from the natural world in which they live, move, and have their being. Meaning and purpose are found outside of nature and not in the natural world itself. Human origins as well as their final destiny are located outside of the natural world. Neither approach does justice to the natural world and the context in which humans and nature interact.

A deepening of reason and expansion of one's self opens up the possibility of a deep-seated harmony with the totality of the natural world to which the self is related. This involves the entire universe, for an emphasis on continuity reveals that at no time can we separate our developing selves from any part of the universe and claim that part is irrelevant. Growth involves a deepening and expansion of perspective to include ever-widening understanding of the natural universe to which we are inseparably bound. This unity can be neither apprehended in knowledge nor realized in reflection. The totality it involves is neither a literal content of the intellect nor an intellectual grasp of nature, but is best seen as an imaginative ideal that is manifested in a deepened attunement to nature. Such an experience brings about not only a change in the intellect but also a change in moral consciousness.

Since humans exist within and are part of nature, any part of nature provides a conceivable relational context for values to emerge. The understanding we have of "human interests," of what is valuable for human enrichment, has to be expanded to incorporate a greatly extended notion of human welfare to include the natural world. To increase our experience of value is not to increase something subjective within us but to increase the value-ladenness of relational contexts within nature. Although the concept of the valuable emerges only through judgments involving human intelligence, value-related qualities occur at any level of environmental interaction involving sentient organisms.

While some environmentalists may question the claim that a distinction in levels of value can be made, and that all of nature has intrinsic value that must be preserved, when push comes to shove and when all the abstract arguments have been made, is it not the case that claims of the valuable must be seen in light of its promotion of or irrepressible harm to human welfare, actual or potential? Does anyone really think that the preservation of the spotted owl and the preservation of the AIDS virus have equal moral claim? Making value judgments of this kind does not involve a reemergence of anthropocentrism, as it is not the case that all value emerges only in relation to humans. Yet neither is it the case that everything in nature has equal value irrespective of its relation to the welfare of humans. Value is an emergent contextual property of situations involving human-environment interactions.

The biological egalitarianism of biocentrism cannot be maintained in practice. Value judgments have to be made relative to those parts of the natural world over which we have some control. Yet this does not mean that humans can ignore the value contexts of sentient organisms within nature. We must make judgments that provide protection for the welfare of humans, yet such judgments must consider to the largest degree consistent with this goal the value-laden contexts involving other sentient organisms. These decisions must be made in terms of conflicting claims that have to be evaluated and not on the basis of the exploitation of nature through egocentric disregard for the valuings of other organisms.

This position does not allow for the emergence of value in nonsentient contexts but neither does it allow for the exploitation of nonsentient entities. It is not possible to envision any aspect of nature that cannot be the object of a conceivable experience of sentient organisms. At no point can an environmental ethic draw the line between human welfare and the welfare of the environment of which it is a part. Everything that can conceivably enter into human experience has the potential for being part of the relational context within which value emerges, and any value as well as any aspect of the context within which it emerges involves consequences and is therefore instrumental in bringing about something further. There is no means-end distinction but rather an ongoing continuity in which the character of the means enters into the quality of the end, which in turn becomes a means to something further.

The debate between instrumental versus intrinsic value is problematic and of no help in making decisions about nature. If everything has intrinsic value, then decisions about uses of nature become somewhat arbitrary. If, for example, every tree has its own intrinsic value and the right to exist, irrespective of its potential for valuing experiences, how can we choose which trees to cut down? Yet common sense tells us we cannot "save" them all, and decisions have to be made relative to specific situations. Value does not lie in the tree itself or in humans themselves, but it emerges in the interactions between humans and nature, and when decisions have to be made, they are made relative to the valuing experiences of human beings.

These decisions are not made by an isolated individual, abstracted from the natural context in which they are embedded. Neither individuals nor nature are the bearers of value; rather, values emerge in the interactions of individuals with nature. Nature gains its value through its interaction with individuals, but the value of individuals cannot be understood in isolation from the relationships that constitute their ongoing development and growth. Decisions must be made relative to the flourishing of humans in an environment that supports and contributes to their development, in all the richness and diversity that constitute human existence.

Managers cannot make morally responsible decisions that involve the environment based on viewing it as purely instrumental, as being there only for exploitation for human purposes. Nor can they find much guidance in holding abstractly that nature has rights or that the ecosystem supersedes the needs of individual societies or humanly structured functions. We cannot save all the trees nor can we be concerned equally with saving all species. What is needed is a recognition that the corporation has its being through its relation to a wider community, which includes the natural environment, and has responsibilities to that wider community.

Responsible corporate decision making, as contextually located and evaluated in terms of consequences, must include environmental considerations when these are relevant. What specific course of action should be followed in specific instances must, of course, emerge from the concrete situation and the unique conflicting demands it involves. But as in all moral decision-making, the more deeply one is attuned to our interactions with the natural environment in which we are embedded, the more a potential exists for seeing and creating alternatives that are viable for enriching human existence.

ECONOMICS AND THE ENVIRONMENT

One major impediment to treating the natural environment in a responsible manner is the way the environment is treated in standard economic theory, as this theory in large part dominates the way we behave with respect to the environment. The market does not respond very well to environmental problems and, if left to its own devices, treats the environment as something external to itself. There seems to be no way the value of the environment or any of its services can be determined through a market process, since there is nothing to be exchanged or traded. People cannot take a piece of dirty air, for example, and exchange it for a piece of clean air on the market, at least given the current state of technology. The same holds true for other components of the environment.

The competitive system limits the ability of corporations to respond to environmental problems on an individual basis, since if they voluntarily clean up their pollution they will most likely price themselves out of the market. Some call this inability of market systems to respond to environmental pollution and degradation market failure, but the use of this term is not entirely accurate. Market systems were not designed to factor in environmental costs and it is not fair to blame the system for not doing something for which it was not designed. Property rights are not appropriately assigned as regards the environment, and nature often lacks a discrete owner to look after its interests. Nature's interests can be violated by market exchanges and, as a common property resource, can be overused and degraded, as it is subject to the "tragedy of the commons," a phenomenon that relates to property held in common for everyone.[25]

Market systems evolved to serve human needs and wants; they are not constructed to protect the environment. The environment is treated as a source of raw materials to be used in the production process and as a bottomless sink in which to dispose of raw materials. The environment has no economic value in and of itself but is worth something only as it can be used to serve some human purposes. The ecological functions of the environment have no value as far as the market is concerned. It is only their economic utility or instrumental value that is of importance in a market economy. Thus the market fails to tell the ecological truth, as it regularly underprices products and services by failing to incorporate the environmental costs of providing them.[26]

Economic growth comes at the expense of the earth's productive assets— its farmlands, forests, fisheries, aquifers, wetlands, and even its climate. The costs of this environmental degradation and pollution are external to normal market processes and are not taken into account in the price mechanism, unless these costs are determined through some other process and imposed on the market system. Only then can environmental values be internalized and reflect themselves in market decisions. This is a major task facing business and society—to find some reasonable and acceptable way to factor in environmental costs along with the other costs of production.

The problem is one of placing an appropriate value on nature so that it can be reflected in market decisions. An interesting attempt to quantify nature appeared in the effort of an international collection of economists, ecologists, and geographers, from twelve prestigious universities and laboratories in three nations, to place a dollar value on nature. In an article that appeared in the May 15, 1997 issue of *Nature*, these experts estimated that the economic value of the biosphere's essential "ecosystem services" such as climate regulation, soil formation, food production, flood control, and water supply averages about $33 trillion annually. To put this number in perspective, the value of the output of the total world economy each year is $18 trillion.[27]

The reactions to this effort were interesting. Some conservationists saw some positive value in this effort, in that putting a dollar figure on what is likely to be destroyed over the next few years if we do not change our ways is a useful tactic to argue for greater conservation efforts. Some argued that it succeeds in speaking in a language that business might begin to hear regarding the value of what we collectively, and thoughtlessly, are destroying. Others, however, felt differently. When asked to comment on this nature-valuation effort, an ecologist by the name of David Ehrenfeld said that "I am afraid that I don't see much hope for a civilization so stupid that it demands a quantitative estimate of its own umbilical cord."[28]

Such quantification only further objectifies nature and leaves out our experience with nature and our so-called subjective relationship with the world. If nature has to be quantified for us to have a sense of its value then we have lost any real connection with nature and see it, as well as ourselves, as nothing more than objects in a quantified universe. Our spiritual and emotional connection to the source and substance of our very being is no less real and no less important for the fact that it cannot be quantified. As stated in one comment on the subject of valuing the environment, "Put me in a redrock canyon and let me watch a mule deer moving beneath the dappled shadow of a cottonwood grove, and I do not need to be told how much what I see and feel there is worth: it is worth nothing—and everything."[29]

Science plays a crucial role in determining standards that should be adhered to in order to protect and promote human health, standards related to clean air and water, exposure to toxic wastes and ultra-violet radiation, and keeping the earth's temperature in bounds. But science is subject to a great deal of uncertainty, which those opposed to such standards use to their advantage, and the findings of scientific studies can be altered by decision-makers to suit their political and ideological interests.[30] Setting reasonable standards that adequately protect humans and the environment and are acceptable as far as their cost is concerned is one of the most difficult problems modern industrial societies face in today's world.

This task cannot be left to government alone, as government is subject to political and ideological pressures that do not allow it to develop a consistent approach to environmental problems. Perhaps business can take the lead and work with other entities in society, including government, to develop an institutional mechanism to figure out these environmental costs and then decide on the best means of imposing these costs on the market, whether it is through standards, taxes, emissions trading systems, or other means. People must be made aware of the environmental costs of their actions and our political, economic, and social systems must change to take into account environmental impacts in every decision.

If McKibben is right, and nature as it once was understood no longer exists, this means that nature has been conquered and is now largely under our control. Perhaps we should even stop using the term natural environment, since there is nothing in this environment anymore that is natural in the sense that it is unaffected by human activities. We are shaping the environment in which we and future generations will have to live and work out our existence, and we need to be aware of this responsibility and take the necessary steps to enhance the environment for the benefit of the entire community of human beings, now and in the future.

Part III

Implications of the Framework for the Corporation

10 The Corporation and Community

This view of the self and society also has implications for our understanding of the corporation, both in terms of our understanding of the corporation itself and its relationship to the broader society. Within the pragmatic framework, the corporation is seen as a social entity rather than strictly an economic entity that has only economic impacts and responsibilities. In economic theory, the corporation is abstracted out of its social context and given an independence that cuts it off from any larger social and moral purpose. However, the corporation is a social community in itself and also part of a larger community. These two aspects of corporate life will be discussed in this chapter.

THE CORPORATION AS A COMMUNITY

According to classical economic theory, the corporation is a legal device that is formed for purely economic purposes. The corporate form of organization was first used for a public purpose, such as building roads or canals in the early years of this country. But in the landmark Dartmouth College decision of the Supreme Court, corporations were held to be voluntary organizations that could be used privately by people to pursue their economic self-interest without any overriding public purpose. People were encouraged to form corporations wherever they thought an opportunity existed that could be exploited for self-interested reasons.

The corporate form of organization enabled risk to be spread across a large number of people and made individuals who invested in the company accountable only for the amount of money they had put into the organization rather than for the whole entity. People could thus minimize their risk and yet join with others in a cooperative enterprise that needed larger sums of capital and resources than they had individually. People could share in a larger endeavor that could exploit economic opportunities that were too large and risky for any one individual to take on by himself or herself. The legal fiction called the corporation enabled this kind of an arrangement to work for the advantage of society.

The corporation was thus formed to create economic wealth by bringing together people with different skills and talents, capital resources of many different kinds, and raw material from many different locations and putting all these elements together to produce goods and services that are useful or have utility for society. Thus people in the corporation are organized to achieve a common purpose, which they may not have in mind when taking a position in the organization. In classical economic theory, the corporation is considered to be a voluntary organization in which people band together as employees, investors, creditors, and the like because of economic self-interest. Nonetheless, their skills, talents, and resources are eventually directed to the common purpose of producing goods and services and creating economic wealth for the society.

Such a view, however, is again based on the understanding of individuals as atomic units that band together with other such individuals for certain common purposes. These individuals have no other connection except for this need to be part of the same organization for self-interested reasons. The corporation has no purpose except to generate economic wealth to serve the economic needs of these individuals and to enhance the economic wealth of the society in general, through paying taxes to communities and governments and fulfilling the material needs of consumers who buy the corporation's products. The individuals who are the parts give meaning and comprise the whole, which is the corporation.

From a pragmatic perspective, however, the corporation is a community, and the individuals who are in such an organization are what they are in part because of their membership in the organization, while the organization is what it is because of the people who choose to become part of the organization. The corporation is a social organization and needs a certain aspect of conformity to its policies and procedures to operate, the generalized other if you will, but at the same time needs input from the unique selves who work for it in order for it to grow and remain competitive. The unique input of individual selves over time makes up the generalized other, the personality or culture of an organization that has developed over the years and changes with new inputs, and this generalized other, in turn, shapes the behavior and attitudes of the individuals in the organization.

Nor are these individuals and their skills and abilities coordinated in some mechanical fashion to accomplish corporate objectives. Such a mechanistic view of the corporation is not consistent with the notion that people who work in the corporation should not have to sacrifice their essential humanness. Managers who treat their employees in an economic sense as just another factor of production are not treating these people as moral beings who are an essential part of the community. Moreover, treating people in a mechanical manner does not lead to an efficient or effective organization. This idea is well encapsulated in the following quotation:

What makes a corporation efficient or inefficient is not a series of well-oiled mechanical operations but the working interrelationships, the coordination and rivalries, the team spirit and morale of the many people who work there and are in turn shaped and defined by the corporation. So, too, what drives a corporation is not some mysterious abstraction called "the profit motive." It is the collective will and ambitions of its employees, few of whom work for a profit in any obvious sense. Employees of a corporation do what they must to be part of a community, to perform their jobs, and to earn both the respect of others and self-respect. To understand how corporations work (and don't work) is to understand the social psychology of communities, not the logic of a flowchart or the organizational workings of a cumbersome machine.[1]

Pragmatism does not think of employees within the corporation as a homogeneous group working in machinelike fashion. It rejects the notions of abstract rationality with which organizations are often viewed, the idea of mechanistic conformity that represents some management ideals and other modernist views inherent in traditional theories of the corporation. Instead, it turns to the pluralistic features of community and the importance of diversity and conflict resolution in the dynamics of community growth. Even the most dissenting voice enters into the ongoing dynamics of community life with the adjustments and accommodations this requires. Corporate dynamics consists of a pluralistic community of voices in communicative interaction.[2]

Having a voice, however, is not enough. Edwin Hartman has pointed out that providing some process whereby members have some sort of voice in a business organization does not guarantee morality in the workplace any more than it guarantees it anywhere else. A good community must encourage the kind of discussion that creates cooperation, mutual support and respect, and general moral progress.[3] The "politics of community" as the embodiment of a pragmatic understanding of authentic community is, by its very nature, what Hartman describes as a good community that thrives in its environment.

Recent trends in the workplace mitigate this sense of community, however, and are destroying the implicit contract that existed between employees and employers. Many changes have taken place in the workplace over the past several decades, as employees and employers have developed new relationships that reflect changing interests and concerns. Rapid change has become more common because of global competition and rapidly developing technology. Companies have downsized by laying off many workers and eliminating layers of middle management. They have outsourced many departments and functions in order to escape paying benefits or to take advantage of much lower costs overseas. Many offices are virtually empty as employees spend their time mainly in the field or work at home. And most companies have had to cut health benefits for employees or abandon their health coverage entirely because of cost pressures. Some have even turned over their pension obligations to the federal government.

These changes in the workplace have resulted in changes in the implied contract between employees and the corporation. By and large, the old contract held that employees had obligations related to satisfactory attendance at work, acceptable levels of effort and performance, and loyalty to the corporation and management. In return for these commitments, employers provided fair compensation for the work done, fringe benefits such as coverage for health care and defined benefit pension plans, the chance for advancement based on seniority and merit, and some degree of job security.

As job security has evaporated because of restructuring, downsizing, outsourcing, and other changes in the workplace, so have prospects for advancement and predictable wage and benefit increases. Management demands for individual commitment and responsibility have largely taken their place. They want people to buy into long-term visions of the company and be committed to corporate goals while at the same time expecting them to cope with an ever-present threat of termination. Such expectations seem to be one-sided and certainly have implications for employee loyalty, particularly since the effects of many of these changes are distributed bimodally. Top executives are well rewarded and are given generous job security provisions and retirement packages, while middle managers, clerical, and production workers face much greater uncertainty.

These changes in the workplace have given rise to new rules regarding the employment relationship with corporations. These rules have been said to include (1) employment no longer implies job security, (2) with no lifetime jobs, corporate commitment to developing employees is on the decline as companies cannot afford to invest in employees who might be with them only a short time, (3) and with no lifetime jobs and little investment in people, it follows that more of the risk associated with a career are being pushed back onto employees. The new era of employment relations forces employees into the status of free agents, responsible for themselves and to themselves.[4]

Instead of lifelong employment, the emphasis is on lifelong employability. While employees still have something of an obligation to provide opportunity for self-improvement, employees have to take charge of their own careers and can no longer rely on a secure place in the corporate organization. They must continually acquire new skills to keep up with the development of new technologies. Employees are expected to share responsibility for their employment and in many places are gaining greater control over what they do in the workplace. Loyalty to the company is said to be dead, and in its place is loyalty to one's profession or job function.[5]

Meanwhile, unions, which provided some sense of community for certain employees, have been in decline for several decades. Unions arose as industrialization took hold in this country and workers found that many problems they were experiencing in the workplace, such as long hours, poor working conditions, low wages, and arbitrary hiring and firing practices, were not being addressed. To deal with these problems, they began to form unions to counter the power of management with an organized labor movement. These unions became a force to be reckoned with and won major benefits for their members in confrontations with management. During a 40-year period from 1935 to 1975, unions grew in number and bargaining power with employers.

Throughout the history of unionism, rights have been the center of controversy and have often involved intense factionalism. The rights of union workers have been pitted against the rights of management, the rights of unions to strike against the rights of society for a smoothly functioning economy, the rights of union workers against the rights of non-union workers. The intensity of this factionalism has manifested itself from time to time in violent situations, as the rights of labor to make its case for better treatment and the rights of management to maintain control of labor have been asserted. In many, if not most of these cases, the process has moved the relationship between labor and management away from any sense of community.

Perhaps in part because of this factionalism, labor unions have declined as a dominant force in American society. Since about 1975, the balance of power in collective bargaining has been shifting back to management. Unions have been declining in numbers and power over this period of time. While there was some increase of union activity in 1994, the resurgence of management strength in collective bargaining is likely to continue, at least for the immediate future. Thus unions are not as able to look after the rights of labor in a changing workplace and do not provide a sense of community for the labor movement that they once did in our society.

Many rights related to the workplace are now protected by state and federal legislation. Many states have laws protecting whistleblowers, right-to-know laws that require employers to identify hazardous substances used in the workplace, and laws restricting the ability of companies to close plants for economic reasons. Other states have made it illegal for companies to force retirement at any age and some have taken steps to modify the employment-at-will doctrine.[6] Federal laws include the right to a safe workplace, the right of handicapped people to meaningful work and reasonable accommodations for their physical challenges, the right to be treated equally in the workplace, and the right to be free from sexual harassment.[7]

Thus it seems clear that the collective bargaining system that has dominated employee relations for several decades has been replaced by a web of public policy measures, which involves governments at many levels imposing substantive terms on the conditions of employment. The notion of employee rights is firmly embedded in American society and has found its way into numerous public policy measures that restrict management's ability to deal with employees in any manner they desire.

The relationship between labor and management has changed, but the tensions between these groups remain.

The forces driving changes in the workplace, such as global competition and rapid technological change, will probably continue for the foreseeable future, making further corporate adjustments necessary. The foundations of the old social contract will continue to erode, making it increasingly clear that the old social contract cannot be preserved or reestablished. The question then becomes, what kind of a new contract will emerge that will be satisfactory to all parties concerned and yet deal with the new realities of the workplace? What moral issues do these changes raise with respect to the relationship between employees and employers? Do companies have a moral responsibility to provide at least some degree of job security for their employees? Can the system function effectively if employee trust and loyalty disappear and responsibility for the employee's well-being is no longer a corporate concern?

Previous administrations took the position that training is a large part of the answer and redefined job security as employment security. It was argued that workers would not accept changes that come from trade agreements, productivity gains, or technological advances unless they were confident that they could get new jobs and thus benefit from these changes. Employment security was defined as having skills and benefits that were portable. While largely unsuccessful in getting any new government-run training programs through Congress, new benefit mandates, such as the Family and Medical Leave Act, were passed, adding to an already long list of employee rights protected by federal laws and regulations. Pressure was also brought to bear on employers to take responsibility in providing the training necessary to keep workers employable.

There are some benefits to this emphasis on employment security rather than job security. What employees need in this kind of economy is opportunity rather than security, and they must have the skills to take advantage of the opportunities that come along. This calls for continual growth on the part of employees, a willingness to learn new skills, an emphasis on continual learning and creativity, and openness to change. Security in a given job or company can lead to stultification, boredom, and creation of a workforce that is resistant to change. On the other hand, an opportunity society can degenerate into a free-for-all, where it's every man for himself and the devil take the hindmost. In this kind of environment, top management has all the security with more than adequate pension plans and severance packages, and employees have all the risk and little opportunity for any kind of security.

No matter what kind of a new contract eventually evolves between employees and employers, there is a need for the kind of trust and responsibility that go with community. In 1994, a report issued by the Committee on the Evolution of Work of the AFL-CIO criticized management by stating that efforts related to work reform amounted to little more than attempts to make workers feel good and work harder. The report acknowledged that distrust between labor and management was endemic to the old system and that any new contract can function effectively only if these deep suspicions are replaced by mutual respect.[8] Some CEOs also emphasized the need for employers and employees to share in both the risks and rewards as an alternative to the disappearance of long-term job security, which was similar to the position taken in the AFL-CIO statement.

Changes going on in the American workplace call for new understandings and new relationships between employees and employers and new roles for government and labor unions. Some of the key elements in dealing with these changes are (1) the need for trust and respect between each employee and employer, (2) the need for open and honest communication within the corporation, (3) the need for participation at all levels of the organization, (4) the need to treat people as human beings rather than abstract factors of production, (5) and the need for commitment to cope with change in a manner that is not destructive for the employee or the organization.

The present situation is one in which past means of interaction between employees and employers is breaking down and new ones must be established. But the past does not necessarily contain guidelines for the future that is emerging. This calls for creative imagination in envisioning possibilities for reconstruction of roles and responsibilities that is sensitive to the conflicting demands of different groups in the corporation that need to be reorganized into workable relationships. Employees and employers must each strive to take the perspective of the other in coming to grips with the diversity of interests to be satisfied. The working out of these new relationships cannot be mandated from on high by either employee organizations or management decrees, but will be an ongoing process that houses an opportunity for real growth on the part of all parties.

The development of a new contract calls for new relationships that can better allow the corporation to function as a true community. This explicitly requires community dialogue, by recognizing all the participants as autonomous, morally responsible individuals whose creative inputs and diverse interests are vital to the adjustment necessary for the ongoing growth of the corporation. What is necessary is the recognition of individual human beings who cannot be dismembered to become a diversity of cogs in a corporate machine, but who can, in their individuality, function as diverse centers of creativity in a unified corporate community.

THE CORPORATION IN COMMUNITY

One purpose of the corporation, of course, is to produce goods and services that contribute to the material well-being of society. If it has done things right and produced things people want to buy and find useful and has done so efficiently, so that people can afford to buy the things the company produces, the company will be rewarded with profits, part of which can be paid out as dividends to stockholders. The price of its stock may also appreciate, in which case the wealth of the investors will also increase. But these economic responsibilities are not the only purpose of the corporation. The corporation is a multipurpose organization that has multiple responsibilities in society.

The business organization also exists to provide meaningful life experiences for its employees, to develop new products and technologies through research and development that can improve society, to engage in activities that enhance the environment and to minimize if not eliminate those activities that result in environmental degradation, to be a good citizen in obeying the laws of the countries in which it operates and where possible to help society solve some of its most pressing social problems. Thus the corporation is truly a multipurpose organization and many of these purposes are noneconomic in nature.

Advocates of social responsibility were trying to get at the interrelatedness of business with the broader community of which it is a part. However, this attempt, as described previously, remained rooted in the same individualistic assumptions as capitalism in general. This rootedness is indicated in the very titles used to characterize the field, "Business *and* Society," or "Business *and* its Environment."[9] The title Business *and* Society implies that there are two separable isolatable entities, business and society, and that the corporation is an autonomous unit, which has a choice of whether to consider its obligations to the society that it impacts. The notion of the social responsibilities of business was problematical from the very beginning of the field and embodied implicit individualistic assumptions.

A more appropriate title for the field is "Business *in* Society," which reflects the relational nature of business to the society of which it is a part and for which it provides many of the meanings and values that inform the society. A corporation, as the individual pole within ongoing community dynamics, has to take the perspective of the society as a whole and incorporate the standards and authority of society, even as it remains a unique center of activity that has a creative dimension that enters into the total social experience. Corporations are inseparable entities within society, and their responsibilities are intrinsic to their very nature as social beings.

Despite the individualistic nature of many definitions, stakeholder theory embodies in its nature a relational view of the firm, which incorporates the reciprocal dynamics of community, and the theory's power lies in focusing management decision-making on the multiplicity and diversity of the relationships within which the corporation has its being and on the multipurpose nature of the corporation as a vehicle for enriching these relationships in their various aspects. But for stakeholder theory to be a viable alternative theory of the firm and its responsibilities, it must shed itself, as social responsibility theory needs to do, of its individualistic assumptions.

Stakeholder theory has been criticized in that it cannot be definitive as to what or who is a stakeholder and various attempts to delimit the list of stakeholders have been problematic. However, stakeholder relations are diffused throughout the community as part and parcel of the various relational networks that enter into well-being. The "weight" to be given to particular stakeholder claims in particular situations does not involve a list of stakeholder relations that can be balanced with some mechanical process, but rather involves an interrelated network integral to the welfare of the community itself, and community welfare as background enters into the specific evaluation of the relative "weights" to be given various stakeholders in specific situations.

Thus there can be, not just as a practical consideration but as a theoretical necessity, no exhaustive list of stakeholders; instead, from the backdrop of community welfare the most relevant stakeholders can be brought into specific consideration within specific contexts. What will count as stakeholder claims is context-dependent, and any decision can be only as good as the holistic moral vision of the decision-maker operating within the contours of a specific problematic context. There can be no set formula for the weighing of stakeholder claims, any more than there can be a set formula for deciding what the right thing to do is from a moral and ethical standpoint.

The multiple purposes of a corporation are often lost sight of in the quest for profits, as managers are encouraged to maximize profits and earn the highest rate of return they can for the shareholders. Such a limited view of the corporation can only arise by severing it from the multiple environments in which corporations function. This single-minded pursuit of profits puts the cart before the horse, so to speak, as profit, while essential to the ongoing activity of the corporation, is a by-product of corporate activity and only serves as one sign that the corporation is functioning well in society. But when the economic purposes of a corporation become the be-all and end-all of its existence, this artificially isolates the corporation from the social context that gives it its very being and stagnates the relationships in which it is embedded, eventually leading to a dysfunctional relationship with society. Profits are a means to building a thriving business, but this thriving involves the thriving of the multiple environments in which it is embedded.

William C. Frederick argues that profit is not an original business value but rather is derivative from its economizing function, which, along with growth and systematic integrity, makes up the three original business values. These three original values, rooted in the nature of the physical world, are essential for all life units, including business firms.[10] He makes the distinction between expansion as merely an increase in the size or scope of operations without improvement in economizing activities, and growth as a manifestation of successful economizing. Business is embedded in a moral matrix and is a dimension of human growth and is intrinsically tied to it through its relational nature. Growth of the business is manifest not just through its economizing activities but also through the many activities that enrich the relational matrix in which it is embedded.

The misplaced pursuit of profit as an end in itself cannot be understood in terms of a narrow concern for oneself, because profit may be pursued by employees in a single-minded way when they themselves are not the immediate beneficiaries. This pursuit is based on a kind of mind-set that views the corporation as no more than an economic entity. Profit need not be pursued in a narrowly self-interested way if that profit is a by-product of promoting a total thriving of the both the corporation and the community of which it is a part. Profit, then, is neither good nor bad in itself, but it becomes one or the other through the way it emerges in relation to the community as a whole.

Moreover, self-interest is not to be disdained any more than profit is to be disdained, but must be understood in something other than an individualistic manner. Self-interest and community interests are inseparably intertwined, and a proper balance between these two dimensions is necessary for effective functioning of the total system. Self-interest pursued under the guidance of the proper balance is at one and the same time community interest. Selfishness is of a different nature. Self-interest becomes selfishness when the individual dimension dominates the "other"; this is not only destructive of the other and destructive of the proper balance that fosters a thriving community, but also destructive of the self, which is engaged in selfish behavior. The self, like the community, thrives through the properly balanced intertwining of the dimensions of the individual and the common other that constitute its internal nature. Such a view applies to institutional behavior as well as to the individual self.

11 Globalization

As business becomes increasingly internationalized and a global economy develops, issues that affect business in the international arena arise out of the changes taking place all over the world because of increased globalization. When countries trade with each other and when they are open for foreign investment and technology, they are also more open to outside influences that may cause them problems. The increased magnitude of international trade and investment that has taken place over the past several decades has led to greater interdependence among individual national economies. These economies have become linked together to form a truly global economy, and companies competing in this arena are engaging in a process of cultural and institutional change that is somewhat unprecedented.

GLOBAL CONFLICT

There are two major trends in the world today that provide a framework for understanding the conflicts going on in many countries around the world because of the changes wrought by globalization. One is the trend towards global assimilation, which is destroying much of the world's cultural diversity through the creation of a truly world market. The other is counter to this assimilation, as ethnic, religious, and other cultural groups militantly define themselves in opposition to this assimilation. This was the theme of the popular book, *The Lexus and the Olive Tree*, which are symbols of the post-Cold-War era of globalization, representing two different forces operative in the world today.[1]

As described by the author, half of the world emerged from the Cold War intent on building a better Lexus, meaning they were dedicated to modernizing, streamlining, and privatizing their economies in order to prosper in the era of globalization. The other half of the world, which was sometimes half of the same country or even half of the same person, was caught up in the fight over who owns the olive tree. Fights over the olive tree are so intense because the olive tree represents everything that roots us, identifies us, and locates us in this world, whether it is a tribe, nation, religion, or a place called home. Olive trees provide feelings of self-esteem and belonging that are essential for human survival. Without a sense of home and belonging, life becomes barren and rootless.[2]

During the Cold War, the most likely threat to one's olive tree was another olive tree, as countries threatened each other with annihilation. The biggest threat to olive trees today, according to the author, is from the Lexus, from all the anonymous, transnational, homogenizing, and standardizing market forces and technologies that are part of economic globalization. The Lexus can be so powerful that it can overrun every olive tree in sight and wipe out ethnic and cultural diversity. But there are other positive things about the Lexus that can empower communities to use the new technologies and markets to actually preserve their olive trees. How this conflict plays out in the different olive trees is critical for the future of globalization.[3]

Terrorist activities can be seen as a part of this conflict, particularly the activities of September 11, 2001, which awakened the United States to a threat that it had largely ignored up to that time. The attacks on the World Trade Center and the Pentagon changed the country overnight and made it aware of its vulnerability. Attention initially centered on one man, Osama bin Laden, who stood as a symbol for everything terrorism represented. After the events of September 11, people all over the country asked why we were so hated in the Arab world and why they wanted to provoke us into a military conflict that they could not win, given America's overwhelming military and technological superiority. What may have been misunderstood, however, is that this action was really part of a struggle over olive trees.

In the imagery of bin Laden and his associates, American culture is regarded as a form of idolatry in its materialistic approach to life, which is based on secularism. Western civilization is a form of evil, according to them, that is being spread around the world through trade between nations, and the World Trade Center was a potent symbol of the Lexus that is changing lifestyles in Arab nations. Equally galling to these terrorists was the presence of the American military on the Arabian Peninsula, so striking the Pentagon was striking at the heart of American military might. But the issue is not the United States as such and our way of life; it is the Arab states that are being influenced by American values.

Countries like Saudi Arabia and Egypt in particular are regarded as idol worshippers, cowering behind the United States and adopting its values. The leaders of these countries are regarded as hypocrites by the terrorists, in having largely abandoned true Islamic values. The attacks of September 11 were designed to force these governments to choose between aligning themselves with the idol-worshipping enemies of God or with the true believers. In the Muslim world, economic globalization and the international balance of power come with an American face. Osama bin Laden's rhetoric divides the world into two camps, the United States and its puppet regimes versus the true believers.[4]

This attempt to polarize the Islamic world was expected to help bin Laden and his followers further the cause of Islamic revolution within the Muslim world itself. They consider themselves an island of true believers, surrounded by a sea of iniquity, and think that the future of Islamic religion, and therefore the world, depends on them and their battle against idol worship. They are motivated to martyr themselves because they believe they are locked in a life and death struggle with the forces of unbelief.[5] They are informed by the Islamic tradition of Jihad, or holy war, to defend the faith against nonbelievers and are engaged in a global struggle against a corrupt and oppressive enemy.

Thus there is a struggle for power going on in these countries, a battle over olive trees, and the terrorist attacks can be seen as a response to the failure of extremist movements in the Muslim world to topple the leadership of Muslim countries. Revolutions in Egypt, Syria, and Algeria have largely failed and governments in these countries have managed to crush or marginalize the radicals. The Lexus seems to be winning in much of the Arab world, but the battle over olive trees will continue as people struggle with the threats globalization poses to their identity and self-understanding. The issue is not primarily one of poverty or lack of education but strikes at the heart of what it means to be a human being with a unique identity.

It is against this backdrop of global change and the conflicts it produces that the global corporation and its activities must be understood. When companies export goods and services to foreign countries or transfer technologies to these countries, they are not just selling products or installing technology—they are also promoting a way of life that involves changes that many of these countries find difficult to accept. This way of life reflects the values of Western industrialized societies, values that relate to a materialistic lifestyle and a secular approach to everyday living.

These values are often resisted by foreign countries, which find themselves faced with tension and conflict over what kind of society they want to become. While many of these countries may be attracted to the increased standard of living that Western societies enjoy, they do not necessarily like the values that go along with acceptance of the lifestyle that accompanies this kind of change. It is important for managers to resist the temptation to think that they are just doing business with these countries. Business is conducted in the larger context of social and cultural values and is a major influence for promoting change in these values. To think of economic development as enhancing the quality of life in developing countries, while destroying the social, cultural, and even natural environments within which people in these countries attain meaningful lives, is to treat business in the abstract and ignore the broader context in which business is conducted.

A GLOBAL COMMUNITY

Neither trend, the engulfment of diverse cultures by globalism or isolationist tribalism, can produce a true global community. And it is the creation of a global community that is going to work for the benefit of everyone involved in the process of globalization, including business organizations. It is difficult to conduct business where there is conflict and the unleashing of self-destructive forces in people who are willing to sacrifice their own lives for what they believe is a just cause. A truly global community must have a way of accommodating diversity, and people who are a part of this community must recognize that while there may be values that all people hold in common, these values do not exist in abstract form but are embedded in a diversity of traditions, cultures, and ways of living represented by different countries. While there must be some common agreement among nations for business to be conducted efficiently and effectively, a nation or culture cannot be expected to accept values that require a suicide of itself through the mutilation of its own history and context of meaningful existence.

If a corporation is part and parcel of community life and emerges within the context of community, then the institutionalized legitimacy of a global corporation is dependent upon its situatedness in a global community. Growth can only occur in a moral context that recognizes the need for both conformity and diversity, which constitute a viable community. Thus, as a citizen of a global community, a corporation has a moral responsibility to respect the diversity and free choice of various cultures, which are essential to the ongoing dynamics of community life. Global corporations have a power potential both for furthering and destroying any drive toward a global community, a community that would bring with it the possibilities for the emergence of truly global corporations.

Any global framework that hopes to avoid the extremes of isolationism or monolithic globalism must definitively reject the long history of individualistic thinking that offers the choice between the collective homogeneous whole at the expense of the individual or the individual at the expense of the collective whole. In this case, the individual unit is the culture with its own unique traditions and meanings, and the collective whole is the uniformity that results from the globalism of market forces. What the dynamics of community require at the global level is the essential dynamics of any community. There must be a balance between conformity and standardization, which is necessary for business to function efficiently, and the need for novelty and unique perspectives that provide meaning and rootedness to individual cultures.

The dynamics of community at the global level, however, are more difficult to maintain because of the lack of global institutions for the adjudication of conflicting claims. The theoretical differences to be adjudicated are also much more difficult. But these differences, like all strongly entrenched differences, can only be resolved by turning to specific situations and the conflicting demands contained in those situations. For a global community to evolve, there must be an evolution of global organs of adjudication, for a community is constituted by the ongoing accommodation between the dimensions of diversity and conformity. A truly global community must provide organs for accommodation and ongoing development capable of transforming alien cultures into a vital pluralistic community, where both conformity to certain norms and novel approaches to life situations are respected.

GLOBAL NORMS AND STANDARDS

Global corporations are changing social, economic, and political landscapes around the world. They are in the process of creating a worldwide culture that is homogeneous in terms of basic values and lifestyles. This internationalization of domestic economies around the world is most directly the result of decisions private firms make to engage in international trade and investment. Growth in trade between nations and international investment means that global corporations have significant economic and social impacts on national economies and political systems. Their activities have become very visible, making them subject to criticism from many quarters.

They have something of a love-hate relationship with many developing countries. On the one hand, many of these countries welcome global corporations because they have the potential to assist these countries in pursuing their own economic growth and development. Yet these same countries view global corporations as a threat to their national sovereignty and autonomy. They do not want to become economically and technologically dependent on institutions that are not subject to their control, and they often find global corporations hard to live with and yet impossible to live without.

Many countries find it difficult to control the activities of global corporations within their territories. The flexibility of these global entities enables them to move capital, goods, personnel, information, and technology across national boundaries. This flexibility allows them to play one country off against another to get the best deal for themselves, just as they sometimes play states off against each other in this country. Since the activities of global corporations affect the level of social and economic development in many countries, particularly developing countries, there is always interest in developing some form of international regulation to control their activities. Third World nations in particular believe that in the absence of international regulation, global corporations would show interest only in profit maximization, without any regard to the developmental needs of host nations. Some of the problems global corporations create for host countries include the following:

- The benefits of foreign investments are poorly or unfairly distributed between global corporations and the host country.
- Global corporations pre-empt the development of an indigenous economic base by squeezing out local entrepreneurs.
- Global corporations employ inappropriate capital-intensive technology, adding to host country unemployment.
- Global corporations worsen the distribution of income in the host country.
- They alter consumer tastes in the host country, thus undermining the culture.
- Foreign investors subvert host country political processes by co-opting the local elites, using their influence to keep host governments in line, and structuring the international system to respond to their needs to the detriment of host authorities.[6]

Expansion beyond national boundaries is much more than a step across the geographical line of a country. It is also a step toward new and different social, educational, political, and economic environments, where different values and cultures mean that there are different ways of conducting business. As conflicts arise between global corporations and host countries, these differences cause problems for managers of global corporations. Most conflicts of this nature arise because global corporations have some degree of economic power because of the decisions they make concerning product lines, location of plants, technology employed, trade flows, treatment of local employees, and other business considerations. These decisions are made with regard to corporate objectives such as profits and market share and are not necessarily made in the interests of the host country.

Investment decisions and operational practices are geared to the need of global corporations to survive and grow by maintaining or increasing world market shares, gaining a competitive edge over rivals, shifting operations to take advantage of access to natural resources or cheap labor markets, and other such factors where policies and strategies are developed that are truly global in nature, scope, and character. Global corporations do not and cannot take the interests of each and every country into account in the decisions they make because the interests of the various countries affected by these decision rarely coincide. Global corporations look after their own interests within a worldwide strategy they develop for themselves.

Yet governments are not likely to let important decisions be made by a foreign private institution without exercising some kind of influence. Host governments influence global corporations in a variety of ways, including regulations to set the rules of the game for the conduct of global corporations. But regulations of this kind are fraught with problems, as the regulations of different countries will most likely clash with global corporations caught in the middle. The regulatory environment varies considerably from country to country. Many regulations governing global corporations are difficult to interpret and are not consistently enforced. Moreover, in large parts of the Third World, there is a distinct absence of regulations or mechanisms for enforcing those regulations that do exist. They often lack the necessary legal and administrative institutions and the technical proficiency to implement and enforce national policies.

Are some kinds of ethical standards, then, part of the answer, standards related to corporate conduct on a worldwide basis? This approach, however, has its problems, as every country has its own standards with regard to the conduct of business, and these standards are often in direct conflict with each other, as well as with the home country, as expressed in custom or formal legislation. These conflicts can arise in almost every area of activity, including anticompetitive conduct, marketing practices, environmental policies, resource exploitation, and hiring practices. Global corporations can be caught between different norms and standards regarding acceptable conduct, making it difficult for global corporations to decide which standards to adhere to in the conduct of their business.

Should a global corporation adopt a "when in Rome, do as the Romans do" policy and adapt its behavior to conform to the standards of each country in which it does business? Or should it adopt a uniform standard for its worldwide operations that it follows in every country with regard to issues such as hiring practices or environmental policies? Should it attempt to do business throughout the world the way business is conducted in the United States, or should it view this approach as cultural imperialism and adopt a more relativistic approach to its conduct in foreign countries?

Some scholars think universal standards exist with respect to many business practices and that such guidelines may be found embedded in several multilateral compacts adopted by governments over the years. Taken as a whole, these guidelines are believed to comprise a framework for identifying the essential moral behavior expected of global corporations, regardless of where they are conducting operations. This set of prescriptions embodies a moral authority that transcends national boundaries and cultural differences, thereby invoking or manifesting universal transcultural standards of corporate behavior that should be adhered to in every country in which a global corporation does business. These guidelines are said to have direct implications for a wide range of specific corporate policies and practices, including pollution control efforts, advertising and marketing activities, childcare, minimum wages, hours of work, employee training and education, adequate housing and health care, severance pay, privacy of employees and consumers, safety and health programs, and other policies and practices.[7]

Other scholars also believe there are general ethical standards that apply to business operating anywhere in the world. Richard T. DeGeorge, for example, believes there are five such standards that are universally applicable because they are necessary either for a society to function at all or for business transactions to take place. These standards include (1) the injunction against arbitrarily killing other members of the community to which one belongs, (2) the positive injunction to tell the truth and its negative corollary not to lie, (3) respect for property, (4) the injunction to honor contracts, and (5) exercising fairness in business contracts.[8] From these basic norms, seven moral guidelines are derived that global corporations should follow when operating in Third World countries.

- Global corporations should do no harm.
- Global corporations should produce more good than bad for the host country.
- Global corporations should contribute by their activities to the host country's development.
- Global corporations should respect the rights of its employees.
- Global corporations should pay their fair share of taxes.
- To the extent the local culture does not violate moral norms, global corporations should respect the local culture and not work against it.
- Global corporations should cooperate with the local government in the development and enforcement of just background institutions.[9]

There is continuing interest in international codes of ethics to deal with differences between countries and promote a uniform way of doing business around the world. The United Nations Centre on Transnational Corporations (UNCTC) provided numerous services for member nations with respect to the operations of what it called Transnational Corporations (TNCs) within their borders. It collected critical data on these world corporations and published incisive critiques of their growing power. It also attempted to develop an international code of conduct to regulate the activities of TNCs with regard to the internal affairs of host countries and to encourage TNCs to facilitate the achievement of the development activities of Third World countries. This code represented the first time a comprehensive international instrument was being developed for regulating a wide range of issues arising from relations between global corporations and host governments.[10]

The code was meant to provide a stable, predictable and transparent framework that could facilitate the flow of resources across national boundaries, enhancing the role of foreign investment in economic and industrial growth. The code was also meant to minimize the negative effects of TNCs by setting out, in a balanced manner, the rights and responsibilities of TNCs and host governments. As a result of this twin focus, it was hoped the code would help reduce friction between TNCs and host countries and enable the flow of direct foreign investment to realize its full potential.[11] However, this effort came to naught when the UNCTC was shut down during the first Bush administration.[12]

In January 1999, United Nations Secretary-General Kofi Annan proposed a Global Compact, in which he challenged world business leaders to build the social and environmental pillars required to sustain the new global economy and make globalization work for all the world's people. The Compact's operational phase was launched on July 26, 2000, at a high-level event at UN headquarters. The Compact is composed of nine principles, drawn from the Universal Declaration of Human Rights, the International Labor Organization's Fundamental Principles on Rights at Work, and the Rio Principles on Environment and Development.[13]

The Compact is not meant to be a regulatory instrument or code of conduct, but global corporations are encouraged to internalize these principles as integral elements of corporate strategies and practices. It is also not a substitute for effective action by governments, but an opportunity for corporations to exercise leadership based on their enlightened self-interest. Companies that commit themselves to support the Compact are asked to post on its website concrete steps they have taken to act on any of the nine principles. The purpose of these postings is to create a databank showcasing what works and what doesn't. Eventually, these postings, together with additional case studies, will form the basis of a comprehensive learning bank, providing useful information on how to promote change consistent with the nine principles and overcome impediments to their implementation.[14]

The Compact's Nine Principles

Human Rights

1. Business should support and respect the protection of internationally proclaimed human rights; and
2. Ensure that they are not complicit in human rights abuses.

Labor

3. Business should uphold the freedom of association and the effective recognition of the right to collective bargaining; as well as
4. The elimination of all forms of forced and compulsory labor;
5. The effective abolition of child labor; and
6. Eliminate discrimination in respect of employment and occupation.

Environment

7. Business should support a precautionary approach to environmental challenges;
8. Undertake initiatives to promote greater environmental responsibility; and
9. Encourage the development and diffusion of environmentally friendly technologies.

Rights have been used as a vehicle for extending moral consideration to people caught up in globalism. The issue of human rights has been of particular concern in relation to certain countries with which the U.S. does business. The Universal Declaration of Human Rights, for example, was meant to declare civil, political, cultural, and economic rights for all people, as well as the rights of children, women, ethnic groups and religions. It was meant to create a global safety net of rights applicable to all persons everywhere, and allows for no cultural exceptionalism.[15]

United Nations Universal Declaration of Human Rights

- The right to property alone as well as in association with others.
- The right to work, to free choice of employment, to just and favorable conditions of work, and to protection against unemployment.
- The right to just and favorable remuneration, insuring for the worker and his family an existence worthy of human dignity.
- The right to form and join trade unions.
- The right to rest and leisure, including reasonable limitation of working hours and periodic holidays with pay.

Rights issues were of particular concern with sweatshops in foreign countries. This term refers to the conditions under which people had to work in factories overseas that were producing goods to be sold in American markets. These conditions involved long hours, poor working conditions, low wages, and in general inhumane treatment of workers with respect to breaks, child labor, and other factors. Pressures were brought against American companies to either improve conditions in these factories or find other suppliers. The issue was often stated as one of balancing labor rights with the need for economic development in these countries.

Another scholar in international ethics as they apply to global corporations uses the rights concept to establish minimum levels of morally acceptable behavior that are the rock bottom of modern moral deliberation regarding the responsibilities of global corporations operating abroad. While the list may be incomplete, it is argued that the human claims it honors and the interests these claims represent are globally relevant. These rights are believed to have universal applicability and apply to people in any country of the world.[16]

- The Right to Freedom of Physical Movement
- The Right to Ownership of Property
- The Right to Freedom From Torture
- The Right to a Fair Trial
- The Right to Nondiscriminatory Treatment
- The Right to Physical Security
- The Right to Freedom of Speech and Association
- The Right to Minimal Education

- The Right to Political Participation
- The Right to Subsistence

Other international codes have been developed by non-governmental organizations, such as the Caux Round Table, which is an organization of business leaders from Europe, Japan, and the United States. This group was formed in 1986 as a means of reducing trade tensions between countries. The Round Table believes that the world business community should play an important role in improving economic and social conditions. The Caux Principles, as they are called, seek to express a world standard against which business behavior can be measured. It is rooted in two basic ethical ideals: living and working together for the common good and human dignity. The General Principles in the code seek to clarify the spirit of these ideals, while the Stakeholder Principles are concerned with their practical application.[17]

The problem with all such international codes is to make them general enough to secure ratification by a number of nations with diverse interests and yet specific enough to have some real meaning in actual situations. Another problem is implementation. Third World countries generally want such codes to be binding and are in favor of setting up some institutional machinery for enforcement purposes, while industrialized countries generally want such codes to be voluntary in nature without any binding authority. This problem of international enforcement authority has undermined many efforts of this nature.

The rights approach, in particular, has been criticized as focusing excessively on individual rights while neglecting the rights of society and the common good.[18] Conflicts between the rights of individuals and the rights of a society to chart its own course and set its own standards are often a factor in trade negotiations between countries. Whose rights take precedence in situations where rights clash? Do sovereign countries have a right to govern themselves as they see fit without outside interference? Or should companies concern themselves with promoting rights of workers in these countries to improve their condition?

International codes of conduct are best seen as attempts to articulate the vague moral sense that expresses itself through various specific rules in various cultural contexts. But the richness of this moral sense both underlies and overflows the culturally variable specifics. And as in all situations that present conflicting interests and needs to be adjudicated, what should result is an ongoing experimental process in which the various interested parties accommodate each other through communicative interactions founded on a deepening and broadening openness of perspectives. Richard DeGeorge says that when nations disagree about what practices are just, what is required is "enlarging one's scope to include other perspectives." And as he elaborates, this widening scope does not imply that one give up one's own ethical perspective, but it also disallows the imposition of one's views even if in a position to do so.[19]

Many global corporations have developed codes of their own to promote universal business principles. They do not believe that a system of government mandated standards is either desirable or sustainable. There are a great variety of products and services, labor markets, competitive conditions, and changing technologies in production systems throughout the world. To develop a set of uniform standards of behavior in the midst of this variety or to create regulations that attempt to foresee all possible situations would make the system onerous, bureaucratic, expensive, and unworkable. Thus it is believed to be better for each company to develop a code that is unique to its own circumstances.

For managers of global corporations, moral guidelines such as those mentioned previously could be taken to represent a growing consensus among the world's peoples about what is thought to be morally desirable action by private enterprises. While these guidelines do not cover all possible issues that are of concern to people nor are they universally adhered to by all countries, they could be taken to represent the general outlines of a globally-oriented system of moral standards governing corporate behavior.[20] These guidelines are important for leaders of global enterprises to take into account when developing policies and strategies for their companies as the internationalization of the world proceeds and grows more complicated.

CHALLENGES

Against this backdrop regarding the role of global corporations in creating a global community in which diversity is respected and celebrated with an underlying recognition of some deeply rooted common values, specific issues such as bribery, marketing practices, labor practices, trade practices, and environmental problems can be seen in a broader context. These issues arise out of the material needs of people all over the world to have a decent level of existence to which global corporations can contribute. The implementation of this vision is not easy nor can it be wished away by adherence to merely economic concerns. The resolution of these issues requires morally perceptive managers who are sensitive to the manifold dimensions of these issues and who are willing to adopt an openness to the perspectives of other cultures and other peoples.

International trade and investment do more than merely increase contact between diverse communities, as they also contribute to an emerging global or world community. The diverse inputs of individual nations are part of an ongoing process of adjustment relative to conducting business according to some common standards or common agreements as to what works in the interests of all parties. The means of adjudication that would enable the resolution of conflicts between countries have not yet been adequately developed, as countries are exploring new and better ways of resolving issues that arise in the world community.

Institutions such as the World Trade Organization (WTO), the International Monetary Fund, the World Bank, the European Union, and the North American Free Trade Agreement (NAFTA), among others, have been created to underpin cooperation among states and consolidate their commitment to liberalize economic policy between nations. The nineteenth century was a world of unilateral and discretionary policy while the late twentieth century was a world of multilateral and institutional policy.[21] What the twenty-first century holds is not clear at this point, as the United States started off with a unilateral military policy that threatens multilateralism.

It seems clear from protests against the WTO, for example, that these institutions are in need of reform along more democratic lines. Secret decisions made behind closed doors are not acceptable to people accustomed to transparent, democratic processes. Interest groups that are used to having their voices heard in their home country are demanding that they also be heard by international institutions. Issues related to environmental problems are not going away nor is concern with labor standards in foreign countries. There will continue to be conflict over these and other issues as globalization proceeds, and global companies will continue to be most visible in this process.

The liberalization of markets by itself does not lift all boats and in some cases does harm to people. What the world lacks is a consensus on how best to create economic growth that is of benefit to all people, not just a favored few in each country. While capitalism has proven itself to be the best way to achieve this growth, it is a peculiar creation of Western culture. While not inherently alien to other cultures, it is at least unfamiliar and unnatural. The enthusiasm for material growth, faith in democracy, and the sanctity of property are Western values not necessarily shared by other societies.

A world community need be neither an absolutism of universal rules imposed on others from "on high" nor a relativism of self-enclosed cultural "choices," but rather depends on an openness involving ongoing dialogue. An emerging consensus regarding international business conduct will come from a deepening attunement to a sense of what human existence is all about and the common values that underlie the diversity of cultural differences. This consensus must be "coaxed out of hiding" through an ongoing dialogue and an accompanying growth process that allows a more adequate understanding of other perspectives and ways of life.

Every human is in interaction with other individuals, and we are all embedded in a single universe upon which experience opens and with which we must successfully interact to survive and grow as human beings. Human existence is inherently communal and embodies universally shared features contoured by diverse sociocultural contexts. As R. Edward Freeman and Daniel R. Gilbert state: "If we share the same kinds of experience—for example, the experience of language, learning, family ties, and meaningful work—we already have a common base from which to look for principles."[22] From this communal basis, Freeman and Gilbert propose a "common morality" applicable to communal interactions everywhere, while allowing for the cultural diversity of moral activities as they emerge within specific sociocultural-historical contexts.

The vague but rich moral sense that guides us in our interactions with each other and the world contains perceptions of global significance, not because these perceptions are clear to reason, but because they are infused with the moral vitality of human impulses. These vague perceptions overflow the abstractive activity of reflective awareness. Frederick puts it this way: "Though varying in shape and force and mode or expression from society to society, the core principles keep reappearing. And for very good reason: they speak to the voice of nature, they tell of an irreducible core of moral meaning."[23] The lifeblood of emerging global organs of adjudication and codes and agreements that these organs elicit is this primal moral vitality, rooted in our natural embeddedness in communal life.

As the world moves toward the development of a true world community, there are few benchmarks to serve as guides, and hence the combination of sensitivity to deeply embedded human values and the creative grasp of possibilities for ongoing development that is consistent with these values is greatly needed. In this ongoing process, emerging rules and standards will need to be continually evaluated for their adequacy in providing guidance in concrete situations, and new problems will, in turn, alter these rules and standards. Though this process may be slow and difficult, only a world community with appropriate institutions for resolving differences between the unique input of individual nations and global corporations and a general or common interest of global proportions can hope to cope with the kinds of issues that emerge in the context of the international business scene.

12 Science and Technology

Ours is a scientific and technological culture. What this means at least in part is that people in our society turn to science for answers as to how the world works and to technological solutions for most of their problems. Science provides us with knowledge of nature, even our own human nature, and gives us the capability of manipulating nature in our own interests. Technology involves the application of scientific findings and gives us the means to use and shape nature to accomplish the objectives of individuals and organizations. Even if we are not professional scientists, we learn to think about the world in scientific terms and are used to thinking of technological solutions. But science and technology are at best a mixed blessing. In addition to solving problems, they oftentimes create new problems with which society has to cope in some fashion. Science and technology impact society and often have unintended consequences.

Business is dependent on science and technology for the development of new products and processes to produce those products. Science discovers new things that can be done with the raw materials that a business organization has available, and new technologies provide the opportunity for business to take these findings and produce new or improved products. Science plays an important role in business organizations, and the way it is used in these organizations is important to society. Technology is employed by business organizations to attain its objectives, and technology can have both good and bad impacts on the society at large. There are inherent responsibilities to the larger community in the use of science and technology because of the moral nature of these endeavors and the possibilities they have to greatly benefit human beings or the potential to do great harm.

BUSINESS AND SCIENCE

Relative to science, these moral dimensions involve the truth claims science makes about certain aspects of our environment and about the effect of certain substances on human health. These truth claims, by and large, have to do with cause and effect relationships. Does smoking cause cancer? Is saccharin a safe food additive? Are certain chemicals used in the workplace dangerous to workers' health? Is asbestos really harmful enough to justify its removal from buildings? Is dioxin really one of the most toxic substances known to humans? Do certain drugs have side effects that are dangerous enough to users that they should be removed from the marketplace? Are breast implants harmful to women? Is global warming real and is it caused by human activities such that immediate steps need to be taken to limit emissions of carbon dioxide and other greenhouse gases? Examples of this nature seem to be endless, as debates about environmental and health matters continue in our society and new evidence is discovered and new research methods developed. The outcome of these debates is crucial to business because of the impact on product development and marketing, to say nothing of the potential liability.

One would think that science could answer these questions conclusively to the satisfaction of all parties, particularly in a society where science is so dominant. Science is supposedly objective and impartial and is concerned with the discovery of so-called facts with respect to questions such as those posed previously. But in most of these situations, the facts are never conclusively established and debate continues. Business tends to come up with its studies that show no significant linkage between a substance and human health or the environment, and government or other private organizations come up with other studies that show such a linkage. Who is right and which studies should be accepted as the basis of decision-making about a product or process?

The Saccharin Controversy

Perhaps an example will illustrate the problem. The safety of our food supply is a matter of serious concern. Substances that are added to food to make it taste better, last longer, sweeten it, or color it are of particular concern and are sometimes controversial. Such a controversy erupted in March 1977, when the Food and Drug Administration (FDA) disclosed that saccharin (called Sweet and Low), a widely-used sugar substitute at the time, could possibly cause cancer in humans and announced plans to ban its use as a food additive. Laboratory experiments in Canada had shown that when rats were fed the "maximum tolerable" dose of saccharin, a larger than expected number of male rats got bladder cancer. These experiments exposed rats to a high dose of saccharin for two generations. Under these conditions, male rats developed significantly more bladder tumors than did rats not exposed to saccharin. This Canadian study was the final confirmation of a series of studies that had shown similar results.[1]

Given these findings, the FDA believed it had no choice under the Delaney Clause of the Food and Drug Act but to ban the additive. This clause was very specific in demanding a "zero tolerance" level for additives that were discovered to cause cancer in humans or animals. The FDA had previously banned other additives, such as cyclamates, safrole, and red dye #2 and other coloring agents. What made the saccharin case different was that it was the only sugar substitute generally available on the market at the time. The ban would have destroyed the $1.1 billion-a-year diet drink industry and deprived diabetics of their only source of sweetening. An unprecedented public outcry against the ban (the FDA received more than 100,000 comments) convinced Congress in November 1977 to pass an 18-month moratorium.[2]

The moratorium legislation called for the National Academy of Sciences to study the situation. They concluded in November 1978 that saccharin was indeed a weak carcinogen, at least in rats. Therefore, the sweetener must also be regarded as a potential, though probably feeble, human carcinogen. Weak in this case referred to the number of cases of cancer, not to the seriousness of the cancer in any one individual. Some scientists pointed out that cancer caused by a "weak" carcinogen is no less deadly to those affected. With this kind of inconclusive evidence and public pressures mounting for its use, when the moratorium did finally end in May 1979, the FDA chose not to revive the ban on saccharin. Warning labels, however, were required on any product containing the product. Congress subsequently extended the moratorium seven times, and in 1991 the FDA formally withdrew its proposal to ban the use of the substance.

All this activity was rendered moot when G. D. Searle received FDA approval to sell its artificial sweetener aspartame (called Nutra-Sweet) in the U.S. market. It had taken eight years for the company to receive approval of this low-calorie sugar substitute. It was initially cleared for use as a table-top sweetener and for use in presweetened cereals, powdered soft drinks, chewing gum, and dessert and topping mixes.[3] Two years later, the FDA approved aspartame for use in carbonated drinks. Subsequently, Coca-Cola Company and Royal Crown Cola Company announced plans to use the sweetener in their diet drinks. More uses of the sweetener followed and sales increased dramatically. Eventually, Nutra-Sweet took over the market and the little pink packets of Sweet and Low disappeared, replaced by the little blue packets of Nutra-Sweet.

In July 1997, the National Institutes of Health (NIH) announced that its National Toxicology Program (NTP) was reviewing data that could delist saccharin from the federal government's Report on Carcinogens. This review was prompted by a request from the Calorie Control Council, an international trade association representing the low-calorie food industry, to have the substance delisted from the report. The Council argued that saccharin's presence on the list was wrong, misleading consumers, and not based on current science. According to the Council, evidence gathered over the past 20 years as well as safe use for over a century clearly demonstrated saccharin's safety. The Council also questioned the studies on which the initial ban had been based.[4]

Some scientists opposed this recommendation and urged the government to keep the artificial sweetener on its list of cancer-causing chemicals.[5] Nonetheless, in May 2000, the NTP announced that saccharin had been delisted, citing the support of leading health groups that had reviewed the scientific research on saccharin and supported its safety. On December 21, 2000, President Clinton signed a bill removing the warning label that had been required. It was not too long after this action that the little pink packets of Sweet and Low made their reappearance on store shelves across the nation without the warning label.

What Are Facts?

What are the facts in this situation? Does the fact that saccharin caused cancer in rats mean that it poses a risk for humans? How relevant are animal studies to humans? Often animals are injected with large doses of a substance to speed up reactions and so as not to miss any potential reactions. These doses are sometimes way off the charts as far as relevance to human consumption is concerned. Are the results, then, relevant to human uses of the substance? Also, the environment in which these studies are done is carefully controlled and the animals are specially bred for this purpose, which is much different from the haphazard environment in which humans live, where they are exposed to many substances in an uncontrolled environment. And how much risk is acceptable? Is a zero tolerance level necessary to adequately protect human health?

Many ethical decision-making models start with a gathering of the facts, assuming that further ethical analysis or decision-making must proceed from a firm knowledge of the facts about certain situations. Without this kind of knowledge, so it is argued, ethical analysis is likely to be off target at best or perhaps irrelevant at worst. Yet this first step of getting the facts is not as simple as it seems. Very often it is precisely the facts that are in dispute, such that a firm establishment of the facts is not possible, as the previous example indicates. Scientists themselves disagree as to what facts are and whether certain kinds of evidence are conclusive with regards to decision-making.[6]

Several years ago, there was a controversy about the safety of ethylene dibromide (EDB), a substance that was widely useful in fumigating grain milling machinery, as a bulk fumigant in grain storage bins, and as a soil fumigant by the citrus industry. Studies were conducted that showed EDB appeared to induce cancer in laboratory animals, and on the basis of these studies and its own analysis of EDB's risk to human health, the Environmental Protection Agency (EPA) eventually banned all uses of EDB and ordered grain products to be removed from grocery shelves that contained what were considered to be harmful residues of the substance. Many reputable scientists, however, disputed the implications of these studies and argued that the results of animal studies could not be extrapolated to humans, and that there were no credible studies connecting cancer in humans to trace elements of EDB in food products.[7]

The smoking controversy has gone on for several decades and is a terribly complex situation, involving all kinds of people and institutions and all kinds of conflicting factual claims and values. We have moved more and more towards a smoke-free society over this period of time, but there are many unanswered questions involved in the controversy. The discovery that second-hand smoke could have harmful health effects on innocent parties changed the nature of the controversy and has led to all sorts of restrictions on where smokers can engage in their habit. The Tobacco Institute, representing the tobacco companies, kept claiming that no one had proven conclusively that smoking causes cancer, because many people who smoke do not get cancer and not everyone who has cancer has smoked. Thus it is obvious, they kept claiming for some years, that there is not a one-to-one correlation between smoking and cancer and thus smoking does not necessarily cause cancer.[8]

While technically the Tobacco Institute is right, the question is what kind of evidence is relevant to making decisions about smoking? We do not have the technological capacity at present of peering inside the human body to see how smoke reacts with human cells to cause cancer. We do not know the mechanism by which this happens. What we have are studies that correlate the inhalation of smoke with the incidence of cancer. While such studies do not prove cause and effect, if enough studies of this kind show a high correlation between smoke inhalation and cancer, and there is no evidence that some other substance caused the cancer, then we begin to infer that there is a cause-and-effect relationship between inhaling smoke from cigarettes and getting cancer.

We live in an uncertain, probabilistic world, where it is generally known that most complex issues of this nature cannot be proven conclusively by science or any other method. But when enough studies show a high correlation between certain variables, we begin to accept the fact that there is a high probability that if we do one thing the other is likely to follow. Thus we begin to believe that if we smoke or inhale second-hand smoke we put ourselves at great risk of getting cancer. This risk is increasingly unacceptable in our society, and thus we have passed many laws limiting our exposure to second-hand smoke in public places like restaurants and airplanes. Even hotels have smoke-free rooms for those that want them.

The so-called facts are not something brutally given in nature and free from the realm of values. While we would like to believe that science collects the facts and objectively analyzes nature to determine the relationships between entities and avoids the "fuzzy" unscientific realm of values, such a view is not very realistic. What we hold as valuable enters into our very perception of the facts. Our judgments about what the facts are, what we will accept as fact, what evidence we believe is relevant to the situation, and what methodology is appropriate to answer questions about nature are all influenced by what we hold as valuable. Values enter into an interpretation of the facts, describing what the facts mean and what implications they have for human life.

Controversies about the facts of a given situation are thus not solely about the facts themselves but are also questions of value. The values we hold about smoking as a human activity, for example, enter into our judgments about the validity of certain kinds of scientific evidence and influence what we accept as true about this question. These values reflect our interests, financial and nonfinancial, that we have in the issue of smoking. Do we own stock in a tobacco company? Do we consider smoking to be a disgusting habit? Or do we gain some amount of satisfaction from smoking? Has a loved one or friend died of lung cancer? Do we believe people ought to be able to do whatever they want? Will our business be adversely affected by a smoking ban? All such interests are reflected in our values as they relate to a specific activity, such as smoking, and the possible effects it has on human health and the environment.

In the EDB case, the EPA had the authority to make the decision about continued use of the substance and based its decision on its judgment about the validity of certain studies and their implications for the risk humans faced from continued exposure to the substance. Its decisions about what the "facts" were in this situation reflected its mission to protect human health and the conservative values inherent in its decision-making process. If business organizations had been making the decision, they undoubtedly would have questioned the validity of animal studies and interpreted the risks in a much different fashion, reflecting the interests of business as a profit-making institution.

Most of the facts about our world, with its complex integrated systems of interrelations, are disputable and changing. They are often in dispute, and how these disputes are resolved reflect the values of the disputants. Facts are no more brutally objective and absolute than the values we hold, and emerge out of human experience the same as values. The way most of these situations work is that evidence begins to mount against a substance, such as asbestos or tobacco, so that over time it becomes apparent to most people that the substance is harmful to human health or the environment. However, it may take years for this kind of conclusion to emerge, and in the meantime, corporations may deny that there are problems with its product until drastic measures are necessary.

For years, Manville Corporation denied that asbestos caused serious health problems, until it had to file for bankruptcy to protect itself from an onslaught of product liability lawsuits. The company emerged from this process a very different kind of corporate entity, subject to governance procedures that were quite out of the ordinary for a public corporation.[9] The discovery that second-hand smoke was dangerous to non-smokers changed the nature of the debate about tobacco, and our society has moved toward a smoke-free society ever since, over the strenuous objection of the tobacco companies. At one point, the Supreme Court came within one vote of deciding that nicotine was a drug subject to regulation by the Food and Drug Administration (FDA).[10]

No one study is definitive in these situations, but some can be pivotal in changing the nature of the debate within corporations, as well as society as a whole. While managers of corporations can never be certain that a particular substance or product is harmful and warrants drastic measures, as the evidence mounts against a substance or product, they should begin to question long-held assumptions and strategies relative to the entity being questioned. Arguments for and against the taking of drastic measures embody conflicting interpretations of the relevance and significance of the data stemming from conflicting value-laden contexts.

As concern about chlorofluorocarbons (CFCs) and their role in depleting the ozone layer mounted, Du Pont Corporation, the world's largest producer of CFCs, initially led producers and users in opposing regulation, citing scientific uncertainty as the primary reason for this opposition. While the company supported the Montreal Protocol, which set production caps for the world's industrialized nations, it initially saw no need to phase out production of CFCs entirely. The issuance of the NASA Executive Summary Report on ozone depletion caused it to reassess its position. This report described a fundamental change in the scientific understanding of the CFC-ozone connection and suggested that implementation of the Montreal Protocol would result in little net depletion of ozone destruction. Soon after this report was released, Du Pont decided to go beyond what the treaty required and stop production of CFCs altogether and accelerate the search for substitutes.[11]

This discussion is meant to strongly suggest that what we believe is factual about the world and what we value are intertwined in manifold ways. Both facts and values emerge out of experience as wedded dimensions of complex contexts, which cannot be so easily reduced into mechanistic laws that show definitive causal relationships between variables. Managers of business organizations need to be aware of which problems need further research that can advance knowledge of a situation and enlighten the discussion because the factual dimensions are still in contention, and where the evidence relevant to a problem is convincing enough that the focus should be on understanding the values operative in the situation that lead to diverse views and recommended courses of action. Only thus can an intelligent decision be made on the basis of what is believed to promote human welfare and human fulfillment.

There seems to be an emerging consensus, for example, about global warming. The evidence relative to two aspects of this situation seem to be beyond contention, namely that carbon dioxide levels in the atmosphere have been on the increase ever since the industrial revolution and that the earth has been warming over the past several decades. Some may want to argue that the way we measure carbon dioxide levels and the earth's temperature are both flawed, but this debate has been relegated to the fringes of scientific opinion. What is the most important question at this point is whether the warming that the earth is experiencing is due to the activities of human beings or due to natural causes, and even here the weight of scientific opinion of the most prestigious scientific bodies comes down on the side of human actions, such as emissions of greenhouse gases.[12]

So the debate at this point is largely about values, about the value of mitigating the extent of future warming by reducing the release of greenhouse gases into the atmosphere and incurring the cost of changing our ways of producing and consuming energy, versus the value of maintaining our current lifestyles and production patterns and incurring the costs of adjusting to a continually warming climate. More research is certainly necessary to understand better how climate patterns work and how they are disrupted, but such research should not be used to confuse the issue and postpone coming to grips with the ramifications of a warming planet and the adjustments that will be necessary if projections about further warming prove to be accurate. We know enough now to realize the options that face us and make value judgments about the kind of world we want to live in and what kind of world we want to leave for future generations.

Moral disagreements of this sort can be resolved by engaging in open and honest dialogue about the kind of options we have and what decisions on the issue involve. Hiding behind either a bogus scientific or moral authority does nothing to promote this dialogue. No one knows the absolute truth about these matters, but we can search for better versions of the truth if we engage in human discourse and are open to new perspectives. We should not let scientific and technical people resolve questions of value under the guise of dealing with "factual" information, nor should we let values be imposed on the situation that are based on something like "free market" ideology or other abstract principles separated from experience. The development of normative principles should be guided by experience, just as empirical studies are guided by values.

Researchers have the luxury of further study if the issue is of interest and money is available. Managers of business organizations do not have this luxury, but at some point they have to make a decision about putting a new product on the market that could have adverse effects on consumers, taking it off the market if there is some question about its safety, cutting greenhouse gas emissions and incurring the costs involved with this action, or changing the production process so that workers are not exposed to a questionable and potentially harmful substance. These are some of the most difficult decisions a manager has to make, as it is obviously not an easy decision to pull a product off the market that has proven to be highly profitable. One can sympathize with the managers of Manville in not being willing to believe asbestos was harmful after years of producing a product that was so useful to society and profitable for the company.

Managerial Responsibilities for Science

Science by its very nature is a community endeavor. The image of the lonely individualistic scientist toiling in his or her laboratory is completely unrealistic. Science involves hundreds, if not thousands, of people working on problems and contributing to an understanding of some aspect of nature. Many scientists have contributed to our understanding of global warming, for example, and, after many years of research, there seems to be an emerging consensus among the scientific community as to the causes of climate change. This consensus is filtering out into society as a whole, so that more and more people are beginning to understand the dynamics of the situation. Science is a community effort, and scientists have a responsibility to the larger community to conduct their research honestly and effectively in the interests of the public as a whole.

Managers, likewise, have a responsibility to use scientific findings in the interests of the community and not just in the interests of their individual enterprise. The decisions they make about the uses of science have impacts on the community, and one of the most important principles they can follow is to do no harm to their customers, their employees, and everyone else affected by their decisions. If scientific research begins to show that a product may be harmful, this research should not be buried or ignored in the interests of making a profit for the company. There have been far too many instances where companies have ignored such research, only to have it eventually disclosed, exposing the company to lawsuits and adverse publicity. Managers apparently are too myopic in these instances, failing to see beyond their narrow self-interests and ignoring the responsibilities they have to the community at large.

It might help if managers of business organizations could become more aware of their own personal values and the values of the institution they work for and where these values are operative in the decision-making process. If the decision involves a substance that is believed to be polluting the environment, for example, management would do well to be honest about its own values and interests and be aware of the values and interests of environmental groups that would like to see the substance banned. These values must be put on the table, so to speak, along with the best scientific evidence that is available. Managers who face this kind of decision need to make themselves aware of all the relevant research and evidence, not just those that support their individual and institutional interests.

Related to this issue is the hiring of scientists to do research supported by the corporation. Managers are obviously not going to be happy to support research that undermines the company's interests, so there is a strong bias in the corporate organization to hire people who are known to be supportive of free enterprise and against government regulation, for example, and who have taken the company line, so to speak, in past research activities. Yet this action will most likely be seen for what it is by the press and opponents, a self-serving action that will be dismissed out of hand by those in opposition to the corporate position. In selecting scientists to do research into controversial issues, the best scientists should be selected to do this research who have the kind of expertise in the area that is respected in the scientific community. And companies should be honest about research they have supported and not try to hide their involvement.

Managers also need to guard against denying there is a problem. They would do well to set up a system of checks and balances in the company itself that can be of use in these situations, some means to raise the hard questions that managers themselves may not want to face. It is best to head off a problem in its beginning stages rather than wait until the only option is to file for bankruptcy to stop the lawsuits or take some other drastic action. The longer a situation continues, the more and more options for managers are closed. Some means must be developed to promote dialogue about the issue within the corporation itself, with all views, even those opposed to corporate interests, on the table.

It is also important for managers to be open with the public about the information they have with respect to the issue under consideration. There is a strong tendency in corporate organizations to disclose only that information that is favorable to corporate interests, but if the company has information that is not so favorable and tries to hide it, this action will most likely come back to haunt the company. In an open society such as ours, with a free press, any such effort will most likely come to light and only further damage the reputation of the company and the possibility of reaching a satisfactory resolution of the problem.

Manville seems to have learned this lesson with respect to its fiberglass product. After having denied the long-term consequences of asbestos hazards and suffered through a painful reorganization as a result of bankruptcy proceedings, the company instituted a product stewardship program when the safety of its fiberglass product came into question. This program involved studying, analyzing, assessing, and above all, communicating to the customer what they knew about the hazards of fiberglass. The company learned that a consistent, conscientious commitment to the truth about a product enabled them to overcome fear, hostility, and cynicism. Customers came to depend on their "you'll-know-when-we-know-policy," and supported the company's action with respect to the product.[13]

Above all, managers would do well to be sensitive to the moral dimensions of these situations. These are not just scientific or business issues, but moral issues that involve protection of human life and human interests. People want new products and the benefits companies can provide, but they also do not want to put themselves at serious risk that involves harm to themselves or their loved ones. People want a safe product, one that they can use and enjoy with confidence. They will reward a company that takes steps to protect them from harm, and conversely, they will punish a company that knowingly and willingly produces a product that harms them in some fashion.[14]

One final word about science must be said. Science is fraught with uncertainty, and its findings are always subject to question. This can be taken advantage of by managers and others who are prone to use science in their own interests. Managers must learn to respect the scientific process and the findings that result from this process. Managers of business organizations are not the only ones who misuse scientific findings, as governments have also been known to alter scientific findings to suit their own interests. But science must be respected for what it is—a community effort that is our best way of getting at the truth of certain situations where natural causes and effects are involved. Managers must be committed to finding this truth, in the interests of the community that they are serving, and must let the science speak for itself without altering it, ignoring it, or misusing it in some fashion to suit the interests of the corporation.

BUSINESS AND TECHNOLOGY

Technology stems from the scientific enterprise. Science discovers new things about nature that can be incorporated into new technologies. These technologies, at their best, can extend the ability of humans to better their lives and improve the environment in which they live. Technology is part of the natural process by which humans who are within and part of nature alter their environment in order to live a more satisfying life. But technology can also alienate people and destroy the environment if not used properly. The problem with technology is not technology itself, because the way technology is applied springs from the ideas and values that operate in conjunction with technological factors and guide the way it is put to use in society. Thus technology provides the means to make life better, but human vision that grasps possibilities for the betterment of human experience is required to guide technology.

Technology is a problem in capitalistic societies because the corporation is the primary institution through which new technologies are introduced. And the corporation, being primarily interested in profiting from a new technology, often asks very limited questions about the impacts of that technology on society and whether it is safe to use as intended. In many, if not most cases, corporations are prone to ask minimal questions about the safety of a new technology, and unless required to do so because of government regulations, do not engage in extensive examination of its impacts on consumers, workers, the public, or the environment. While this pattern has changed in some organizations, concern about safety and whether the technology will actually better human existence and the environment is still not of the highest priority in many organizations. The main concern is whether it will make a profit for the corporation.

Technology and Management

This problem is well illustrated in many cases where concerns of engineers and other technical people in corporations clash with managerial concerns over the way a particular technology is being employed. Differences arise from time to time between engineers and technical people over the safety or workability of a product or technological device, and managers who often overlook such concerns in the interests of organizational objectives. There are many cases where engineers or technicians have raised questions about problems with some product or technology, and these concerns have been ignored or circumvented by managers in the interests of profits, schedules, or some other organizational concern.

In a situation that happened some years ago, involving production of a new plane for the Air Force called the A7D, the brake designed by the senior engineer of a subcontractor was not large enough to safely stop the aircraft upon landing. While initially the problem was believed to be with the materials used in the brake assembly, eventually it was determined that the fault lay in the design itself, as the brake repeatedly failed in laboratory tests, no matter what materials were used. Yet management refused to deal with this technical reality and created a fictional reality of their own by having technicians falsify the test data that was sent to the Air Force and the prime contractor. They did not want to incur the expense and delay that a redesign effort would take and apparently believed that the brake would work in the actual aircraft despite the test results. When the brake did not work in actual flight, however, and almost resulted in a major accident with possible loss of life, it then had to be redesigned. The technical people involved in the incident became whistle-blowers and eventually disclosed to investigators what had actually happened with regard to the original brake. They were the ones who paid the cost of this fiasco, however, while management personnel either stayed in place or were even promoted.[15]

In the Dalkon Shield case, involving A. H. Robins Company, a technician had showed in a simple experiment that the tail used to extract the IUD could wick, meaning that infectious agents could enter a woman's body by this route, causing pelvic inflammatory disease. But this evidence was ignored by management because the company had a product that was making them a good deal of money, and they didn't want to hear about potential health problems. Yet these problems couldn't be wished away and eventually came back to haunt the company in the form of lawsuits, which eventually led to bankruptcy and takeover by another company.[16]

One of the most devastating cases of all in this regard is the Challenger space shuttle disaster. Engineers had raised a question long before the disaster occurred about an O-ring problem with the solid booster rocket joints. Apparently, the design of the field joints did not work as intended and the seals were not able to seal effectively to prevent leakage. Blow-by had been noticed on several of the previous launches when the booster rockets were recovered, and a seal task force had been formed to study the problem. The O-rings had even been reassigned from a Criticality 1-R rating, where there was redundancy with a secondary seal, to a Criticality 1 rating, where there was no backup because it was believed that the secondary seal would be ineffective should the primary seal fail in flight. This information, however, was not passed on to the highest levels of NASA management, and the criticality rating was continually signed off on by a lower level of NASA management so launchings could proceed on schedule while the problem was being studied.[17]

On the night before the launch of the Challenger, temperatures were much lower than had been experienced on any previous launch. Initially, the prime contractor, Morton Thiokol International (MTI), recommended against the launch because the temperature was outside of their experience base and there was concern the primary seals would lose all resiliency and lead to an explosion on the launch pad itself. Under pressure from NASA, however, MTI reversed its decision, leaving the engineers out of the decision-making process, except for the head engineer, and making what was called a management decision to support the launch and please a customer. Perhaps the most revealing event in this flawed decision-making process occurred when Robert Lund, the head of engineering for MTI, was asked by the rest of the managers to take off his engineering hat and put on his management hat, and in the role of management he supported the launch decision. The rest is history, as the O-ring seal did fail, but rather than explode on the launch pad, the leakage from the solid booster rocket acted like an acetylene torch, burning through the external fuel tank and causing it to explode in mid-air, killing all the astronauts on board.

All these examples have some common elements. The differences between a decision based on technical concerns and a decision based on management or organizational concerns led to vastly different courses of action. Supposedly, an engineering decision is based on certain technical realities that the engineers and technicians believe are true relative to a brake assembly, an IUD, and an O-ring seal that could leak and cause serious problems. Engineers and technicians are concerned that a technology work properly, that it is safe, and that there will be no unexpected problems. Their reality is a technical one, and the values that guide their decisions are related directly to the technology itself.

Managers, however, live in a different world and base their decisions primarily on financial realities, budget considerations, schedules, customer desires, and similar kinds of organizational concerns. These concerns are no less real, but they are of a different nature than technical realities. The numbers related to finances, budgets, and schedules put pressures on managers that are of a different nature than the concerns of engineers and technical people. These numbers mean different things than the numbers engineers and technical people deal with; they are not related directly to the technology itself, and lead to different kinds of decisions that sometimes have disastrous consequences, as the examples illustrate.

In modern corporate organizations, managers control the decision-making process and have the final say regarding the employment of a particular technology. They are responsible for making a profit, staying within budget, meeting schedules, satisfying customers, and other organizational objectives. If these pressures become great enough, some managers are inclined to create technical fantasies by falsifying test data, as in the A7D case, or ignore technical concerns, as they did in the other cases. This difference between the concerns of engineers or technicians and the concerns of managers constitutes a critical problem in the modern corporate organization regarding the management and use of technology.

While technical realities do not always take priority in the decision-making process, they do take priority in the real world. When a faulty brake design is finally field-tested on an actual aircraft, it fails, and the reality of this failure can no longer be ignored or falsified. The tail on the IUD does wick, causing many cases of pelvic inflammatory disease, and the company faces so many lawsuits that it seeks bankruptcy for protection. The O-rings do fail to seal properly under low temperatures, and while the Challenger does not explode on the launch pad as expected, it later explodes in mid-air, killing seven people and putting the Shuttle program on hold for many months.[18] While profits are necessary for an organization to survive and grow and schedules must be met for customers to be pleased, the organization will not continue to be profitable and the customer will certainly not be pleased if the technology doesn't work as promised.

Defining the Problem

How can this problem be addressed and what kind of problem is it in the final analysis? It could be seen as a structural problem that is inherent in the capitalistic system, where the corporate organization has to serve certain kinds of values that are antithetical to the demands of technology. It could also be seen as an organizational or policy problem that requires changes in the organization to give engineers more of a say in decision-making or to facilitate whistle-blowing on the part of engineers or technicians. There are several ways to view this problem, which lead to different approaches.

One scholar who dealt with this problem on a structural level was Thorstein Veblen, who is best known for his book about conspicuous consumption and the theory of the leisure class. But perhaps his most insightful work has to do with the structure of the corporate organization and the system in which it functions. In this regard, he developed an analytical model that involved a distinction between what he called the machine process and the business enterprise, two aspects of what he considered to be a single, continuous activity.[19] Today we might call the machine process technology or the technical system and the business enterprise the management or administrative system.

As described by Veblen, the machine process is a high-level abstraction that consists of an interlocking, detailed arrangement that is based on an impersonal and mechanical cause-and-effect relationship which runs in standard terms of quantitative precision, requiring disciplined habits of thought. However, this machine process is managed and controlled by another entity, what Veblen calls the business enterprise, which is able to control the machine process through control of the capital goods that are used in the machine process. Thus the owners of capital are given the final right to determine how this capital shall be used and combined in the production of goods. These decisions as to how capital shall be employed are made on the basis of the pecuniary return to these owners, who are concerned about industrial efficiency only to the extent it increases profitability. The machine process is thus capitalized on its business capacity and not on its industrial capacity.

Seeing problems developing in this arrangement, Veblen predicted that the business enterprise would eventually be undercut by the machine process on which it depended because the vested interests of the business enterprise would constitute more and more of an extraneous interference and obstruction to the industrial system in the interests of making a profit.[20] These vested interests would so badly misallocate resources as to enter a stage of increasingly diminishing returns and reduction of the national dividend beyond limits of tolerance. This development constitutes the "secular trend" that he called "the cultural incidence of the machine process." Eventually, Veblen predicted, a revolution in industrial society will take place in which the engineers draw together, work out a plan of action, and decide to disallow absentee ownership out of hand.[21]

Veblen provides us with a useful distinction inherent in the capitalistic system that aids in understanding the dilemmas illustrated by the examples at the beginning of this section. The point, which Veblen so ably described, is that the machine process and the business enterprise, or the technical system and the management system, have different operatives, different requirements, different objectives, and the decisions in each realm are based on different values. Since the management system is in control of the technical system, however, it is the values of this system that prevail when push comes to shove in particular instances, and the requirements of the technical system are sometimes ignored in the interests of reaching management goals and objectives. In the final analysis, management values and concerns dominate engineering or technical considerations.

John Kenneth Galbraith's analysis of this situation is much less revolutionary than Veblen's and is focused on the need for organizational or policy changes. Galbraith makes a case for involving more engineering and technical people in the decision-making process of the modern corporate organization. His understanding of decision-making within the corporation is encapsulated in his concept of the "technostructure," which refers to all persons who can contribute specialized information to group decision-making in the organization. The technostructure consists of management, technical specialists, scientists, and other knowledgeable people who may be involved, depending on the type of decision.[22]

Galbraith's point is that the complexity of modern technology makes it impossible for top management to possess enough knowledge to make a decision that will work in the corporation's best interests. They have to rely more and more on technical specialists within the organization and include them in the decision-making process, thus moving decision-making and control from the top of the organization down into lower levels, involving more and more employees. In this way, power has shifted to some degree to those who possess important knowledge about technology rather than just status or position.

Based on Galbraith's analysis, a corporate organization would give engineers and technicians more authority in decision-making regarding technology. The reporting structure might be changed so that engineers report to other engineering personnel, who will be more likely to understand their concerns and respond to them in an appropriate manner. In the A7D case, for example, low-level technical people reported to management rather than other technical specialists and thus were able to be pressured by management into falsifying test data. An organization could also have more engineering people become managers and thus have more of a say in the decision-making process. Some companies consider themselves to be engineering companies, where many, if not most, managers have an engineering background. Where this kind of management prevails throughout the organization, one would expect technical values to carry more weight.

There has been some movement in this direction, as companies have had to involve more engineering and technical people in decision-making because of the complexity of modern technology. Yet as many examples clearly illustrate, engineering people can be shut out of the decision-making process when a management decision has to be made involving a particular technology. Moreover, even if technical people are given more clout in management decision-making, and even if the reporting structure is changed so that engineering has more authority at top levels of the organization, when a critical decision has to be made, the top engineer may be asked to put on his management hat and make a management decision. For this reason, making engineers managers does not seem to solve the problem. Even with an engineering background, managers have to make management decisions and concern themselves with finances and schedules and other management considerations. They thus tend to become part of what Veblen called the business enterprise and are subject to its values and requirements.

Should whistle-blowing be encouraged, making it easier for engineering and technical people to bring their concerns to the attention of top management? An enabling and empowering environment could be created where dissent is not equated with disloyalty. In order to implement this idea, many companies have instituted policies that encourage whistle-blowing and have established hotlines for employees to report activities that may involve criminal conduct or corporate policy violations. But again, this seems to be only a partial solution to the problem, as whistle-blowers can be silenced if necessary and management objectives can take precedence over the objections of whistle-blowers that may be based on technical considerations. Hotlines have their own problems and many people are skeptical about their usefulness, as such practices may be destructive of community and trust, which are essential to a successful organization.[23]

A New Look at the Problem

This problem of technical versus managerial values is not a structural problem of capitalism that can be solved by developing some new kind of system in which private property or absentee ownership is abolished, as Veblen suggested. Socialistic systems fared even worse than capitalistic systems in efficiently and effectively managing technology and were almost totally unresponsive to concerns about environmental problems. While Veblen provides us with a useful distinction inherent in the capitalistic system that aids in understanding the conflict between the technical and business aspects within a corporation, his analysis misses the mark in providing an understanding of the moral dilemmas faced by organizations with regard to technology.

Whereas he recognizes that profit alone provides an inadequate measure of serviceability to the community, his entire analysis views the machine process as a self-sufficient mechanistic system with its own self-sufficient ideal of maximum material productivity. The machine process as described by Veblen is a benefit to the welfare of the community at large only if its welfare is equated with maximum productivity. Veblen seems to recognize that technology cannot be understood as an instrument for bringing about goals external to the process, but because the process is viewed abstractly, the goals themselves are similarly limited.

Nor is the problem simply an organizational or policy problem that can be addressed by giving engineers and technical people more authority in corporate organizations, as Galbraith argues. The problems surrounding the misuse of technology lie in a lack of understanding of technology's inherently moral dimensions, and this lack of understanding is in turn related to the abstraction of technology from the contextual situations in which it functions and from its role in enhancing human existence. Technology cannot be understood as an instrument for bringing about goals that are external to the contexts in which it operates, and the context in which technology functions is imbued with values that demand consideration. Thus technology as it actually operates in concrete situations has a contextually dependent moral quality. Technology creates a moral situation, and this situation should provide the context for decision-making.

How many times have we heard about some new technological development proceeding so quickly so as to outstrip our ability to deal with the moral implications of new applications? Some complain that while technology has advanced dramatically in our society, our moral aptitude in dealing with it has not, as if to say that technology and morals are separate realms of concern. But this complaint is radically mistaken, as it fails to see that a technological accomplishment, the development and adoption of a technological device, always and already constitutes a moral decision. The technologies we decide to implement in our society and the way we use them are decisions that are fundamentally moral in nature.

There is no separation between technology and morality, as if technology proceeds on its own, so to speak, and then morality has to play catch-up and question whether particular technologies ought to be allowed to proceed, and if so, whether they ought to be highly regulated. The decisions about a technology that have already been made are moral decisions that have set a particular direction for the employment of that technology. The question is whether that particular direction will be of benefit to society and whether people making the decisions about this technology are aware of the moral dimensions of their decisions. On what basis are these decisions being made and what values are dominant in the decision-making process?

The values that are basic to the success of a corporate organization are primarily economic in nature, and these values are dominant in the decision-making process regarding technology. Even with the management revolution and the separation of ownership from control in the modern corporation, to be described in the next chapter, economic values are still dominant. Veblen saw this dominance as a problem and believed that values more directly related to what he called the machine process would eventually have to become dominant if society was to reap the benefits from this process. But contrary to what Veblen implied, engineers cannot run the corporate organization solely on technical factors, any more than managers can run it solely on economic factors. Both of these ways of measuring the success of the organization are abstractions from the context in which technology is employed.

Technology itself is experimental, and while engineers and technicians may raise questions about the safety and workability of a particular technology, there is no certainty that they are right and that their concerns should thus override managerial considerations. But they may, at least, introduce an element of "reasonable doubt" into the decision-making process that should be taken into consideration. What managers may be doing in ignoring these concerns is conducting a real-world experiment that will, one hopes, falsify the concerns of the engineers and technicians.

All technology is in some sense experimental, as even under the best of conditions no one can be certain what effects a technology is likely to have on people and society. After all the testing has been done, even if done accurately, and after all the problems that are discovered in testing have been dealt with rather than ignored, when a new technology is introduced into the real world it can have unforeseen consequences that may adversely affect people and society. The question for all concerned is where to draw the line between reasonable risks and those that are unacceptable. We are currently in the midst of a world-wide experiment regarding climate change. Is continuing our reliance on fossil fuels, knowing the effect carbon dioxide may have on global warming, a reasonable risk, or is it unacceptable, making major changes in our lifestyle and in the way we produce energy necessary?

Part of the problem is that the people who are most directly affected by an experiment of this nature are not fully informed as to the nature of the experiment in which they are participating. The final decision as to whether to go ahead with the experiment should involve those who put their lives at risk and not rest solely in the hands of either managers or engineers, who are not directly participating in the experiment. When there are "reasonable doubts" concerning the outcome of such experiments, at the very least the individuals involved should know the nature of the risks they face when involved in such experiments, so they can make an informed decision not to participate if these risks are judged to be unacceptable.[24]

Technology thus has impacts on a larger community that need to be taken into consideration. When consumers can make individual decisions about the use of a new product, they need to be fully informed about the possible adverse effects. Thus the advertisements about prescription drugs seen on television that disclose possible side effects are a step in the right direction, even though these side effects are downplayed by a soothing voice. But what about technologies that are implemented on a larger scale, where individual marketplace decisions may not have much of an impact, technologies that are implemented in a society where consumer choices may not be involved? Should the government act on behalf of its citizens and make decisions about stem cell research or institute a carbon tax to reduce carbon dioxide emissions, for example?

Elected officials, whether at the federal, state, or local level, tend not to be schooled or experienced in science and scientific thinking, as the kinds of skills it takes to be a politician are not the same as those involved with science and technology. Yet many of the decisions made by these politicians affect the implementation of technology in our society. An entity called the Office of Technology Assessment (OTA) was created by Congress in 1972 to provide scientific and technological information to policymakers on a wide range of issues. The OTA drew heavily on specialized studies by the National Academies, university researchers, corporate leaders, and nongovernmental organizations. It used such studies to clarify reasons for debate about leading issues of the day involving technology and define alternative public policy positions. The OTA, however, was shut down in 1995, as Congress thought its work was no longer valuable or timely enough to be helpful. Since that time, something of a vacuum has existed that has been partially filled by the National Academies, advisory boards, expert advice, and other such activities.

The problem with government involvement is that the decisions of Congress or a governmental agency are subject to political pressures. The Food and Drug Administration, for example, which was created to assure the safety and effectiveness of new drugs put on the market, has had a checkered history regarding its ability to carry out its mission of protecting the public from unsafe and ineffective drugs. It is subject to political pressures from Congress, which controls its budget, from the President, who makes high-level appointments to the agency, and from business that lobbies against government regulation. These pressures compromise its mission on many occasions and have caused many changes in the agency's policies and practices over the course of its history.

Despite government involvement and despite changes in corporate governance mentioned in the next chapter, managers of corporate organizations are in a position where they make the final decision about the employment of new technologies in our society. This is an awesome responsibility and involves considerations that go way beyond whether the new technology can make a profit for the organization. The experimental nature of technology and the possible impacts on the larger community make this responsibility one that has to be taken seriously by managers. Perhaps they should do more in the nature of technology assessment themselves and have a group in the corporation that does nothing but deal with the impacts of a new technology on the environment and society.

One such experiment going on at the turn of the century involves genetically engineered crops, which are transforming American agriculture. About half of the corn crop in the country, three-fourths of the cotton crop, and 85 percent of soybeans are estimated to have been genetically altered in some manner. Monsanto is at the forefront of this endeavor by discovering how to insert a Roundup-resistant gene into crop plants (Roundup is its best selling herbicide) so that they can be doused with the weed killer without any damage to the crop plant itself. Monsanto has licensed these genes to a wide variety of seed companies, who breed the gene into plants and sell the seeds to farmers. The company made its name in chemicals, but this new effort has been so successful that the company made more money from these seeds than herbicides. In 2006, 70 percent of its $3.5 billion profit came from seeds.[25]

Alfalfa is another crop that was genetically altered in this fashion, and on May 3, 2007, a federal district judge banned the sale or planting of Roundup Ready alfalfa until the Department of Agriculture conducts a full environmental impact statement on use of the genetically altered crop, the first time such a review has been required for a genetically altered crop. This ruling could have significant implications for all such crops, as evidence is mounting that these crops have led to the growth of "superweeds" that have mutated to survive Roundup, and this development threatens to involve new costs for farmers and the environment. The impact of these crops on human health is also not understood, as these altered genes have transformed the food that consumers eat by contaminating traditional and organic crops.[26]

It appears that these genetically altered crops underwent only cursory review before they were introduced into society. But even if an environmental impact statement does not justify the release of genetically altered alfalfa, it will be difficult, if not impossible, to put the genie back in the bottle, so to speak. Getting genetically altered crops out of the environment is not exactly like recalling a defective automobile. The seeds spread everywhere and infect a traditional crop, which eliminates the choice farmers have to grow non-genetically engineered crops. Called transgenic "creep," it is believed that it is already underway in alfalfa. The fear is that eventually the distinction between genetically engineered and conventional and organic crops will disappear, regardless of whether anyone wants such an outcome.[27]

There should be severe sanctions for managers who willingly and knowingly place people in experimental situations without disclosing the full nature of the experiment to those who will be most directly affected. Farmers and consumers should know the risks involved in introducing genetically altered seeds into the environment and the potential this has to alter our food supply. One thing that might help managers in this endeavor is to envision themselves or their loved ones in the experimental situation engendered by the technology and ask if the risks to which they are subjecting others would then be acceptable. Their decisions might well be different if they were to personalize the decision, rather than view it in terms of dehumanized and decontextualized abstractions.

Neither managers nor engineers can be expected to be moral heroes who have to put their jobs and careers on the line to raise questions about the workability and safety of a particular technology. Rather, what may be needed is open dialogue through which they share their knowledge and concerns with the rest of the organization and with the public at large when appropriate. Everyone involved with a technology needs to ask the question as to whether the results of experimental testing conducted thus far on a particular technology are sufficiently conclusive to warrant a real-life experiment. They need to ask themselves if they are willing, should that experiment fail, to take responsibility for the decision and show the public that it was rationally and morally justified based on the best available evidence.

Technology demands moral sensibility, as technology creates and operates within moral situations. Economic considerations are an abstraction from a real situation involving technology, and real situations always have considerations that go beyond mere economics. Moral sensibility doesn't ignore technological factors, doesn't falsify technical data, and doesn't reduce the conflicting demands of an actual situation to abstract possibilities in which human lives and deadlines and profits become nothing more than equal weights in a probability matrix. Business interests and technological interests alike need to be understood in the network of actual contexts in which they are embedded, and there needs to be recognition that business interests, technological interests, and community interests are inseparably intertwined.

Technologies, as inherently experimental, must be constantly evaluated, and the evaluation of the consequences of various technologies, a grasp of the goods and ills that result from their implementation, requires that advanced technological know-how be accompanied by advanced enhancement of the skills of moral decision-making, the skills of sensitivity, creativity, and imagination. This activity is not an abstraction from the business of using technology to further organizational goals and interests, but is inseparably intertwined with the attainment of them. Managers must learn to deal with technological issues in the contextual, value-laden situations in which technology is embedded and see their responsibilities in this regard more broadly.

Managers thus need to give appropriate attention to technology when real questions of safety and workability are raised by engineers and technicians. They must not allow themselves to get caught up in the world of profits, budgets, and schedules and ignore these technological questions. They cannot be just managers in distortive abstraction from their concrete functioning as human beings embedded in a moral context. The organization in which they work must develop a culture where community interests come first, community interests in a safe and workable technology that will enrich the lives of people exposed to the technology.

13 Governance

The term corporate governance refers to the structure, participants, and processes by and through which corporations are managed. This chapter thus deals with the questions of who controls the modern corporation, who makes the crucial decisions about the use of corporate resources, and who decides what the corporation does and what activities it pursues. These questions are important because of the emphasis on property rights in a capitalistic system. The owners of the corporation, i.e., its stockholders, should ultimately control the corporation and be the major factor in the governance process. They supply the financial capital the corporation needs and have legal ownership of a certain number of shares in the corporation. Thus they collectively own the corporation and should have confidence that it will be used to further their interests.

When companies were small, the governance process was simple, as the participants were few because of the absence of other owners. Owners of small companies managed their businesses themselves and acted in their own personal interests. As companies grew in size, however, and particularly as they incorporated and became public companies, the governing process became more complicated and divorced from ownership. The size and complexity of the modern corporation have muddied the waters regarding governance of the modern corporation. The role that stockholders and management play in the governance process is a critical question that warrants some discussion.

THE SEPARATION OF OWNERSHIP AND CONTROL

The traditional view of corporate governance is obviously individualistic in nature and rests on the rights of stockholders. The way the process is supposed to work in large public corporations is that shareholders meet once a year to hear a performance report from management, elect a board of directors and dispose of other business on the agenda that may need stockholder approval. The board acts as an intermediary between the shareholders and the management of the company. The board of directors is supposed to act in the interests of the shareholders and elect the officers of the company to run it on a day-to-day basis. They are also to meet periodically with management to exercise an overseer function to protect the interests of the shareholders. Management, in turn, exercises a derived authority over the rest of the employees to direct their activities to accomplish corporate objectives and is something of an agent of shareholders.

The legitimacy of this process rests on the notion that the property rights of the owners are supreme. These property rights are supposedly the most important right in a capitalistic system, and control of one's property is paramount. There is nothing like a stakeholder notion in this traditional view of corporate governance, nor is there any notion of the corporation being responsible to a larger community. Stockholders have legal rights to exercise their control over the corporation through the voting mechanism described previously and by challenging, if necessary, the actions of corporate management in the courts when circumstances leave them no other alternative. The ultimate right of shareholders, of course, is to dispose of their property by selling their ownership certificates.

That the traditional model of corporate governance did not work out in practice should come as no surprise to anyone acquainted with the modern corporation. Share ownership of most major corporations is so widely dispersed throughout society that no one person owns a large enough block of stock to make a difference in the voting outcome at an annual meeting. This dispersion means stockholders do not think of themselves as owners of the corporation but as investors who hope to make an adequate return on their investment. If they feel this return is not adequate, they do not go to the management of the company or the board of directors and demand better performance. They go to their stockbroker or access their on-line account, sell the stock and invest in some other company that seems to hold more promise.

As far as voting rights are concerned, millions of dollars are spent each year to send out proxy statements to shareholders to vote for board members or for other matters that may find their way on the ballot. Most investors, however, either throw them away or simply send the signed statements back to the company without even reading them carefully. They are not interested in taking any kind of an active part in management of the company. All they are interested in is how well the stock is performing. Yet this expenditure is necessary to maintain the myth of shareholder control and to fulfill the legal obligations of the company.

Because of this dispersion of stock ownership and a change in the way shareholders perceive themselves, the owners of large corporations do not have control over the use of corporate resources. Individually, they have little or no power to affect change. Yet it is difficult to organize them in significant numbers even to attend an annual meeting and exercise the collective power they have in theory. Thus there has been a change in corporate governance regarding the modern corporation, a change that was described several years ago in the well-known thesis of Adolf Berle and Gardiner Means regarding the separation of ownership and control in the modern corporation.[1]

These authors studied share ownership of the 200 largest nonfinancial corporations in the country and determined that no dominant stock interest owned even as much as 5 percent of the stock in over half of these corporations, which they concluded was the minimum needed to exercise some influence. This study was later updated by Robert Larner, who could find no dominant stock ownership, which he defined as at least a 10 percent ownership by an individual or group that could vote as a unity, in 85 percent of the top 200 corporations.[2] Thus there is some empirical support for the idea that stock ownership is widely dispersed in most public corporations and that there has been a separation of ownership and control.

The assumption is, of course, that the absence of a dominant ownership interest created a vacuum of power that has been filled by management. They not only came to run the company on a day-by-day basis but also came to exercise ultimate control over the use of corporate resources and have complete control over corporate activities. This separation of ownership from control, according to Berle and Means, created a condition where the interests of owners and managers may, and often do, diverge. In addition, many of the checks and balances that formerly operated to limit and guide the use of corporate power disappeared. Corporations had become large social and political institutions that could cause great harm to the public at large.

After the publication of the Berle and Means book, Congress passed the Securities Act of 1933 and the Securities Exchange Act of 1934, which were its first major efforts to introduce reforms into corporate behavior. These acts were designed to make the operations of large corporations more transparent to the owners and provided a means to protect shareholders from outright fraud. It required registration of securities with the Securities and Exchange Commission and established rules for the provisions of information to shareholders. These laws took a large step toward acknowledging the interests of society in providing a check to unrestrained corporate power and supported the notion of shareholder rights that went along with stocks bought on public exchanges.

Nonetheless, management continued to rule the corporation and became self-perpetuating by controlling the proxy machinery in selecting the proxies that appear on the ballots sent to shareholders. They naturally selected proxies who would elect directors who would, in turn, reappoint the existing management. The board of directors became ineffectual in protecting shareholder rights and also came under the control of management. Some companies had boards composed of a majority of inside directors, officers of the company who are beholden to top management for their positions. Those outside directors who were on the board were most often friends of management, such as officers of other corporations, investment bankers, and the like, who shared the same values as management and were not likely to raise any serious opposition to management's policies and decisions. These boards rarely questioned the recommendations of top management and left them to run the company as they chose. Boards were often in the dark about the condition of the company, as the chief executive officer (CEO) of the company was in many cases also chairman of the board and set the agenda for board meetings and controlled information going to board members.

What developed over time was a small group of unknown managers who control the resources of large corporations in our society and exercise vast power over almost every aspect of life in this country. They constitute a class of people who give themselves large rewards for the functions they perform and appear to be beholden to no one but themselves. They continue the ritual of annual meetings and board meetings that have no real purpose other than to perpetuate the myth of stockholder control. This trend was termed *managerialism* in a book published in 1941 by James Burnham, who argued that the legitimacy of this managerial class was not dependent on the maintenance of capitalist property and economic relations.[3]

Burnham argued that traditional notions of capitalism were disappearing and socialism remained an abstract Marxian ideal. What was emerging in industrial societies all over the world was a managerial society, where managers of large organizations were achieving social dominance and becoming the ruling class in society. These were the people who actually manage, on the technical side, the processes of production. The functions of management in a technological society were becoming more distinctive, complex, and specialized, and more crucial to the whole process of production. The legitimacy of this class was not dependent on ownership of private property but upon the technical nature of the processes of modern production. Thus the notion of property rights has been usurped by management in the modern corporation, and the legitimacy of the system is in question.

CORPORATE RAIDERS

There are, or course, exceptions to this view of management control that appear from time to time, and one such exception appeared in the 1980s, which saw an increase in takeovers of even large companies by outsiders. Huge amounts of money available through junk bond financing and bank credits allowed outsiders called raiders to take over some of the largest companies in the country. No company was safe from these takeover attempts, and even when raiders weren't successful, target companies were often forced to restructure their organizations to ward off the takeover bid or to seek a friendlier merger partner.

Raiders such as Carl Icahn, who took over TWA, and T. Boone Pickens, who forced Gulf Oil to merge with Standard Oil of California, justified their actions by claiming to represent a grass-roots movement of shareholders who wanted to shake up entrenched management and restructure corporations to be more productive and provide greater returns to shareholders. They claimed a strongly knit corporate aristocracy existed in America producing a welfare state consisting of an army of unproductive workers. These raiders wanted to be seen as folk heroes taking on "corporcracy" itself and forcing managers to take shareholder interests into account by making them more accountable in the use of corporate assets.[4]

Investment banking houses on Wall Street put together many of these deals and managed the exchange of equity for debt that enabled these takeovers to proceed. From 1980 to 1985, the capital of these banks more than tripled to $22 billion, and their assets, which consisted mostly of trading inventories of stocks and bonds, increased to nearly $400 billion.[5] Investment banks, such as Drexel Burnham Lambert, founded the junk bond market that enabled raiders to attain huge amounts of unsecured loans and thus mount their takeover attempts on huge companies. Eventually, these investment banks began to suggest deals instead of just responding to the needs of an outside raider and then take equity positions in companies for which they arranged leveraged buyouts and other financing. Some became outright owners of major companies by pooling their own money with pension funds and other institutions with deep pockets.[6]

From the standpoint of corporate governance, these takeover attempts forced management of many large corporations to adopt strategies to resist outsider takeovers of their companies. In some cases, they arranged deals of their own to buy the company they managed through leveraged buyout arrangements. They used the same tactics as the raiders to enrich themselves by buying back all of the company's shares, freeing themselves from the shareholder pressure and from the threats of raiders. Some critics saw a positive development in this trend toward leveraged buyouts. It was hoped that when management became a significant equity holder and had their own interests more directly at stake, they might run the company more efficiently than when they were merely agents of shareholders. The leveraged buyout might reestablish closer ties between commerce and finance and resolve the conflict between owners and managers over the control and use of corporate resources.[7]

If management didn't propose a leveraged buyout, they had to adopt other strategies to ward off takeovers by corporate raiders. In some cases, they sold off lackluster divisions and laid off employees to boost cash flow and increase their stock prices, making the company less attractive to takeover attempts. In other cases, they agreed to buy back the raider's shares at a premium over-market price, so-called greenmail that was not available to other shareholders, and allowed the raiders to amass fortunes. Regardless of the strategies used, however, the effect was to focus management's attention on the short-term performance of the company. Once the company's stock was put into play in the takeover game, managers had to sacrifice long-term plans for the company.[8] Management of even the largest corporations was thus subject to external pressures from raiders to use corporate resources in new ways for short-term objectives.

The heyday of the raiders was in the 1980s and may have peaked in 1989 in the battle for RJR Nabisco, which resulted in a $25 billion buyout by Kohlberg-Kravis-Roberts. After this, the junk bond market collapsed, along with the bankruptcy of Drexel Burnham Lambert, the leading firm in the junk bond market, and the conviction of the leading proponent of junk bonds, Michael Milken, on charges of insider trading. Companies also began to adopt antitakeover provisions, so called poison pills, to make the company less attractive. States also got into the act by adopting statutes designed to repel raiders. The state of Delaware, where about 56 percent of the Fortune 500 companies were incorporated, passed a law that barred hostile acquirers from merging with target companies for three years except under certain conditions.[9] Thus in the 1990s, takeover activity slowed significantly.

But the takeover movement never stopped completely. Carl Icahn remained active and in 2007 was, in his fourth decade of dealmaking, in a fight with the management of Motorola, which he believed was not yielding the value shareholders deserved. There was some belief that he was more formidable than before, having built a team of associates to help him find targets and mount his crusades against companies. Since greenmail is no longer possible because of changes in corporate charters and state laws, the focus is on increasing shareholder value. The rise of hedge funds has helped him in this regard, and these funds are in some sense performing the role junk bonds did in earlier days. When Icahn targets a company, these hedge funds typically follow along and are far more willing to vote against management. [10]

Another individual who appeared on the scene in later years was Keith Rupert Murdoch, who had built up a $70 billion media conglomerate seen by nearly 75 percent of the world's population. Murdoch published 175 newspapers and owned 35 television stations in the U.S. alone, which reached 40 percent of its citizens. In 2007, he offered to buy out Dow Jones, the parent company of the *Wall Street Journal*, by paying $60 share, for a total of $5 billion for the company. While making assurances that he would uphold the *Journal's* editorial integrity, many feared that he would intrude on the editorial independence of the paper's newsroom and make its news coverage more pro-business and conservative. There was also concern that he would interfere with any coverage that was disadvantageous to his business interests.[11]

FAMILY CONTROL

This incident brings up another aspect of corporate governance, namely that there are some corporations where certain families, that in many cases founded the company, maintain control of the company. In the case of Dow Jones, the Bancroft family controlled 52 percent of the company's voting power, and initially opposed the buyout offer. But since Murdoch's offer of $60 a share was 67 percent more than the stock was worth at the time the offer was made, the family reconsidered and agreed to meet with Murdoch to discuss his offer. They also declared a "receptivity to other options," effectively putting the company in play for other bidders. They may have begun to question the viability of an independent newspaper company in a world where readers and advertisers are increasingly using Web-based news sources, making the business much more competitive.[12]

Families such as the Bancroft family are able to maintain control of a company through the use of dual-class stock structures, where the ownership of Class B shares carries super voting power. In the case of Dow Jones, the Bancroft family controlled 76 percent of the votes through this arrangement. Several other major corporations are controlled by families in this fashion, including Ford Motor Company, Google, Estee Lauder, and Polo Ralph Lauren, where Class B shareholders control 88 percent of the votes.[13] Families that have a substantial interest of this kind can be expected to vote their stock more or less uniformly and take an active interest in the running of the company because they have such a large stake in its performance. Thus they would seem to have the power to influence management policies and even replace management if necessary.

But this potential for control may not be exercised for many reasons. The Bancrofts remained aloof from the company's day-to-day management and respected the integrity and independence of the paper as part of their philosophy of governance. Perhaps members of families have no interest in overseeing the business for other reasons and are more interested in enjoying their wealth. Unless someone in the family has a good business sense and an active interest, the potential for control may not be utilized. Even if a family desires to do so, it is not always easy to influence or replace an entrenched management. Family ownership, even in companies where they control a majority of the votes, does not necessarily translate into direct control over the use of corporate resources.

ACTIVIST SHAREHOLDERS

The activist shareholder movement began in the 1960s, as small shareholders interested in pursuing social goals found a way to make their voice heard at annual meetings. The Securities and Exchange Commission (SEC) amended the proxy rules, allowing small shareholders to place resolutions concerning social issues on corporate proxy statements. This action opened a door for public interest groups to buy a few shares of stock in a company and introduce resolutions dealing with social issues. These resolutions became quite numerous in the late 1970s and 1980s, confronting management with questions about social responsibility, including company policies with respect to South Africa, production of nuclear weapons, marketing practices related to infant formula, minority employment, purchasing practices, and a host of environmental issues ranging from clearcutting of forests to the use of chlorofluorocarbons.

In the 1990s, corporate governance issues became more important to activist shareholders, as questions about executive pay and other governance issues received increasing attention. In 1991, some 124 corporate governance issues were planned, up 30 percent from the previous year. Most of these governance issues considered rescinding poison pill takeover defenses and implementing confidential voting procedures to guard against management pressure. Several proposals also attacked golden parachutes, the practice of management awarding itself excessive payments in the event of a takeover.[14] In 1992, there were 74 proxy proposals to restrict executive compensation and another 32 to force greater disclosure of executive pay packages or hold special votes on these packages.[15]

During the 1970s, the SEC supported this movement toward shareholder activism. In February of 1978, it reversed its earlier "one percent rule," which permitted a company to omit a resolution that was not "significantly related" to the company's business. In reversing this rule, the chair of the SEC said, "There are some issues that are so important that quantitative tests are irrelevant." The commission also ruled that a company must forward a copy of its statement opposing a resolution to the sponsors of the resolution ten days before the preliminary filing of the proxy with the SEC, so that the sponsors have a chance to challenge any alleged factual misstatement in the response.[16]

In 1992, the SEC gave shareholder activism another boost when it issued new proxy rules that gave shareholders more freedom of speech. Under the new rules, pension funds, financial institutions, and individual investors could talk to each other about their stakeholdings without getting clearance or meeting filing requirements previously in effect. They could announce how they would vote on directors and proposals and more easily vote for and run as individual board members. They could also gain access to corporate shareholder lists to gain support for their views without actually soliciting proxy votes.[17]

Besides this support from the SEC, shareholder activists also received support from organizations like the Interfaith Center on Corporate Responsibility, which was formed at the beginning of the 1970s to help Roman Catholic groups leverage their stock holdings to raise issues with corporate management. Other groups were formed, such as a community organization in Rochester, New York that convinced the owners of 39,000 Kodak shares to sign over their proxies so they could be used to vote against the management of the company for failing to hire enough minorities. The campaign to get companies to cut off doing business with South Africa started off slowly but picked up steam when churches and universities joined forces in using the power of their investments to put pressure on companies.

Shareholder resolutions introduced by activist shareholders never received anything approaching a majority vote and they were not, of course, popular with corporate management. Especially irksome were small shareholders that repeatedly submitted the same proposal. While their impact on corporate strategy may have been minimal, these activists at least enlivened usually staid annual meetings and made management think twice about the social consequences of business practices. Activists claimed a moral victory in voicing social concerns and a tactical victory in being heard. Shareholder activism proved to be more than just a passing fad and became a permanent feature of corporate governance in the United States and abroad.

In 2007, shareholder resolutions seemed to make more of an impact than ever, as more and more of these resolutions were negotiated away in meetings between shareholders and boards ahead of the annual meeting. Some 22 percent of all proposals were withdrawn because of successful negotiations. Those that did make it to the ballot won well over a majority of the vote in some cases. A proposal that all directors be reelected each year rather than hold staggered elections, for example, received 72 percent of the vote on average. Activists and directors were having more dialogue than ever, leading some to say that 2007 would be a breakthrough year for shareholder activism.[18]

Most of these resolutions had to do with corporate governance. The most widely adopted resolution in 2007 had to do with majority voting, where directors must be elected by more than 50 percent of the shareholders voting rather than just by a plurality. Some 57 percent of the resolutions dealing with this issue were withdrawn before the annual meeting because deals had been made with the companies or they agreed to adopt the resolution. Another issue that was embraced quickly would give shareholders the right to make a nonbinding vote on executive compensation packages. This resolution gained an average vote of 43 percent at the 66 companies where it was introduced. Other issues were on the horizon, as a ruling was expected on whether to give large shareholders "proxy access" or the right to nominate their own candidates to the company's slate of directors.[19]

INSTITUTIONAL INVESTORS

Anyone acquainted with the stock market knows that financial institutions own substantial blocks of stock in many corporations. This phenomenon was noted in 1970, as at least one scholar argued that financial institutions, not individual investors, were the dominant influence in the stock market. The market had entered the era of the institutional investor holding an ever-growing share of corporate stock. In 1970, mutual funds, pension funds, and insurance companies, all with varying degrees of bank involvement, owned more than a third of all stocks listed on the New York Stock Exchange. At that time, some 10 million people were purchasing $5 billion worth of shares a year of over 200 mutual funds. In 1967, these funds reported assets of over $50 billion, which was 50 times their 1948 holdings. In 1940, only four million jobholders were covered by pensions, and the reserves of these pensions totaled less than $2.5 billion. But in 1970, more than 28 million people were covered by pensions and the assets had swollen to $80 billion, half of which was invested in common stock.[20]

Institutions continued to grow in size and importance as they increased their holding in corporations. By 1989, institutions owned at least one-half of the stock of 27 of the top 50 U.S. corporations and at least one-third of the stock of 47 of the top 50 companies. Pension funds alone owned 10.6 percent of General Motors' common stock and 9.1 percent of IBM Corporation. Thirteen of the top 20 pension funds were controlled by state or local governments. The five largest pension funds controlled $202 billion or about 8 percent of total pension fund assets of $2.5 trillion.[21]

Couple the holdings of these financial institutions with the holdings of universities, churches, and foundations, and institutions had the potential to influence the policies and practices of many corporations. This potential, however, was initially not exercised, as institutions acted much like individual investors. Because their main concern was financial return, if they disliked a stock because of its low return, they shifted into another. They rarely opposed management on any issue and routinely sent in their proxies, as did individual investors. Most institutional investors believed that their fiduciary duties precluded real activism.

This passive role changed as takeovers and leveraged buyouts grew in significance. Pension fund managers in particular believed they had a fiduciary duty to earn their beneficiaries the best return possible and were successful in many takeover situations by tendering their shares to outside raiders hostile to management. Potential for larger returns put managers of these institutional funds at odds with company management that wanted to establish takeover defenses. Institutional financial managers began to oppose poison pills and other such takeover defenses.[22] In 1987, 60 shareholder resolutions were filed asking companies either to rescind their poison pills or at least put them to a vote of the shareholders.[23]

What began as a rebellion in the 1980s grew into an organized movement in later years. Pension fund managers, joined by some money managers of mutual funds, adopted a watchdog role over corporate management. Some of the big public-employee pension funds teamed up with nongovernmental organizations in pursuing social issues. They became leaders in mounting proxy fights to withdraw from South Africa. They forced Exxon after the Alaskan oil spill to name an environmentalist to its board of directors and wanted to discuss how the company's environmental problems were affecting the value of the stock owned by them. These institutions thus came to concern themselves with social as well as economic issues, particularly when social issues had a financial impact.[24]

Because stock ownership became more concentrated in these institutions, perhaps more than at any time in the country's history, any business that needs money will have to live up to the expectations of pension fund managers. And since they focus on the short term, having to show immediate gains quarter by quarter, pension fund managers are pushing managers of larger corporations to forgo long-run considerations in deference to immediate earnings and stock prices. This threatens America's long-term economic future, according to Peter Drucker, as the basic wealth-producing capacity of corporations is ignored.[25]

Institutional share ownership continued to grow at the beginning of the new century. At the end of 2005, institutional investors, defined as pension funds, investment companies, insurance companies, banks, and foundations, controlled $24.1 trillion in assets, which was a substantial increase from the low of $17.3 trillion in 2002. These assets grew 19 percent from 2002 to 2003, another 11.7 percent from 2003 to 2004, and another 5.1 percent from 2004 to 2005. In 2005, these investors held a record 61.2 percent of total U.S. equities, which was an increase from the 51.4 percent held in 2000. Institutional ownership of the 1,000 largest U.S. corporations increased from 61.4 percent in 2000 to a peak of 69.4 percent in 2004, and then declined slightly in 2005 to 67.9 percent. The so-called activist investors, state and local pension funds, increased their percentage of U.S. equity markets from 2.9 percent in 1980 to 9.8 percent in 2005, while funds that rarely participate in activism declined in their percentage share. These activist funds were affected by the Enron and WorldCom scandals and were asserting themselves as never before.[26]

In the early 2000s, a new factor appeared on the scene. Hedge funds grew in 2000 and 2001 as the stock market increased in value, and by 2005 were said to control more than $1 trillion in assets. One advantage they had over other institutional investors was the ability to move quickly and exploit opportunities to force a change in corporate management. They could quickly buy up the stock of a corporation, for example, to become a major shareholder and then press for whatever changes they deemed necessary.[27] In some cases they might pressure to sell off parts of their business that were not doing well, and in other cases might even lead the charge to replace top management.

BOARDS OF DIRECTORS

The Board of Directors is supposed to look after the interests of shareholders, but has been criticized as being no more than a ceremonial function that "rubber stamps" the views and policies of management. Board members were accused of being dominated by top management, who set the agenda for board meetings and were the sole source of information for many board members. As a result of these criticisms, many changes were made to make the board more responsive to the interests of the owners and less subservient to management.

One of the first changes was relative to the composition of boards, by changing its membership to include more outside directors, either by expanding the board or dropping some inside members. And these outsiders were not necessarily quasi-insiders, such as the company's legal counsel, banker, major supplier, or retired officer. Instead they often had no ties to the company itself, making them truly independent. Representation of women and minority-group members also increased. With more women and minorities reaching senior management levels, corporations were tapping more of them for board openings.

Another change was the development of more board committees and making them independent of management. One important committee is the audit committee, which in some cases is composed entirely of outside directors. The purpose of this committee is to monitor the company's accounting procedures and ensure the accuracy of information appearing in the annual report. Another critical committee is the nominating committee, which takes the power of nominating new board members away from management. Most large companies also created compensation committees to evaluate the performance of top management and determine the terms and conditions of their employment. It was hoped that these committees would help to curb the continuing rise in the salaries of top management, and particularly prevent large pay increases from being granted by the board when the company had not done well and other stakeholders did not get a fair return. However, this committee has not been successful in controlling executive pay and it has continued to climb.

Board members were also held more accountable for their actions. Board membership had been something of a pleasant and undemanding hobby for many members, but as shareholder suits against corporate officers and directors increased during the 1980s, board members began to take their responsibilities more seriously. Insurance coverage for directors and officers became more expensive as these suits increased. A landmark decision was handed down by the Delaware Supreme Court in 1985 that accelerated this trend towards accountability. The court ruled that ten former directors of Trans Union, a railroad-equipment leasing company, were finically liable for selling their company too hastily and for too little. The lawsuit filed on behalf of 10,000 shareholders claimed that the directors had spent just two hours discussing a purchase offer of $55 a share, which was accepted, when the company actually had been worth much more. The directors were held responsible for the difference between what was actually accepted and a "fair value" for the company. Depending on what the court determined this value to be, each director may have been potentially liable for millions.[28]

Independent board members began to meet with managers present, which gave members more opportunity to speak openly about the performance of the management team and make suggestions for change. After the scandals at Enron and other companies, the New York Stock Exchange urged boards to have a "lead" or presiding director who would provide information to the rest of the board members and organize its sessions. This took away control of the board from management, who had previously set the agenda and controlled the information the board received. Also, accountants and compensation consultants began to report to the board rather than management, giving the board more responsibility.[29]

OTHER ASPECTS

There are several other aspects to corporate governance that deserve to be mentioned. Private equity had been a factor in the $25 billion buyout of RJR Nabisco, but this deal stood for two decades as the biggest buyout in history. By 2006, however, private equity funds were again a factor, as they were able to raise huge sums of money to buy out companies like Hertz and the Hospital Corporation of America (HCA) company. A strong motivation for these buyouts came from the fact that taking a company private meant that it could avoid the hassles of dealing with activist shareholders or institutional investors. The CEOs of these companies have to answer only to their private-equity investors, who share the same goal of making money. Some observers say that private equity is the new model for corporate ownership in the twenty-first century.[30]

In 2006, there were $415 billion worth of private-equity deals, including HCA at $32.7 billion, Equity Office at $38.9 billion, and TXU Energy at $43.8 billion. The latter was a Texas utility company where Kohlberg Kravis Roberts was one of the buyers taking the company private, the same group involved in the takeover of RJR Nabisco two decades earlier. Wall Street investment banks entered the private equity business, which further compromised their judgment as corporate advisors. In some cases, managers were active in these deals, as they stood to make huge gains from taking their company private, often keeping shareholders and directors in the dark until it was too late to stop the buyout.[31]

An emphasis on increased disclosure is another aspect of corporate governance that deals with many aspects of corporate behavior. The purpose of such an emphasis is to make the corporation more responsive to stockholder interests and perhaps to society as a whole. Reforms in this area can be seen as attempts to make the present system more effective by providing shareholders more information on which to base their investment decisions. The primary force behind disclosure is the Securities and Exchange Commission (SEC); however, the establishment of the Financial Accounting Standards Board (FASB) in 1972 continues a self-regulatory process to establish uniform standards of accounting. The purpose of the FASB is to develop standards for financial measurement and reporting. As a quasi-legal body, the board must obtain the cooperation of industry, accountants, government agencies, statement users, and the general public in order to set standards that will be accepted and followed.

There have been several issues over the years where increased disclosure of information was seen as the solution. One such issue concerned line-of-business reporting, which was a requirement imposed by the SEC that made business report sales and earnings for every component of a company with over 10 percent of sales and earnings. Supposedly, this information would help investors determine the lines of business that are the most profitable, therefore influencing their investment decisions. Other areas of disclosure include a 1974 SEC ruling that required companies to disclose a five-year history of financial statistics, a 1978 SEC requirement that all proxy statements disclose the economic and personal relationship of members of the board of directors, the requirement of the Foreign Corrupt Practices Act of 1977 for disclosure of foreign payments, and a court ruling that required disclosure of early merger negotiations that may sometimes be of "material" interest to shareholders.

Of more recent origin is the Sarbanes-Oxley Act, passed in 2002, in response to the corporate scandals at Enron, WorldCom and others, which had overstated earnings, among other things, to mislead investors and the public. These actions resulted in huge losses to employees and shareholders and caused a crisis in investor confidence. The intent of the Act was to protect investors by improving the accuracy and reliability of corporate financial disclosures. It created new standards for corporate accountability as well as new penalties for wrongdoing. It holds the CEO responsible for the accuracy of financial reporting and specifies new internal controls and procedures designed to ensure the validity of financial records.

The major provisions of the Act (1) mandated that the board audit committee consist solely of independent board members and be responsible for hiring and overseeing auditors, (2) required executives to certify reports with criminal penalties for reckless certification, (3) mandated new disclosures regarding a firm's internal controls, and (4) created a new regulatory agency to oversee accounting.[32] The Act applies to all public companies in the U.S. that have registered equity or debt securities with the SEC and accounting firms that provide auditing services to these companies.

Finally, there is the issue of executive compensation, which has been around for some time and is high on the agenda of shareholder issues. Executive compensation was already on the agenda in 1977, when the SEC issued a ruling pertaining to the disclosure of executive compensation, requiring such disclosures to include not only salaries and bonuses, but also deferred compensation, fringe benefits, and non-salary compensation known as "perks," which were usually buried in the footnotes of annual reports. These requirements were later watered down in another SEC ruling.[33]

The issue was back on the agenda in the early 1990s, as there was a political furor over increasing compensation unrelated to corporate performance. Traditionally, the SEC considered executive pay to be part of the ordinary business of a company to be decided by the board of directors, and would not allow executive pay proposals to be put in proxy resolutions. But in 1992, it began to side with shareholder activists and allowed nonbinding shareholder votes on pay proposals.[34] This action opened the door for new disclosure rules about executive pay, proposals that went into effect a year later. Proxy statement charts were required to explain compensation for the five highest-paid executives and include a separate graph to show stock and dividend performance. The board's compensation committee was also required to prepare a signed rationale for top executive pay. These requirements were instituted to allow investors to decide if a company's performance justified the pay packages proposed for senior management.[35]

The issue of stock options granted to senior management came up already in 1993, when the FASB moved to force companies to deduct the value of stock options from their earnings. At the time this action was taken, stock options were the only major type of compensation that was not deducted from reported earnings. This proposal was aimed at top management, where many stock option packages were deemed to be excessive. Business opposed this requirement and the FASB eventually agreed to delay implementation.[36] There were many different proposals as to the most accurate way to value options, since their value at the time they were issued was difficult to determine. Thus options continued to be issued at no cost to the company and their use grew significantly, fueling a continuing rise in executive compensation.

Supporters of stock options argued that they would give CEOs a greater stake in the company and thus be more of an incentive for them to work harder to increase the value of the company. Normally, options gave the CEO the right to buy shares of the company's stock at the closing price on the date the options were granted. They could exercise these options after they vested. If the stock price increased, as it did for most companies in the 1990s, CEOs made millions and stock options became the preferred means of compensation. But some CEOs were not satisfied with this arrangement and backdated their options by picking a date for determining the price when the stock was selling at a lower price than the date of the grant, guaranteeing them an instant profit. This was a no-lose situation, which meant that CEOs stood to gain even if the company was underperforming.

The SEC investigated these activities and after a year or so began issuing penalties that turned out to be much smaller than anyone expected. The first companies to settle, the Mercury Interactive unit of Hewlett-Packard and Brocade Communications, paid just $28 million and $7 million respectively in penalties. The commission actually reduced the penalty for Mercury by 20 percent from the $35 million the company originally agreed to pay to settle its backdating charges. The SEC believed that options backdating was a much less serious offense than accounting fraud, which deliberately misleads investors about the company's financial condition, and the cost to shareholders was much lower as was the impact on earnings.[37]

Throughout the last several decades, CEO pay has continued to grow despite efforts to rein it in and tie executive pay more closely to performance. In 2006, according to an analysis by The Corporate Library, the average CEO of a Standard & Poor's 500 company earned $14.78 million in total compensation. This represented a 9.4 percent increase from the previous year. According to some estimates, the ratio between the compensation of top executives and the average pay of workers increased from 42 in 1980 to more than 400 in 2005, a ratio that is unprecedented, particularly when compared with that of other countries.[38]

But it isn't only an average worker who is losing ground to top management. A widening gap also exists between different levels of management. At Office Depot, for example, the CEO's compensation was $2.2 million in 1997, more than double that of the second-ranked executive and two-thirds greater than the fifth-ranked executive. In 2007, the CEO of the same company made $12 million, more than four times the compensation of the second-ranked executive and over six times that of the fifth-ranked executive. The same is true of many companies, even those that once had more even-handed practices. Overall, the CEOs of the largest companies in the nation earned on average about 80 percent more than the third-highest paid executives in the 1960s and 1970s, according to a study jointed conducted by MIT and the Federal Reserve. By 2000, this gap had swollen to 260 percent.[39]

How much money do these people need? What are they worth? Is this compensation the result of competition for the best talent or the result of bottomless greed? Consider the following examples. Steven Jobs, the CEO of Apple Computer, was paid only $1 in salary but he collected $646.6 million from sales of company stock, making him the highest paid CEO in 2006.[40] Is he actually worth this much to the company or is it simply that he is able to manipulate the board to his advantage? Some of these options, it was alleged, may have been backdated, and the company was investigated by the SEC in this regard. At Federated Department Stores, the CEO was paid $16 million in 2006, and also received 40 percent off of everything he bought at Federated Stores, like Macy's and Bloomingdale's, while the rank-and-file employees received only 20 percent off such merchandise.[41]

These examples strongly suggest that the imperial CEO is alive and well in corporate America, as the rich get richer and the poor poorer, hardly indicative of a community that values every member. The American dream of getting ahead and every generation being better off than the one before is fading for many citizens. One study finds that males in their 30s are worse off than their fathers' generation, which is a reversal of fortunes from just a decade ago. The typical family's income has lagged far behind the growth of productivity, also a reversal from most of the period since World War II. Between 2000 and 2005, productivity rose 16 percent while median income fell 2 percent, challenging that notion that a rising tide lifts all boats. Some people don't have a boat, and if they do, it is leaking badly.[42]

These trends of ever-increasing executive compensation and declining incomes for many workers will keep this issue on the agenda for some time. CEOs have become a symbol for the inequalities that have increased in the society as a whole, as the middle-class loses more and more ground. Corporations have outsourced many jobs, leaving Americans unemployed, opted out of their pension programs, and shed their heath care coverage for employees, while all the time rewarding their top executives ever-increasing compensation packages. Compensation committees have been unable to control executive pay, and it is not clear at this point how this issue is going to be resolved. It is a challenge to top management to be more responsible and realistic about their worth to the organization and recognize that they are part of a community, all the members of which are necessary for the success of the organization. All employees need to be treated fairly and compensated adequately for the jobs they perform.

STAKEHOLDER GOVERNANCE?

For much of the last century, chief executives of large corporations held unilateral power over their companies, with unquestioned authority to do whatever they wanted with the resources at their disposal. Boards rarely opposed the will of management, even at poorly performing companies, and institutional investors and activist shareholders, while effective at times in pursuing objectives at odds with management in some companies, did not mount an effective overall challenge to management control. Top management determined how corporate resources were used and enjoyed increasing levels of pay and benefits that enabled them to live a lifestyle that most people could not even imagine. They became a new class of royalty, if you will, that was able to extract huge sums of money from corporations for their services.

Changes began to take place at the beginning of the twenty-first century, and with the collapse of the stock market, the terrorist attacks, and, in particular, the scandals at Enron, WorldCom, Adelphia, and Tyco, among others, public perceptions of top management plunged. New laws were passed, institutions began to be more aggressive, and attorneys general of some states became more active. Some managers began to change their attitudes, recognizing that they needed the approval of the public at large in order to succeed. Some began to take their boards more seriously. Firings of the Chief Executive Officer (CEO) increased dramatically, beginning in 2004, and continued in later years.

Consider this fact: A decade ago, two-thirds of all CEOs stayed in their jobs at least until they reached the early retirement age of 62. Today, nearly two-thirds of CEOs don't. Instead, they are subject to constant reevaluation and the possibility that at any time, they may be dumped. Four times as many of the world's top CEOs were forced out of their jobs in 2005 as in 1995 . . . Boards are rapidly becoming more independent, as directors who won their jobs in an older, CEO-centric regime retire. Institutional shareholders are becoming more aggressive, challenging directors and corporate policies more often. Hedge funds and private-equity funds are accumulating larger piles of cash, putting even the largest public companies within their reach. Corporate-focused nongovernmental organizations are raising more money and growing stronger, as wealthy people with activist inclinations feed the movement toward social entrepreneurship. Politically ambitious attorneys general still see attacking corporate crime as a quick way to make a reputation. Underlying it all, the public continues to view corporate leaders with deep cynicism and distrust.[43]

The power of the CEO has been greatly diminished because of these trends, and according to Alan Murray, writing in *Revolt in the Boardroom*, the CEO now has to share power with boards of directors, government regulators, pension and hedge fund managers, accountants, lawyers, and nongovernmental organizations. All of these groups want a say in the corporation's affairs, and the forces driving these changes show no sign of abating. Something new is emerging with respect to corporate governance that some hope will result in a more democratic and socially responsible institution.[44] While this may be overly optimistic, perhaps it is safe to say that there is an emerging stakeholder model of corporate governance with more of a community of interests that have to be taken into account by management. The era of the imperial CEO seems to be ending.

Some are not so sure, however, about the implications of these changes. Nanette Byrnes, in a review of Murray's book, points out that when CEOs do a good job of running the company, they are largely left alone, and cites several examples to prove the point. Some aspects of the revolution Murray describes may already be reversing, as CEO turnover levels have already slowed.[45] Robert B. Reich, writing in *The American Prospect*, argues that shareholders and fund managers cannot be depended on to constrain the growth of CEO pay because they don't care about it as long as company performance isn't hampered.[46] And finally, Geoff Colvin, writing in *Fortune*, argues that shareholder democracy is not like democracy as ordinarily understood. He cites a study of shareholder voting that showed that on issues that have significant shareholder opposition, management frequently wins if only by a tiny margin. There are many features built into the system of shareholder voting that favor managers, such as the ability to monitor results as voting takes place and taking action to influence votes that haven't been cast. These features give management a significant advantage to shape the outcome in their favor.[47]

Whatever one thinks is happening with respect to corporate governance, it seems that the values of community and responsibility could be more of a factor in the process. Managers are not just agents of shareholders; they are leaders of a community of employees that must work together to achieve success. If shareholders are not able to exercise any influence in the governance process and boards are ineffective, managers are then free to do pretty much as they please and take as large a slice of the pie for themselves as they can get away with. They have responsibilities to all the employees of the corporation to act in their interests, in seeing that they are treated fairly and equitably and are able to lead fulfilling lives, and they have responsibilities to the larger society to see that they are enhancing the multiple environments in which people live, work, and try to put together a meaningful existence for themselves. Top management needs to justify its compensation to the larger community in which the corporation is embedded and be accountable to that community.

14 Management

Initially in this book, the case was made that the traditional understanding of capitalism is based on individualism and rights, and it was argued that this philosophical base of capitalism needs to be expanded to include the notions of community and responsibility. Efforts to broaden the responsibilities of business to include at least some notion of community and responsibility, such as social responsibility and stakeholder theory, were then discussed. These efforts proved to be largely unsuccessful because they ran aground on the shoals of this individualistic philosophy. While there was a broadening of responsibilities through the public policy process, which supposedly reflects community interests, this effort ran up against the limitations of a rights-based approach. Likewise, ethical approaches have been limited in affecting corporate behavior because of their individualistic emphasis.

The next task was to discuss a different approach to the self that was not individualistic in nature and did not consider rights to be inherent in the individual. This philosophy was based on the notion of a social self that developed as part and parcel of a community, with rights along with their attendant responsibilities being derived from the community itself. The implications of this social understanding of the self for capitalism, market systems, the environment, the corporation, globalization, and science and technology were then discussed. An examination of corporate governance shows that while there has been some change towards a stakeholder approach, management is still the key player when it comes to deciding how corporate resources are going to be used in society. This brings us back to the central question posed at the beginning of the book. Can business and management become a profession in every sense of the word, comparable to the traditional professions of law and medicine?

THE RISE AND FALL OF MANAGERIAL CAPITALISM

The emergence of management as an identifiable function within the corporation was congruent with the rise of the modern corporation. These enterprises grew in size and complexity by combining the various stages of production within a single industrial establishment. The integration and synchronization of these stages allowed output to be controlled and managed in a manner that was not possible in an economy composed of many smaller enterprises. Thus the economy changed after the Civil War, from one composed mostly of small organizations in competition with each other to one dominated by the large corporations we see in today's economy, which operate in a different competitive environment.

An example of this kind of integration is provided by the aluminum industry. The making of aluminum products involves a number of stages, starting with the mining of raw ore containing aluminum called bauxite, the processing of bauxite into a concentrated white powder called alumina, a smelting process to convert this alumina into aluminum ingots, the transforming of these ingots into aluminum products including sheet and plate products, aluminum wire, rod, and bar, and different kinds of fabricated shapes, and finally, the distribution and sale of these products. Rather than having different companies at each stage of this process competing with each other that would then sell their output to another company at the next stage, a company like Alcoa combines all these processes into a single enterprise and manages and coordinates the entire process.

The management of this kind of organization involves a great many administrative tasks, such as directing the labor force, organizing the production process, defining procedures to get the work done, and numerous tasks of this nature. The performance of these tasks fell to an emerging function within the corporation called management, which was not identified as either labor or capital, but which over time came to control the modern corporation as discussed in the last chapter. These managers had a great deal of discretion regarding the use of corporate resources and were not subject to the discipline of the market in the same way as smaller enterprises. This led Alfred Chandler, a professor at the Harvard Business School, to argue that the visible hand of management had replaced the invisible hand of the market. Managers were making administrative decisions about the employment of resources that would have been made by the market in a more competitive environment composed of smaller less integrated enterprises.[1]

Managerial capitalism thus involved the emergence of a managerial class that did not derive its legitimacy from ownership of stock, but from its ability to administer and coordinate the tasks that needed to be done in large and complex organizations. It took over the authority that entrepreneurs had who may have started the business and from the owners of the corporation, who had certain property rights. Managers controlled the corporation and called the shots, and their authority within the corporation was unquestioned. Their legitimacy, however, was always in question, and the argument that they derived their authority from stockholders through the board of directors was largely fictional. They came to control the board of directors, and until recent times, shareholders were largely shut out of the governance process. But by what right did they take over control of the corporation?

> But one must also concede that both the Founding Fathers and Adam Smith would have been perplexed by the kind of capitalism we have . . . They could not have interpreted the domination of economic activity by large corporate bureaucracies as representing, in any sense, the working of a "system of natural liberty." Entrepreneurial capitalism, as they understood it, was mainly an individual—or at most, a family—affair. Such large organizations as might exist—joint stock companies, for example—were limited in purpose and usually in duration as well. The large, publicly owned corporation of today which strives for immortality, which is committed to no line of business but rather seeks the best return on investment, which is governed by an anonymous oligarchy, would have troubled them, just as it troubles and puzzles us. And they would have asked themselves the same questions we have been asking ourselves for almost a century now: Who "owns" this new leviathan? Who governs it, and by what right, and according to what principles?[2]

This legitimacy question continued to haunt management, as they needed to find some basis for the authority they exercised over the use of corporate resources. One of the ways this was attempted, according to Rakesh Khurana, an associate professor of organizational behavior at the Harvard Business School, who published an extremely interesting history of business schools in the United States, was the establishment of business schools within the American university. The primary purpose of these schools at their inception, according to Khurana, "was to legitimate and institutionalize the new occupation of management."[3] The achievement of this purpose was attempted by presenting management as an emerging profession, like the traditional professions of medicine and law, and thus dedicated to serve the broader interests of society rather than the more narrowly defined interests of either capital or labor.[4]

Khurana calls this effort to establish business as a subject of professional education the professionalization project, and it was at the center of concerns for business schools for several decades.[5] This professionalization project began to be abandoned after the end of World War II and was accelerated with the publication of the Gordon and Howell and Pierson reports, funded by the Ford Foundation and Carnegie Foundations respectively, both of which were extremely critical of business school education as being too vocationally oriented and consequently lacking academic respectability. These reports argued that management had become more of a science with the development of decision-making tools during the war years and provided generous funding to promote reforms of teaching and research along these lines.[6]

These efforts were based on the notion of a science-based professionalism, but this notion contained a contradiction that eventually led to the abandonment of the professionalization project altogether. For if management is truly a science that can be reduced to a set of fundamental scientific principles, what need is there for management to be viewed as any kind of a profession with broader responsibilities to society? Many of the writings of the day reflected this contradiction. For example, Oliver Sheldon, in a book entitled, *The Philosophy of Management*, argues for the development of a managerial creed, a code of principles that is "scientifically determined and generally accepted," that would act as a guide for the daily practice of the profession.[7] The primary focus of the creed would be to promote an efficient use of resources to increase the society's standard of living. Management thus derives its legitimacy from applying scientific principles in running corporate organizations to accomplish this objective.

The aim of those who are practicing the management profession, says Sheldon, should be to develop a "Science of Industrial Management," which is distinct from the science it employs and the technique of any particular industry. Standards to guide managerial practice can be determined by the analytical and synthetical methods of science. Yet if the practice of management can be circumscribed by a set of scientific principles, what need is there for a philosophy of management or a professional creed for management? If management is a science in this sense, it becomes nothing more than the applications of scientific principles to concrete situations. It involves no considerations of responsibilities to the larger community or any ethical reflection that is a part of a true professional activity.

What finally ended the professionalization project for good was the emergence of what Khurana calls investor capitalism as a replacement for managerialism. Managers were seen as standing in the way of the efficient operation of competitive markets and were accused of mismanaging corporate assets. Takeovers were justified on this basis, and to ward off hostile takeovers, managers had to improve performance of their companies by divesting themselves of unrelated businesses, cutting out layers of middle management, outsourcing noncore functions, downsizing, and other measures to improve their economic situation. Loyalty to workers, products, communities and the like went out the door, as the only thing that mattered was the creation of shareholder value.[8]

According to Khurana, the rise of agency theory supported this change to investor capitalism and ended any concern about the professionalization of management. Agency theory holds that managers serve as merely agents of shareholders and are bound to manage corporate assets in their interests. They are in a sense nothing more than hired hands (hence the title of the book) and have no permanent responsibilities to any collective interests like society. Agency theory is clearly based on individualism and does not incorporate any notion of a collective responsibility, but instead views managers as distinct individuals dissociated from one another that have no responsibilities to any collective entity, including the organization itself. The organization is simply a nexus of contracts among individuals with no sense of community. Such a view is opposed to any notion of professionalization.[9]

> . . . the promise that business schools would socialize managers into a culture of professionalism—thereby legitimating managerial authority in the face of competing claims to corporate control from the socially disruptive forces of capital and labor— . . . gave rise to the university business school in the first place. The autonomy and authority of professional managers would be rooted not only in expert knowledge but in their obligation not to represent the interests of either owners or workers—much less of themselves—but to see that the corporation contributed to the general welfare. Agency theorists, however, dismiss any such framing of managerial work as tenderhearted do-gooding. Agency theory also excludes from consideration any notion of collective identity—a fundamental attribute of professions in any sociological framing of the phenomenon—let alone collective responsibility. On the contrary, it frames managerial agents as distinct and dissociated from one another, defining an organization as simply a nexus of contracts among individual agents.[10]

Khurana goes on to say that managers were thus cut loose from any moorings to the organizations they led and to the communities in which these organizations were embedded. In the final analysis, they were cut loose from shareholders themselves, as shareholders were unable to prevent these managers from taking a greater and greater share of corporate wealth to enrich themselves at the expense of shareholders and other employees of the corporation, regardless of their performance. It also opened the door to a series of corporate scandals involving misstatement of earnings, backdated stock options, and a host of other malpractices in a number of companies, all of which undermined public trust in the integrity and fairness of the capitalistic system.[11]

Managers have become loose individuals who do not feel constrained by any social values such as fairness or equity and have no allegiance to anyone else but themselves. When relationships are anchored only in utilitarian self-interest, managers can play fast and loose with other individuals in relationships that involve trust and responsibility.[12] To counter these trends, Khurana advocates reviving the notion of professionalism as it applies to management, as professions are a vital part of the economic and social order, and when they are compromised or corrupted, society is harmed. But any new professionalization project must be rooted in community rather than individualism, for professions derive their basic structure and logic from communities, according to Khurana.[13] What should also be pointed out is that community would involve a sense of responsibility on the part of management to something other than themselves.

TOWARD A PROFESSIONAL MODEL FOR MANAGEMENT

What would a professional model for management look like that is based on community and responsibility rather than individualism and rights? The problem with a professional model for business, as was stated by Levi in the first chapter, is the conflict between the professional demand for service and the exclusively business demand for profits.[14] The true professional is committed to serve his or her client, and while profits are necessary for lawyers and doctors to continue to serve their clients, profits are not the overriding objective as they are for business. The businessman has to keep his eye on the reward, and the overriding objective of business is to make a profit and increase the economic wealth of the nation. Whatever goods business produces or services business provides are secondary to this objective. Levi thinks this is largely a matter of emphasis, a kind of mentality that pervades the business community; it is not necessarily a function of the capitalistic system itself.

Levi did not seem too optimistic that a change in this mentality would ever take place, as it would go against the way Western civilization thinks of business activity and would require a rethinking of the purpose of business as well as society and a rethinking of the nature of the self as has been attempted in this book. It is not just business that has this kind of mentality; it is pervasive throughout the entire society. As Levi states, the ethical behavior of any segment within society is generally not without roots in the more general aspiration of that society as a whole.[15] This is one of the most important insights that he provides and must be kept in mind as the discussion about business as a profession proceeds. The notion that wealth is primarily if not exclusively economic in nature is widely shared in Western industrialized societies. The creation and acquisition of material wealth are what these societies are all about, and money is what an acquisitive society values above everything else.

Money can be counted, it is quantifiable, and it is therefore something of a precise measure of economic wealth. Individuals and households can determine precisely how much they are worth and what income they have to support themselves. Assets can be evaluated in terms of money and then counted and added up to determine economic wealth. The nation as a whole adds up the goods and services that are produced in the entire economy to determine if the economy is healthy and growing, so that it is getting richer in terms of economic wealth. The nation measures its success in this manner just as individuals and households. Money is the measure of all things good and bad and is as precise an indicator as can be hoped for to give one a sense of what one is worth.

Business managers are, of course, a part of this money-oriented society and it is not surprising that they should seek profits as the overriding goal of their organization. Money is the measure of their success and the success of the organization. Profits are taken to be an indicator of how well the company has contributed to the well-being of society, even if those profits come at the expense of people's health and the environment. If a company is profitable, it is generally taken that the organization has performed a useful role in society and is given society's blessing to continue in existence because it is believed to have served the public good in some sense. But profits in themselves are not the problem; it is the profit motive that I think Levi is concerned about.

What is the difference, for example, between a for-profit and not-for-profit organization? Even the latter has to make a profit in order to have money to continue in existence. The difference then has to be in whatever motivates the people in the organization. Managers in a for-profit organization are motivated by the desire for profit, while managers of not-for-profit organizations are supposedly motivated by other objectives. But isn't it time that we grew out of this idea that profits are what motivate people to work in business organizations? Most employees do not work for the profit of the organization; they just want a good job that provides them with an adequate standard of living. Managers who work only to increase the profits of the organization are cutting themselves off from more rewarding and satisfying goals related to doing something that goes beyond mere profit-making.

To be a profession in the true sense of the word, management must put profits in a broader context, and recognize that their major objective is to serve the clients of the organization, the people who consume their products, work for it, and invest in it, and who depend on it for various things in the community. To be a true profession, managers must change their focus to one of putting the client foremost in their decisions. If they do this and produce products that truly enhance people's lives and provide good jobs for their employees with adequate wages and are concerned about their impact on the environment, profits will follow in a society that keeps money in its proper perspective.

One of the first and most important tasks relative to thinking of business as a profession is to place the corporation in the context of society. This involves a de-centering of the corporation; a recognition that the corporation is not the center of the universe around which society revolves, but that the corporation is but one element, albeit an important one, of the total social context in which humans work out a meaningful and fulfilling existence for themselves.[16] Business exists to serve society and enhance the well-being of the members of that society; the society does not exist to serve business and its interests. This involves a change of worldview on the part of business people who tend to think of the organization as being at the core of the universe.

All of the elements that go towards the making of this worldview are consistent with each other and inform our understanding of capitalism and the role of the corporation in society. An emphasis on individualism and rights is consistent with the notion that the use of private property to increase material wealth is the most important undertaking in society, and that society must see to it that the organization that is the primary generator of this wealth, namely the corporation, is given priority in its concerns. The economy is separated from the rest of society, and along with production and consumption, which keep the economy going, it is seen as an end in itself with no further moral justification.

This idea that society and all its elements exist to serve corporate interests has to change in order for business to be seen as a profession. Managers of these organizations have to broaden their perspective to think of society in their decisions and how the corporation can enhance the well-being of society's members in ways that involve more considerations than just the creation of economic wealth. As stated previously, economic wealth is something of an illusion and a fiction and merely reflects the value society places on economic entities. Business must serve a wider spectrum of values and interests than just economic ones, and this broader perspective must be considered when managers formulate business policies and practices.

Society, however, is itself something of an abstraction, as people who constitute the society have different goals and values, making the determination of a common good somewhat difficult. It is at this point that another element of the traditional professions comes into play, namely the notion of the client. It is through these clients that the values of society can be discerned, as the aggregate interests of these various clients can be seen as constitutive of the common good for society as a whole. Thus it is important for managers to think in terms of clients and attempt to determine their interests and the impacts that the actions of the corporation have on their existence.

But who are the clients of business organizations? The traditional view of business would hold that the stockholder is the major client, that managers are agents of the owners and have a primary responsibility to earn the highest rate of return that can be earned on the owner's investment in the business. But a case could be made that the major client is the consumer, as business exists to produce goods and services to satisfy consumer demand. Thus the focus should be on producing goods and services that make the lives of consumers better and more satisfying. One could also make a case for employees being the major client, as they spend the better part of their waking hours working for the company and the enhancement of their experience should be the focus of corporate activity.

It seems then that business has multiple clients, but this is actually no different from the traditional professions. Private hospitals have stockholders to satisfy; lawyers have staff to keep happy, as do large doctor's offices with many nurses and clerical personnel. Every decision will probably affect all of these clients to some degree, but most decisions will most likely affect one or more clients to a greater degree than the others. Thus a stakeholder model would seem to be an appropriate way to approach the client question, but as was seen in an earlier chapter, if stakeholders are viewed through an individualistic lens, they are not seen as integral to the functioning of the organization. The corporation must be seen as a community within a community to overcome this individualistic view, with multiple responsibilities to the various members of that community to enrich the total community experience.

Management must then be concerned with producing goods and services that are going to better the lives of consumers and provide them with enriching experiences, with providing its employees with meaningful experiences and the opportunity to grow and develop as human beings during the time they spend working for the corporation, and in providing stockholders with an ample return on their investment. It is not a matter of balancing these various interests against each other, but of giving all of them attention at the same time. They are all part of the same community nexus and these interests are tied together in seeking a better life with more enriching experiences. And it is not just the human community that is of concern, but also the natural world that must be taken into consideration in corporate decisions, as outlined in an earlier chapter.

Business can and should take the lead in many of these concerns and not simply rely on market demand for products. There is no question that the market responds to consumer demand, and if, for example, more people were to demand high-mileage vehicles and refuse to buy low-mileage sports utility vehicles, more of the former would be produced. The fact is that people enjoy sports utility vehicles and are not willing to give them up without being coerced or faced with high gas prices. While we may profess concern for the environment, this is not always reflected in our market behavior. If more people were to demand products that are environmentally friendly and produced under sustainable conditions and take the time to investigate and buy such products, more of them would appear.

Currently, there is concern about the health of the American population, and obesity is seen as a major problem causing all kinds of health problems. Those in the fast food business in particular can and have taken the lead in providing more healthful food, but if more people were concerned about their health and took more interest in eating healthy, more nutritious food would appear on the market, and the calorie-laden cheeseburgers and muffins would disappear. It seems rather ludicrous for people to sue McDonald's for serving high-calorie fast foods when all people have to do is stop eating such food. Yes, companies do all they can through advertising and other marketing techniques to persuade people to buy their products, but ultimately the decision is the consumer's whose decisions reflect his of her interests and values, and business functions within the values and interests of society at large.

But what people may be asking for in such lawsuits is for business to take the lead in changing their behavior and do for them what they cannot do for themselves. Business has enormous influence over people's behavior with its advertising techniques and can use this power to persuade people to adopt better or different lifestyles by using products that are more healthful or environmentally friendly. They do not always have to produce what people want but can change those wants and desires. A good society is more than the aggregation of people's existing wants and desires, but involves a vision of what a better society would look like and how we can get there.

ACCOUNTABILITY

The word capitalism traditionally refers to the physical capital, such as machines and factories, the company has at its employ and the financial capital the company has available to finance its operations and potential expansion. But capitalism need not be limited to these factors; it can also include things like human capital and natural capital. Human capital refers to the human resources the company needs to do its work, and natural capital means the natural resources that the company uses in its operations, not only the resources used directly in its products but also the resources that are used or affected in the production process, like air and water and the climate as a whole.

The annual report in its traditional sense has been a means of accounting to shareholders for the use of their investment in the company and focuses largely on data that convey this information. But there is no good reason it could not become a means of accounting to the society at large for the use of society's resources. Thus it would include not only financial information relative to the firm's financial situation, but also information on the state of its physical capital, how well the company had used its human resources, how well it had served consumers, and how it had used society's environmental resources.

Thus companies would have to report statistics relative to job safety and health, for example, and statistics on the diversity of its workforce. The report should include information about its products and whether there had been any problems with respect to adverse effects of its products on consumers. It would also be necessary for companies to report on the use of physical resources and what the company had done to minimize its pollution and dispose of toxic wastes properly. Many companies already report such information, either in a separate report or in the annual report, but such reporting would have to become standardized as much as possible and required of all public companies registered on the stock exchanges.

Such a change in the notion of accountability is consistent with de-centering the corporation and seeing it as part of society and accountable to society for what it has done to enhance the well-being of that society. And a society that was oriented to a broader conception of itself than just the accumulation of economic wealth would be interested in how the corporation was affecting its total existence. Money is not the measure of all things, and other measures, such as those mentioned, are important to indicate how the corporation is impacting the entire society. There has been on ongoing effort, sometimes called social accounting, to persuade the corporation to include such measures, so there is already a good deal of experimentation that has been done to invent meaningful measures for human and natural capital, for example, and if these dimensions were taken more seriously and required of all corporations, better measures would undoubtedly be developed.

SELF-REGULATION

If management were able to change across the board and become truly professional and society were to broaden its perspective beyond economic wealth and see itself as a community that is something more than individuals competing with each other, managers would most likely be given greater leeway to police and regulate themselves. Society might come to trust business at a new level and change its image of the greedy businessperson who will do anything to make a profit. Managers might be allowed through business and trade associations to monitor competition in an industry and police themselves if competition appeared to be disappearing because of the action of a few merger-minded executives. They might be able to reach agreement on environmental standards where these were deemed necessary and find some acceptable manner by which to factor environmental costs into the prices of their products. And they might be trusted to set and enforce safety and health standards for workplaces.

They might even agree that with regard to some issues, government has a role to play in making public policies that become matters of law and formal regulation, but rather than have their self-interest in mind when working with government, they might be able to think of the larger community interest and provide needed information to government regulators. For example, it might be in the interest of business as well as society to keep agencies like the Food and Drug Administration in business to assure that our food and drugs are safe to eat and use as directed. This might be too onerous a task for business to take upon itself, and perhaps the government is best equipped to do the testing and investigation necessary for this function. But business could cooperate with government in developing testing methods and providing information when necessary.

When it comes to self-regulation, the example of business school accreditation offers a relevant example. Business schools across the country are accredited by an organization called The Association for the Advancement of Collegiate Schools of Business (AACSB), which is largely made up of deans from the various schools that are members of the organization. Accreditation is something that is eagerly sought by most business schools because of the advantage it gives them in recruiting students and faculty. The accreditation process and the standards used in evaluating schools are entirely under the control of this organization. The government does not have anything to do with setting standards or with seeing that they are enforced.

The AACSB does this on its own, and from time to time changes the standards and the way they are enforced. Since this is an organization of deans by and large, it seems evident that the schools thus regulate themselves and set the standards by which they are going to operate. Accreditation committees made up of these deans visit the schools personally to evaluate them, and use this experience, along with information submitted by the schools, in making the final decision about accreditation. The AACSB has a staff that helps in this process, but it is the deans that make the final decision. Having been a part of this organization for a few years and attended several of their meetings, I was duly impressed with the manner in which this self-regulatory process worked and the professional manner in which business was conducted.

Business executives are reluctant to criticize each other, but if they were members of an organization, such as the AACSB, perhaps they would find this organization useful to police and censure those organizations that did not meet the standards set by the organization. This is what a professional organization does; it sets standards and then sees to it that members of the organization adhere to these standards. It does not rely on the government to enact laws and issue regulations and ensure that these laws and regulations are being followed through the legal system. Think of the money and time that society would save if business were to regulate itself in this manner.

Perhaps the AACSB accreditation process could serve as a model for self-regulation of business, where CEOs would meet and set standards for their member organizations and police their members to make sure the standards were met and taken seriously. But it will take a major change in the society as a whole for something like this to happen. Changes of this kind have to be based on a vision of community and the responsibilities we have to each other as members of a community. Individualism and rights are not going to get us there. The latter leads to factionalism and irreconcilable clashes that can only be resolved, if at all, in some kind of political context that may lead to continued conflict, as we have seen with respect to many, if not most, regulatory efforts.

THE PROFESSIONALIZATION OF BUSINESS SCHOOLS

What would it take for the professionalization project to be revived in business schools and what would a professional model for business look like? Currently the business school curriculum reflects the traditional philosophy of individualism and rights in its courses, as the stated or unstated purpose of most courses is still the maximization of shareholder wealth despite many years of social responsibility, ethics, and stakeholder management. There has been no significant change in the economic, social, and moral philosophies that inform the courses that are taught in the traditional business school. Even business ethics, to the extent that it is based on the "good ethics is good business" idea, reflects this traditional philosophy.

If management is no longer considered to be a profession, but managers are nothing more than hired hands, then in what sense can business schools be considered professional schools at the same level as schools of law and medicine aligned with the mission of the university as a whole? Have they become nothing more than highly sophisticated trade schools to prepare students for careers in organizations whose sole purpose is to create wealth for themselves as agents and for shareholders as principals?[17] Is one of the primary purposes of gaining a business school education to develop a social network that can give access to a job in one of the top companies in the country, if not the world? Is the MBA program more like an exclusive fraternity or country club that gives students an advantage in the labor market, as Khurana suggests?[18] If so, this has implications as to what business schools are doing.

> If academic credentialing and providing a social network are now the primary functions of business schools, then the role of the institution is that of a gatekeeper rather than a transmitter of knowledge and values . . . a student invests in higher education simply to purchase a signal that is received by prospective employers as an indication of the likelihood that he or she is committed to a business career and will perform productively.[19]

Others have criticized the MBA program as being an enculturation process, where students learn to accept the basic values found in corporate culture and become committed to the goals and practices that are needed to achieve marketplace success.[20] An Aspen Institute study found that students entering an MBA program who may have initially believed that customer needs and product quality were top priorities of the company changed their top priority to shareholder value by the time of graduation.[21] Students see the MBA degree as opening up opportunities to climb the corporate ladder that are not available to non-degree people. They do not have to start in the mailroom or on the factory floor but can start on the middle rungs of the ladder, so to speak.

> The business schools' most important purpose is to serve the corporate labor market by screening, disciplining, training, and mentally conditioning its graduates so they may be minimally ready for life within the corporate system. Never mind that most of the knowledge acquired by MBA students is irrelevant to the actual conditions and challenges to be encountered in the workplace, as countless critics have demonstrated. Getting in the corporate door is what it's all about.[22]

Nothing else really matters, including corporate social responsibility, ethics, ecology, or any other subject not directly related to this central objective of maximizing shareholder wealth. Once in the corporation, one has to play the game to get ahead, and the game consists of meeting financial goals, not being socially or environmentally responsible or making a contribution to society. As Khurana states: "Notions of sustained effort to build companies that create useful products and services, provide employment, and contribute to their communities are less and less a part of the aspirations of American business school students."[23]

The place to change this attitude would seem to be in the business schools themselves, where business school students are trained and enculturated. Change has to start somewhere; it will not happen by magic, and the educational process is one place where students can be encouraged to think differently about their lives and occupations and adopt values that they come to believe will lead to more fulfilling and enriching lives for themselves and society. Reviving the notion of management as a profession that makes managers the primary link between the narrow concerns of business and the broader concerns of society is seen to be essential for business schools to gain respectability within the university and regain a sense of mission and purpose that goes beyond that of a trade school.[24]

> If university business schools . . . are to continue to play any role in the education of managers that could not be filled equally well by corporate training programs or for-profit, purely vocational business schools, they belong in the forefront of the discussions now taking place among informed and thoughtful citizens all around the globe about the shape that capitalism should take in the twenty-first century.[25]

To effect this change and regain a sense of professionalism, business schools must change their worldview, consistent with what was said at the beginning of this chapter. According to Robert Giacalone and Kenneth Thompson, "We teach students to perpetuate business' importance and its centrality in society, to do so by increasing wealth, and to assume that by advancing organizational interests, they advance their own and society's overall best interests."[26] The corporation must be de-centered and placed in the context of society at large. Business exists to serve society and not the other way around. This entails the adoption of a different philosophy of business based on community and responsibility that would be reflected in the courses that are taught in the business school curriculum.

What would have to change to reflect a different philosophy based on community and responsibility is not so much a matter of content but is rather a matter of emphasis.[27] The rationale or objective of courses would have to be restated and taught with a different focus. For example, marketing courses would have to focus on how products could be sold in such a way as to maximize consumer satisfaction and take into account the interest of consumers of bettering their lives, rather than an exclusive focus on how the consumer can be persuaded to purchase the company's products so that a profit can be made for the company. Advertising would have to focus on providing the consumer with the information they need to make an informed decision that will work to make their lives better, rather than trying to manipulate the consumer to buy things they may not want or need in order to better the company.

Likewise, strategy courses would have to focus on how the company can do better things to enhance the entire society, rather than on how to beat the competition and attain a greater market share. Finance courses would focus on using financially resources efficiently and effectively in bettering society, rather than on maximization of shareholder wealth. Organizational behavior courses would have to be concerned with providing experiences in the workplace that enhance workers' lives, rather than with how to make them more productive. And accounting courses would have to broaden their perspective to focus on accounting for the use of society's resources as a whole and not just on financial concerns, and develop means for reporting on the use of human and physical resources in a meaningful and accurate manner that could be audited in the way financial information is audited.[28]

Other courses that are not now a part of most business schools could be added, such as a course in science and technology to give business students a better understanding of how science works and the importance of technological concerns in decision-making. An important course would be one that deals with ecology and environmental concerns to provide an understanding of the way in which nature is connected with human well-being and how corporate activities affect the environment. While liberal arts courses are important to broaden a student's perspective, these kinds of courses would show the relevance of science and technology and the environment to business concerns. While ethics should be a part of every course where appropriate, a separate course that focuses on conflicts of interest, fraud and deception, and other strictly ethical issues is a necessity.[29]

The final course to be added, if it is not already in the curriculum, is a leadership course that should come in the final semester. This course could focus on the qualities of leadership and stress how leadership is different from just managing a corporate organization. It could look at how leaders in business, politics, and other areas have used their power to effect change in the organization and society. The most important project in this course would be to require a paper that would make students articulate their philosophy of management. Every student in an MBA program graduates with some kind of philosophical understanding of management, but in most cases this is unarticulated. This project could serve as kind of a capstone to the entire MBA experience and would give students the opportunity to reflect on their business education and set down on paper what it all means. This could be the most important project in the entire curriculum.

Such a curriculum would most likely have little appeal to MBA students who are currently in the program or to faculty currently teaching who see maximization of shareholder wealth as the overriding objective of business organizations and profits as their major responsibility. But over time, such a curriculum could appeal to different people who have an interest in serving society and devoting their lives to something more than just making profits for the organization in which they spend the majority of their lives and thereby gaining more power and economic wealth for themselves. This curriculum should have an appeal to more socially-minded students who want to do something more fulfilling for themselves and recognize that their well-being is tied up with the well-being of society as a whole.

The changes suggested in this chapter are quite idealistic and are not likely to take place, if at all, any time soon. The intent of this chapter and indeed of the entire book has been to lay out what it would take for management to be considered a profession in the best sense of the word. It would take a rethinking of capitalism and a corresponding change of attitude towards the business institution and the role it plays in society. Such a change, if it occurs at all, will be a long time in the making. The change from an emphasis on individualism and rights to community and responsibility involves a challenge to the basic understanding of what it means to be an American and goes against the grain of thinking that has informed the self-understanding of Americans for centuries.

Since capitalism as traditionally understood has been so successful in providing for our material needs, there is not an urgent need to rethink its fundamental tenets and direction. Yet as environmental challenges mount and as the world's resource base shrinks, there will be added pressures to make adjustments to cope with these problems. It would seem that a professional approach to these problems that recognizes the limitations that a profit-driven system has in resolving these issues might be worth considering. Yet this involves changes in the entire society, not just in business alone, changes that require a different understanding of what constitutes a good life and human fulfillment.

Critics can continue to harp on the evils of a consumer culture and keep on presenting information about impending environmental crisis, but until a new vision of human enrichment is presented that appeals to the emotions, change is not going to happen. The materialistic lifestyle that has been in place for years in Western societies and now is taking hold in China and India is appealing, and talk about adopting a different lifestyle that is not so materialistic falls on deaf ears and fails to motivate people. Efforts to introduce spiritualism into the workplace have limited appeal, as do efforts to promote different kinds of behavior in the marketplace.

In all these cases of exhortation, pleading does not come merely to emotional appeals or persistent haranguing. There are facts that people need to be reminded of, connections and implications that must be clarified, deceptions and fallacies that have to be exposed. But none of this will do much good as long as most people remain enthralled by consumption. To dislodge them from that persuasion, they need to be presented with or reminded of an alternative vision of life.[30]

As argued in this book, any new vision of life in a capitalistic society must incorporate an emphasis on community and responsibility, the idea that we live as part of a community of human beings and nature and have responsibilities to each other and to the natural world in which we exist. If the philosophical base of capitalism were to be expanded in this fashion, perhaps we would be able to place production and consumption in a different context and expand our notions of capitalism to include more facets of our existence. The professionalization of management is part and parcel of this change and would result in a different approach to the role of business in society. Management, in some sense, is the key to it all, making the kind of education that managers receive of critical importance.

Notes

NOTES TO THE INTRODUCTION

1. Warren G. Bennis and James O'Toole, "How Business Schools Lost Their Way," *Harvard Business Review*, 83 (2005): 96–104.
2. Rogene A. Buchholz and Sandra B. Rosenthal, "The Unholy Alliance of Business and Science," *Journal of Business Ethics*, 78 (2008): 199–206.
3. Bennis and O'Toole, "How Business Schools Lost Their Way," 102.
4. William A. Levi, "Ethical Confusion and The Business Community," *Ethics and Standards in American Business*, ed. J.W. Towle, (New York: Houghton Mifflin, 1964), 20–29.
5. Ibid, 27.

NOTES TO CHAPTER 1

1. Adam Smith, *The Wealth of Nations* (New York: Bantam Dell, 2003).
2. Richard Bronk, *Progress and the Invisible Hand* (London: Warner Books, 1998), 7.
3. "For Smith, the promotion of national wealth through the market was a goal worthy of the attention of moral philosophers because of its place in his larger moral vision. Smith valued commercial society not only for the wealth it produced but also for the character it fostered. He valued the market in part because it promoted the development of cooperative modes of behavior, making men more gentle because more self-controlled, more likely to subordinate their potentially asocial passions to the needs of others. In his own way, *The Wealth of Nations*, like Smith's *The Theory of Moral Sentiments* (1759), was intended to make men better, not just better off." Jerry Z. Muller, *The Mind and the Market: Capitalism in Modern European Thought* (New York: Knopf, 2002), 52.
4. Smith, *The Wealth of Nations*, 572. Italics mine.
5. Bronk, *Progress and the Invisible Hand*, 90.
6. John Locke, *Two Treatises of Government* (Cambridge, UK: Cambridge University Press, 1988).
7. See David Bohm, *Wholeness and the Implicate Order* (London: Routledge & Kegan Paul, 1980).
8. Thomas Michael Power, "Trapped In Consumption: Modern Social Structure and the Entrenchment of the Device," in *Technology and the Good Life*, eds. Eric Higgs, Andrew Light, and David Strong (Chicago: University of Chicago Press, 2000), 271–93.

9. Kenneth Minogue, "The History of the Idea of Human Rights," in *The Human Rights Reader*, eds. Walter Laqueur and Barry Rubin (Philadelphia: Temple University Press, 1979), 14–15.
10. Milton Friedman, "The Social Responsibility of Business is to Increase its Profits," *New York Times Magazine*, September 13, 1970, 122–26.
11. William A. Levi, "Ethical Confusion And The Business Community," in *Ethics and Standards in American Business*, ed. J. W. Towle (New York: Houghton Mifflin, 1964), 28.

NOTES TO CHAPTER 2

1. See William C. Frederick, "From CSR1 to CSR2: the Maturing of Business and Society Thought," Graduate School of Business, University of Pittsburgh, 1978, Working Paper No. 279, 1.
2. See Melvin Anshen, *Managing the Socially Responsible Corporation* (New York: Macmillan, 1974).
3. See Milton Friedman, "The Social Responsibility of Business is to Increase its Profits," *New York Times Magazine*, Sept. 13, 1970, 122–26.
4. See Committee for Economic Development, *Social Responsibilities of Business Corporations* (New York: CED, 1971), 29–30.
5. Keith Davis and William C. Frederick, *Business and Society: Management, Public Policy, Ethics*, 5th ed. (New York: McGraw-Hill, 1984), 33–34.
6. Rogene A. Buchholz and Sandra B. Rosenthal, "Control Data Corporation," *Business Ethics: The Pragmatic Path Beyond Principles to Process* (Upper Saddle River, NJ: Prentice Hall, 1998), 136–38.
7. S. Prakash Sethi, "Dimensions of Corporate Social Responsibility," *California Management Review*, 17 (1975): 58.
8. Friedman, "Social Responsibility," 122–126.
9. F. A. Hayek, "The Corporation in a Democratic Society," *Management and Corporations, 1975* (New York: McGraw-Hill, 1960), 106.
10. Theodore Levitt, "The Dangers of Social Responsibility," *Harvard Business Review*, 36 (September–October 1978): 41–50.
11. Gerald D. Keim and Roger E. Meiners, "Corporate Social Responsibility: Private Means for Public Wants?" *Policy Review*, 5 (Summer 1978): 83.
12. Friedman, "Social Responsibility," 122–26.
13. Keim and Meiners, "Corporate Social Responsibility," 83.
14. Manuel G. Velasquez, "Why Corporations Are Not Morally Responsible for Anything They Do," *Business and Professional Ethics Journal*, 3 (Spring 1983): 1–18.
15. See Paul MacAvoy, "Economic Efficiency the Priority," *The Wall Street Journal*, January 20, 1983, 7.
16. Milton Friedman, *Capitalism and Freedom* (Chicago: University of Chicago Press, 1962), 133.
17. Neil W. Chamberlain, *The Limits of Corporate Responsibility* (New York: Basic Books, 1973), 4, 6.
18. Robert C. Solomon, *Ethics and Excellence: Cooperation and Integrity in Business* (New York: Oxford University Press, 1993), 149.
19. William C. Frederick, one of the founders of the field of Business and Society and a leading proponent of corporate social responsibility, concludes the following: "This much we can conclude about the social responsibility movement in the United States: both external and internal advocates of corporate social action have been, and remain, highly constrained in what can be accomplished through the corporate structure. Corporate philanthropy,

while part of a life support system for many important community activities, cannot begin to serve many of the community's most urgent social needs. Corporate social responsiveness appears mainly as a defensive tactic utilized by an elite group of socially aware companies; it is not generally perceived or treated as a broad-scale societal strategy capable of leading humanity to a resolution of its most severe problems." William C. Frederick, *Corporation, Be Good!: The Story of Corporate Social Responsibility* (Indianapolis, IN: Dog Ear Publishing, 2006), 62.

NOTES TO CHAPTER 3

1. Tom Donaldson and Lee Preston, "The Stakeholder Theory of the Corporation: Concepts, Evidence, and Implications," *Academy of Management Review*, 20 (1995): 65–91.
2. William C. Frederick, "Social Issues in Management: Coming of Age or Prematurely Gray?" Paper presented to the Doctoral Consortium of the Social Issues in Management Division, The Academy of Management, Las Vegas, Nevada, August 14, 1992.
3. Archie B. Carroll, *Business and Society: Ethics and Stakeholder Management*, 3rd ed. (Cincinnati: Southwestern, 1996), 74.
4. Max Clarkson, ed., *The Corporation and Its Stakeholders: Classic and Contemporary Readings* (Toronto: University of Toronto Press, 1998), 2.
5. See Carroll, *Business and Society*, p. 68 for an expanded stakeholder map and p. 80 for a map related to a given corporation on a specific issue.
6. Tom Donaldson and Lee Preston, "Foreword: Redefining the Corporation," in *The Corporation and Its Stakeholders: Classic and Contemporary Readings*, ed. Max Clarkson (Toronto: University of Toronto Press, 1998), vii.
7. R. Edward Freeman, "A Stakeholder Theory of the Modern Corporation," in *The Corporation and Its Stakeholders*, ed. Max Clarkson (Toronto: University of Toronto Press, 1998), 125.
8. A. M. Marcoux, "Business Ethics Gone Wrong," *Cato Policy Report*, 22 (2000): 1.
9. Freeman, "A Stakeholder Theory," 132.
10. Ibid.
11. Marcoux, "Business Ethics Gone Wrong," 1.
12. Ibid.
13. Freeman, "A Stakeholder Theory," 132.
14. Ibid.
15. Ibid., 126–28.
16. Donaldson and Preston, "The Stakeholder Theory of the Corporation," 87.
17. Andrew C. Wicks, Daniel R. Gilbert, and R. Edward Freeman, "A Feminist Reinterpretation of the Stakeholder Concept," *Business Ethics Quarterly*, 19 (1994): 479.
18. Ibid.
19. Ibid., 476–77.
20. Ibid.
21. Ibid., 493.

NOTES TO CHAPTER 4

1. *Occupational Safety and Health Act*, Public Law 91–596.

2. Thomas R. Dye, *Understanding Public Policy*, 3ʳᵈ ed. (Englewood Cliffs, NJ: Prentice Hall, 1978), 23.
3. John Rawls, *A Theory of Justice* (Cambridge, MA: Harvard University Press, 1971), 266.
4. Gerald Sirkin, *The Visible Hand: The Fundamentals of Economic Planning* (New York: McGraw-Hill, 1968), 45.
5. James Buchanan, *The Demand and Supply of Public Goods* (Chicago: Rand McNally, 1968), 8.
6. See Michael J. Mandel, "How Much Is A Sea Otter Worth?" *Business Week*, August 21, 1989, 59, 62.
7. Aaron Wildavsky, *Speaking Truth to Power: The Art and Craft of Policy Analysis* (Boston: Little, Brown, 1979), 253–54.
8. There is a school of thought called public choice theory, which looks at government decision-makers as rational, self-interested people who view issues from their own perspective and in light of personal incentives. While voters, politicians, and bureaucrats may desire to reflect the "public interest" and often advocate it in support of their decisions, this desire is only one incentive among many with which they are faced and is likely to be outweighed by more powerful incentives related to self-interest of one sort or another. See Steven Kelman, "Public Choice and Public Spirit," *The Public Interest*, 87 (Spring 1987): 80–94 for an interesting critique of the public choice school of thought.
9. Lee E. Preston and James E. Post, *Private Management and Public Policy: The Principle of Public Responsibility* (Englewood Cliffs, NJ: Prentice Hall, 1975), 11.
10. Kenneth W. Chilton and Ronald J. Penoyer, *The Hazards of "Purse Strings" Regulatory Reform: Regulatory Spending and Staffing Under the Reagan Administration, 1981–85* (St. Louis: Washington University Center for the Study of American Business, 1984), 8.
11. David Vogel, "Business and the Reagan Administration," *Business in the Contemporary World*, October 1988, 52–55.
12. The Vice-President, Office of the Press Secretary, Statement by Vice-President George H. W. Bush, Press Release, August 11, 1983, 2.
13. Vogel, "Business and the Reagan Administration," 55.
14. William G. Laffer, III, *George Bush's Hidden Tax: The Explosion in Regulation* (Washington D.C.: The Heritage Foundation, 1992), 1–2.
15. Melinda Warren, *Federal Regulatory Spending Reaches A New Height: An Analysis of the Budget of the United States Government for the Year 2001* (St Louis: Washington University Center for the Study of America Business, 2000), 1–3.
16. Susan Dudley and Melinda Warren, *Moderating Regulatory Growth: An Analysis of the U.S. Budget for Fiscal Years 2006 and 2007* (Arlington, VA and St. Louis, MO: Mercatus Center at George Mason University and Washington University Murray Weidenbaum Center on the Economy, Government, and Public Policy, 2006), 6–10.
17. Murray L. Weidenbaum, *The Future of Business Regulation* (New York: AMACOM, 1979), 22, 25.
18. Melinda Warren, *Government Regulation and American Business* (St. Louis: Washington University Center for the Study of American Business, 1992), 4.
19. Murray L. Weidenbaum, *Progress in Federal Regulatory Policy, 1980–2000* (St. Louis: Washington University Center for the Study of American Business, 2000), 11–12.
20. Cass R. Sunstein, *Radicals in Robes: Why Extreme Right-Wing Courts Are Wrong for America* (New York: Basic Books, 2005), 15.

21. Ibid., 10–11.
22. Ibid., 3–11
23. Ibid., 26.
24. Ibid., 243.
25. Ibid., 245. See pp. 15–16 for an enumeration of specific actions the Rehnquist Court has taken in this regard.
26. See Simon Lazarus, "Repealing the 20ᵗʰ Century," *The American Prospect*, December 2007, 19–22.
27. Richard Bronk, *Progress and the Invisible Hand* (London: Warner Books, 1998), 59.

NOTES TO CHAPTER 5

1. Michael Lerner, *The Politics of Meaning: Restoring Hope and Possibility in an Age of Cynicism* (Reading, MA: Addison-Wesley, 1996), 35.
2. Max Weber, *The Protestant Ethic and the Spirit of Capitalism* (New York: Charles Scribner's Sons, 1958).
3. Ibid., 35–40.
4. Ibid., 90–92.
5. Ibid., 39–40
6. The Marxist interpretation of history holds that religion is a part of the superstructure built upon the organization of the productive forces of society. Thus religion is a product of the economic organization of society and is in no way an active agent in giving shape to economic development.
7. David C. McClelland, *The Achieving Society* (New York: Free Press, 1961), 48.
8. Richard LaPiere, *The Freudian Ethic* (New York: Duell Sloan, and Pearce, 1959), 16.
9. Gerhard W. Ditz, "The Protestant Ethic and the Market Economy," *Kyklos*, 33 (1980): 626–27.
10. Bob Goudzwaard, *Capitalism & Progress: A Diagnosis of Western Society* (Toronto, Canada: Wedge Publishing Foundation; Grand Rapids, MI: William B. Eerdmans Publishing Co., 1979), 61. In a related passage, Michael Lerner states that: "A materialist worldview emerged that validated only that which could be experienced by the senses. And in place of any ethical concerns of the community, this new social order insisted that the ultimate reality was the pleasure and satisfaction of each individual. The lone individual became the center of the universe, and if we built families and communities, it was only because the lone individual had found it in his or her interest to do so. All connections between human beings hereafter would be based on contract: free individuals choosing to make a connection with others. The sole goal of the state, in this scheme, was to ensure that there was a realm of free contracts in which no one would interfere." Lerner, *The Politics of Meaning*, 37.
11. John Gilchrist, *The Church and Economic Activity in the Middle Ages* (London: Macmillan, 1969), 123. Protestantism, as an institution could never exercise the kind of control and domination over secular forces as did the Medieval Catholic Church. The nature of the Protestant principle did not allow for this kind of control. The kind of revolution it introduced supported political and economic forces in establishing their own ground and authority. The challenge the Protestant movement presented the Catholic Church in questioning its claim to universal and eternal truth and the revolutionary philosophy that informed it, did not allow Protestantism to then turn around

and exercise the same kind of domination and control in the nature of a universal authority. Protestantism as an institution and a movement could not exercise a universal constructive approach to the ordering of life and still be true to the critical principles that informed its emergence. Economic forces had to be given their own course along with the development of secular sources of meaning and purpose. See Richard Niebuhr, *The Kingdom of God in America* (New York: Harper and Row, 1937), 28–30.

12. Goudzwarrd, *Capitalism & Progress*, 22.
13. Christopher Lasch, *The Culture of Narcissism: American Life in an Age of Diminishing Expectations* (New York: Norton, 1978), 52–53.
14. The University of Michigan Survey Research Center asked 1,533 working people to rank various aspects of work in order of importance. Good pay came in a distant fifth behind interesting work, enough help and equipment to get the job done, enough information to do the job, and enough authority to do the job. See "Work Ethic," *Time*, October 30, 1972, 97. See also *Editorial Research Reports on the American Work Ethic* (Washington, D.C.: Congressional Quarterly, 1973); Harold L. Sheppard and Neal Q. Herrick, *Where Have All the Robots Gone* (New York: The Free Press, 1972); Special Task Force to the Secretary of Health, Education, and Welfare, *Work In America* (Cambridge: MIT Press, 1973); and Judson Gooding, *The Job Revolution* (New York: Walker & Co., 1972).
15. Clyde Kluckhohn, "Have There Been Discernible Shifts in American Values During the Past Generation?" in *The American Style: Essays in Value and Performance*, ed. Elting E. Morrison (New York: Harper& Bros., 1958), 207.
16. Ibid., 184.
17. Ibid., 207
18. Ibid., 192.
19. Daniel Bell, *The Cultural Contradictions of Capitalism* (New York: Basic Books, 1976), 70.
20. Ibid., 21.
21. Ibid., 64–65.
22. Ibid., 71–72.
23. Ibid., 75.
24. Daniel Yankelovich, *New Rules: The Search for Self-Fulfillment in A World Turned Upside Down* (New York: Random House, 1981).
25. Ibid., 3.
26. Ibid., 9.
27. Ibid., 39.
28. Ibid., 10.
29. Christopher Lasch, *The Culture of Narcissism*, 53.
30. Ibid., 53.
31. Ibid., 68–69.
32. Robert H. Tawney, *Religion and the Rise of Capitalism* (Gloucester, MA: P. Smith, 1962), 228–29.
33. Clarence E. Ayres, *Toward A Reasonable Society* (Austin, TX: University of Texas Press, 1961), 280.
34. Tom Donaldson and Patricia Werhane, *Ethical Issues in Business: A Philosophical Approach*, 4th ed. (Englewood Cliffs, NJ: Prentice Hall, 1993), 17. Italics mine.
35. Manuel Velasquez, *Business Ethics: Concepts and Cases* (Englewood Cliffs, NJ: Prentice Hall, 1992), 104–106. Italics mine.
36. J. B. Callicott, "The Case Against Moral Pluralism," *Environmental Ethics*, 12 (1990): 115.

37. Robbin Derry and Ronald M. Green, "Ethical Theory in Business Ethics," *Journal of Business Ethics*, 8 (1989): 521.
38. The principles of justice that Rawls advocates are based on a social contract agreed to by members of society in a so-called original position. This original position is something of an intellectual exercise to show how principles of justice can be derived in an impartial and unbiased manner. In this exercise, principles of justice are worked out behind a so-called veil of ignorance where the members of a society do not know their race, social standing, economic resources, gender, or anything else of this nature about themselves. Without this kind of knowledge they are then supposedly free from particular kinds of interests that they would be prone to protect if they had this kind of knowledge. Since they do not know what their station or role in society will be, it is assumed that they can come to a more just agreement regarding the rules they want to live by when they step out from behind this veil of ignorance and take their place in society. This agreement is thus worked out by atomic individuals prior to their membership in any kind of society. Rawls's position is rooted in the self-interest-driven principles of abstract justice formed by atomic pre-social individuals operating behind a veil of ignorance. This position emphasizes the primacy of the individual and assumes that individual units are prior to and can exist independently of any kind of social or community relationships. See John Rawls, *A Theory of Justice* (Cambridge: Harvard University Press, 1971).

NOTES TO CHAPTER 6

1. There has been a movement in existence for several years that goes by the name of communitarianism, which challenges the primacy of the unfettered individual and tries to temper the excesses of American individuality in the interests of the larger society. According to this movement, the rights of the individual must be balanced with responsibilities to the needs of the community. An understanding of the general welfare of the common good must take group interests and identities into account, while standing apart as more than their aggregate. In the words of Amitai Etzioni, the founder of this movement: "The term highlights the assumption that individuals act within a social context, that this context is not reducible to individual acts, and most significantly, that the social context is not necessarily or wholly imposed. Instead, the social context is, to a significant extent, perceived as a legitimate and integral part of one's existence, a We, a whole of which the individuals are constituent elements." Amitai Etzioni, *The Moral Dimension: Toward A New Economics* (New York: The Free Press, 1988), 5.
2. R. Edward Freeman, "The Politics of Stakeholder Theory: Some Future Directions," *Business Ethics Quarterly*, 4 (1994): 419.
3. Charles Taylor, *The Ethics of Authenticity* (Cambridge, MA: Harvard University Press, 1991), esp. 95 and 117.
4. Classical American Pragmatism incorporates the writings of its five major contributors, Charles Pierce, William James, John Dewey, George Herbert Mead, and Charles I. Lewis. That these philosophers provide a unified perspective on self and community is assumed in this chapter, but this claim is defended at some length in Sandra Rosenthal, *Speculative Pragmatism* (Amherst, MA: University of Massachusetts Press, 1986).
5. George Herbert Mead, *Mind, Self, and Society*, ed. Charles Morris (Chicago: University of Chicago Press, 1994), 154.
6. Ibid.

7. John Dewey, "Authority and Social Change," in *The Later Works, 1925–1953*, Vol. 11, ed. Jo Ann Boydston (Carbondale and Edwardsville, IL: University of Southern Illinois Press, 1987), 133.

8. Ibid. Dewey notes that the "principle of authority" must not be understood as "purely restrictive power" but as providing direction.

9. George Herbert Mead, *Movements of Thought in the Nineteenth Century*, ed. Merritt Moore (Chicago: University of Chicago Press, 1936), 375–377.

10. Ibid., 353–354. A person may be a member of more than one community, for there are diverse levels and types of communities. Any community consists of many subgroups, and although individuals may feel alienated from a particular society, they cannot really be alienated from society in general, because this very alienation will only throw them into some other society.

11. John Dewey, "The Public and Its Problems," in *The Later Works, 1925–1953*, Vol. 2, ed. Jo Ann Boydston (Carbondale and Edwardsville, IL: University of Southern Illinois Press, 1984), 330, 332.

12. William James, "Great Men and Their Environment," in *The Will to Believe and Other Essays, The Works of William James*, ed. Frederick Burkhardt (Cambridge, MA: Harvard University Press, 1979), 170, 170n, 171.

13. John Dewey, "Ethics," in *The Middle Works, 1899–1924*, Vol. 5, ed. Jo Ann Boydston (Carbondale and Edwardsville, IL: University of Southern Illinois Press, 1978), 327.

NOTES TO CHAPTER 7

1. See Karl Polanyi, *The Great Transformation* (Boston: Beacon Press, 1944).

2. The existence of economics points to another major difference between business and the traditional professions of law and medicine. These latter professions have no home discipline that provides them with the rationale and justification for their existence. They are strictly practical activities that need no other justification beyond their duty to serve their client's interests. Business, however, does have a home discipline in economics that prescribes the role business is to play in society and describes how the firm functions in a capitalistic society to create economic wealth.

3. Alan Durning, *How Much Is Enough?* (New York: Norton, 1992).

4. Mark Sagoff, "What Is Wrong With Consumption?" Paper presented at the Ruffin Lectures, The Darden School, University of Virginia, Charlottesville, VA, April 14–17, 1997.

5. Durning, *How Much Is Enough?*, 13.

6. Alan Gewirth, *The Community of Rights* (Chicago: University of Chicago Press, 1996), 1–2.

7. Ibid., 2–3.

8. George Herbert Mead, *Movements of Thought in the Nineteenth Century*, ed. Merritt Moore (Chicago: University of Chicago Press, 1936), 375–77.

9. John Dewey, "Authority and Social Change," in *The Later Works, 1925–1953*, Vol. 11, ed. Jo Ann Boydston (Carbondale and Edwardsville, IL: University of Southern Illinois Press, 1987), 133.

10. Thomas Donaldson, *Corporations and Morality* (Englewood Cliffs, NJ: Prentice Hall, 1982), 41. Italics in text.

11. As an example, envision, on the one hand, a person taking care of a sick spouse because of an intellectualized "external" sense of duty and, on the

other hand, a person taking care of a sick spouse because of the internalization of a caring and attuned relationship to that person.

NOTES TO CHAPTER 8

1. See, for example, John Kenneth Galbraith, *The New Industrial State* (Boston: Houghton Mifflin, 1967).
2. Alfred D. Chandler Jr. and Richard S. Tedlow, *The Coming of Managerial Capitalism: A Casebook on the History of American Economic Institutions* (Homewood, IL: Irwin, 1985), 346.
3. Ibid., 358–59.
4. Ibid., 369.
5. Irwin M. Stelzer and Howard P. Kitt, *Selected Antitrust Cases: Landmark Decisions*, 7ᵗʰ ed. (Homewood, IL: Irwin, 1986). 9.
6. Michael Krantz, "The Main Event," *Time*, June 1, 1998, 33–37.
7. Mike France and Jay Greene, "Settlement or Sellout?" *Business Week*, November 19, 2001, 112–14.
8. Steven Levy, "What Was That About?" *Newsweek*, November 12, 2001, 42–43.
9. Zachary Schiller, "The Great American Health Pitch," *Business Week*, October 9, 1989, 115–22.
10. "Taking a Bite Out of Food Hype," *U.S. News & World Report*, February 19, 1990, 12.
11. Diane Duston, "Food Labels Must Tell All, Stricter U.S. Standards Say," *Times-Picayune*, December 3, 1992, A-1.
12. The European Union created a market to control carbon dioxide emissions in 2005 by establishing a cap and issuing tradable allowances based on this cap. At the time of writing, Congress was considering seven proposals to set up a similar program in this country. See Bret Schulte, "Putting A Price On Pollution," *U.S. News & World Report*, May 14, 2007, 37–39.
13. United States Environmental Protection Agency, *Environmental Progress and Challenges: EPA's Update* (Washington, D.C.: U.S. Government Printing Office, 1988), 28
14. United States Environmental Protection Agency, Office of Air and Radiation, *The Plain English Guide to the Clean Air Act* (Washington, D.C.: EPA, 1993), 15.
15. "Pollution Swap," *Time*, May 25, 1992, 22.
16. Jeffrey Taylor, "CBOT Plan for Pollution-Rights Market Is Encountering Plenty of Competition," *Wall Street Journal*, August 24, 1993, A8.
17. United States Environmental Protection Agency, Acid Rain Program 2003 Progress Report, *Clean Air Markets—Progress and Results*, 2005, www.epa.gov/airmarkets/progress/arpo3.html.
18. Marjorie Kelly and Richard Rosen, "The failure of electricity deregulation," *The Denver Post*, May 6, 2007, 1E. For a counter-argument, see Nicholas G. Muller, "The real story on electric deregulation," *The Denver Post*, May 17, 2007, 7B.
19. Ibid.
20. Ibid.

NOTES TO CHAPTER 9

1. Bill McKibben, *The End of Nature* (New York: Random House, 1989).

2. Ibid., 25.
3. Ibid., 38.
4. Ibid., 137.
5. Roderick Frazier Nash, *The Rights of Nature: A History of Environmental Ethics* (Madison, WI: University of Wisconsin Press, 1989), 125.
6. Peter Singer, "The Place of Nonhumans in Environmental Issues," in *Moral Issues in Business*, 4th ed., eds. William Shaw and Vincent Barry (Belmont, CA: Wadsworth, 1989), 471.
7. Ibid., 474.
8. Nash, *The Rights of Nature*, 140–41.
9. Ibid., 126.
10. Christopher D. Stone, "Should Trees Have Standing?—Toward Legal Rights for Natural Objects," in *Moral Issues in Business*, 4th ed., eds. William Shaw and Vincent Barry (Belmont, CA: Wadsworth, 1989), 475–79.
11. Nash, *The Rights of Nature*, 128–29. Oftentimes, rights given to animals are used as surrogates to protect other aspects of nature that are not given moral consideration. For example, the Endangered Species Act gives rights to species that are threatened with extinction. In the controversy over the spotted owl that took place in the Northwest part of the United States, the rights given to the owl when it was placed on the endangered species list were used to prevent logging of old growth forests. Protecting the species means protecting its habitat. The same thing may be happening with regard to the polar bear in the Artic region. Placing it on the endangered species list may be a way to force the U.S. government to deal with climate change in order to protect the bear's habitat.
12. Kenneth E. Goodpaster, "From Egoism to Environmentalism," in *Ethics and Problems of the 21st Century*, eds. Kenneth E. Goodpaster and K. M. Sayer (Notre Dame, IN: University of Notre Dame Press, 1979), 21–33.
13. Nash, *The Rights of Nature*, 152.
14. Ibid., 153.
15. Ibid., 160.
16. Holmes Ralston III, "Just Environmental Business," in *Just Business: New Introductory Essays in Business Ethics*, ed. Tom Regan (New York: Random House, 1984), 325–43.
17. Holmes Ralston III, *Philosophy Gone Wild: Essays in Environmental Ethics* (Buffalo, NY: Prometheus Books, 1987), 121.
18. Ibid., 141.
19. Ibid., 103–104.
20. Sara Ebenreck, "An Earth Care Ethics," *The Catholic World: Caring for the Endangered Earth*, 233 (July/August 1990): 156.
21. Nash, *The Rights of Nature*, 10.
22. Ibid., 150.
23. Some approaches to deep ecology seem to recognize this relational aspect of humans and the environment. See Christian Diehm, "Identification With Nature: What It Is And Why It Matters," *Ethics and the Environment*, 12 (2007): 1–22.
24. Gary T. Gardner, *Inspiring Progress: Religion's Contribution to Sustainable Development* (New York: W. W. Norton, 2006), 147.
25. See Garret Hardin, "The Tragedy of the Commons," *Science*, 162 (December 13, 1968): 1243–1248.
26. See Lester R. Brown, *Plan B: Rescuing a Planet Under Stress and a Civilization in Trouble* (New York: W. W. Norton, 2003), especially 199–222.
27. See T. H. Watkins, "The Worth of the Earth," *Audubon*, 99 (September–October 1997): 128; Donella H. Meadows, "How Much Is Nature Worth?" *Business Ethics*, 11 (July/August, 1997): 7.
28. Watkins, "The Worth of the Earth," 128.

29. Ibid.
30. See David Michaels, *Doubt is Their Product: How Industry's Assault on Science Threatens Your Health* (New York: Oxford University Press, 2007); Chris Mooney, *The Republican War on Science* (New York: Basic Books, 2005).

NOTES TO CHAPTER 10

1. Robert C. Solomon, *Ethics and Excellence: Cooperation and Integrity in Business* (New York: Oxford University Press, 1992), 150.
2. Some contemporary theories of the organization see organizational dynamics in terms of power tensions and creative confusions. These tensions between empowerment and disempowerment are necessary in order for organizations to sustain themselves. This approach represents the "politics of power" as opposed to the "politics of community involved in pragmatic theory. See John Hassard, "Postmodernism and Organizational Analysis: An Overview," in *Postmodernism and Organizations*, eds. John Hassard and Martin Parker (London: Sage Publications, 1993), 20–22.
3. Edwin Hartman, *Organizational Ethics and the Good Life* (New York: Oxford University Press, 1996) 174–76.
4. Allan A. Kennedy, *The End of Shareholder Value: Corporations at the Crossroads* (Cambridge, MA: Persus, 2000), 94.
5. Ibid., 95.
6. In 2007, some states were even considering laws that would make bullying in the workplace an "unlawful employment practice" and give victims of such bullying the right to sue an employer who does not take steps to prevent bullying from happening. See Michael Orey, "Legal Notes," *Business Week*, May 14, 2007, 14.
7. With all these laws, it is hard to find an American worker who does not fall into at least one and sometimes several of these protected categories. This trend is something of a counter-trend to the threat of termination leading to less job security as the threat of litigation makes employers less likely to terminate even problem workers. See Michael Orey, "Fear of Firing," *Business Week*, April 23, 2007, 52–62. Such a situation, however, is hardly conducive to the creation of a true community.
8. *The New American Workplace: A Labor Perspective* (Washington, D.C.: AFL-CIO Committee on the Evolution of Work, February 1994), 8.
9. This point is developed in some detail in Sandra B. Rosenthal and Rogene A. Buchholz, "Business and Society: What's in a Name?" *The International Journal of Organizational Analysis*, 5 (1997): 180–201.
10. These values make up his first cluster of values listed under the general category of "economizing values" or those that support prudent and efficient use of resources. These are intertwined with the other two sets of values fitting into the respective categories of "ecologizing" and "power-aggrandizing." The tensions and conflicts between and among the three sets of value clusters, economizing, ecologizing, and power-aggrandizing, are seen as evolutionarily inevitable. See William C. Frederick, *Values, Nature and Culture in the American Corporation* (New York: Oxford University Press, 1995).

NOTES TO CHAPTER 11

1. Thomas L. Friedman, *The Lexus and the Olive Tree* (New York: Farrar, Strauss, and Giroux, 1999).
2. Ibid., 27.

3. Ibid., 29.
4. Michael Scott Doran, "Somebody Else's Civil War," *Foreign Affairs*, 81 (January–February 2002): 41.
5. Ibid., 26.
6. Jack N. Berhman, *Essays on Ethics in Business and the Professions* (Englewood Cliffs, NJ: Prentice Hall, 1988), 59–60.
7. See William C. Frederick, "The Moral Authority of MNC Codes," paper presented at the Conference on Socio-Economics, Harvard Business School, March 31–April 2, 1989, p. 2. See also William C. Frederick, "The Moral Authority of Transnational Corporate Codes," *Journal of Business Ethics*, 10 (1991): 165–77.
8. Richard T. DeGeorge, *Competing With Integrity in International Business* (New York: Oxford, 1993), 19–21.
9. Ibid., 45–46
10. Berhman, *Essays on Ethics*, 111.
11. Ibid., 114.
12. Gerald Piel, "Globalopolies," *The Nation*, May 18, 1992.
13. UN Global Compact Office, "The Global Compact: What It Is—and Isn't," January 17, 2001. www.corpwatch.org/campaigns.
14. Ibid.
15. Thomas M. Franck, "Are Human Rights Universal?" *Foreign Affairs*, 80 (January/February, 2001): 193.
16. Thomas Donaldson, *The Ethics of International Business* (New York: Oxford University Press, 1989), 80–82.
17. The Caux Round Table, *Principles for Business*, 1994. www.cauxroundtable.org/principles.html.
18. Franck, "Human Rights," 196.
19. Richard T. DeGeorge, "International Business Ethics," *Business Ethics Quarterly*, 4 (1994): 4.
20. DeGeorge, *Competing With Integrity*, 24.
21. Martin Wolf, "Will the Nation-State Survive Globalization?" *Foreign Affairs*, 80 (January–February 2001): 184.
22. R. Edward Freeman and Daniel R. Gilbert Jr., *Corporate Strategy and the Search for Ethics* (Englewood Cliffs, NJ: Prentice Hall, 1988), 40.
23. William C. Frederick, *Values, Nature, and Culture in the American Corporation* (New York: Oxford University Press, 1995), 293.

NOTES TO CHAPTER 12

1. "Saccharin: Where Do We Go From Here?" *FDA Consumer*, April 1978, 18.
2. Ibid., 17.
3. G. D. Searle Gets Approval to Start Aspartame Sales," *Wall Street Journal*, July 16, 1981, 2.
4. Calorie Control Council, "Latest News: Saccharin Gets a Clean Bill of Health," U.S. National Toxicology Program and International Agency for Research on Cancer Review of Saccharin, Washington, D. C., December 28, 2001.
5. See Center for Science in the Public Interest, "'Saccharin Still Poses Cancer Risk,' Scientists Tell Federal Agency," Press Release, October 28, 1997.
6. See John Carey, "When Medical Studies Collide," *Business Week*, August 6, 2007, 38, for the story of contradictory reports about echinacea, a herbal remedy that was claimed to help ward off colds. The article points out the difficulty of reaching firm conclusions in the area of medical research.

7. See "The EDB Controversy: Scientific Uncertainty," in Rogene A. Buchholz, et al., *Management Responses to Public Issues: Concepts and Cases in Strategy Formulation*, 3ʳᵈ ed. (Englewood Cliffs, NJ: Prentice Hall, 1994), 100–121.
8. See "The Smoking Controversy: Changing Values," in Rogene A. Buchholz, et al., *Management Responses to Public Issues: Concepts and Cases in Strategy Formulation*, 3ʳᵈ ed. (Englewood Cliffs, NJ: Prentice Hall, 1994), 77–99.
9. See "Manville Corporation: Product Liability," in Rogene A. Buchholz, et al., *Management Responses to Public Issues: Concepts and Cases in Strategy Formulation*, 3ʳᵈ ed. (Englewood Cliffs, NJ: Prentice Hall, 1994), 122–38.
10. See David Kessler, *A Question of Intent: A Great American Battle With a Deadly Industry* (New York: Public Affairs, 2001).
11. See Forest Reinhardt, "Du Pont Freon Products Division," in Rogene A. Buchholz, et al., *Managing Environmental Issues: A Casebook* (Englewood Cliffs, NJ: Prentice Hall, 1992), 281.
12. "Over the past 20 years, evidence that humans are affecting the climate has accumulated inexorably, and with it has come ever greater certainty across the scientific community in the reality of recent climate change and the potential for much greater change in the future." William Collins, et al., "The Physical Science behind Climate Change," *Scientific American*, 297 (August 2007): 65. The 2007 report of the Intergovernmental Panel on Climate Change (IPCC) placed the probability that human activities have caused global warming at greater than 90 percent. The 2001 report put the probability at greater than 66 percent.
13. Bill Sells, "What Asbestos Taught Me About Managing Risk," *Harvard Business Review*, 72 (March–April 1994), 76–90.
14. As of July 2007, Merck faced 27,250 claims over the harm done by its Vioxx product. The company's strategy is to fight each suit separately, and so far 10 out of 15 verdicts have been decided in its favor. But a new threat emerged that could increase the company's liability. Its success in fighting lawsuits was based on the argument that people had to take the drug for 18 months or longer for it to pose cardiovascular risks. But new studies began to show that there was an increased risk from even short-term use of the drug. See Arlene Weintraub, "Is Merck's Medicine Working?" *Business Week*, July 30, 2007, 67–70. Also in July 2007, Purdue Pharmaceuticals, the maker of OxyContin, and its three top executives were ordered to pay $643.5 million for misleading the public about the dangers of the painkiller. See "Pharmaceuticals: No Jail of Purdue Executives," *The Week*, August 3, 2007, 37.
15. See Kermit Vandiver, "Why Should My Conscience Bother Me?" in *Business Ethics: Readings and Cases in Corporate Morality*, 2ⁿᵈ ed., eds. William M. Hoffman and Jennifer Mills Moore (New York: McGraw-Hill, 1990), 116–125.
16. See "A. H. Robins: Product Safety," in Rogene A. Buchholz, et al., *Management Responses to Public Issues*, 3ʳᵈ ed. (Englewood Cliffs, NJ: Prentice Hall, 1994), 276–300.
17. See Mark Maier, *A Major Malfunction: The Story Behind the Challenger Disaster* (Binghamton, NY: SUNY, 1992), 2–44. See also Diane Vaughan, *The Challenger Launch Decision* (Chicago: University of Chicago Press, 1996).
18. The breakup of the shuttle Columbia had many of these same characteristics of engineering concerns versus managerial concerns. See Michael Cabbage and William Harwood, *Comm Check . . . The Final Flight of Shuttle Columbia* (New York: Free Press, 2004).

19. See Thorstein Veblen, *The Theory of the Business Enterprise* (New York: Augustus M. Kelley, 1965); *The Instinct of Workmanship* (New York: Augustus M. Kelley, 1964); *The Engineers and the Price System* (New York: Augustus M. Kelley, 1965); and *Absentee Ownership* (New York: Augustus M. Kelley, 1964).

20. "The growth of business enterprise rests on the machine technology as its material foundation. The machine industry is indispensable to it; it cannot get along without the machine process. But the discipline of the machine process cuts away the spiritual, institutional foundations of business enterprise; the machine industry is incompatible with its continued growth; it cannot, in the long run, get along with the machine process." Veblen, *The Theory of Business Enterprise*, 375.

21. "So soon—but only so soon—as the engineers draw together, take common counsel, work out a plan of action, and decide to disallow absentee ownership out of hand, that move will have been made . . . The obvious and simple means of doing it is a conscientious withdrawal of efficiency; that is to say the general strike, to include so much of the country's staff of technicians as will suffice to incapacitate the industrial system at large by their withdrawal, for such time as may be required to enforce their argument." Veblen, *The Engineers and the Price System*, 166–67.

22. John Kenneth Galbraith, *The New Industrial State* (Boston: Houghton Mifflin, 1967), 13–17

23. March Mason, "The Curse of Whistle-Blowing," *Wall Street Journal*, March 14, 1994, A14.

24. What is ironic about the Dalkon Shield situation is that the product was introduced at a time when adverse side effects of birth control pills were beginning to manifest themselves. Thus the time was ripe for a new birth control device that was deemed to be safe and effective to capture a large market share, and the executives at A. H. Robins were well aware of this market potential. The use of the pill was itself something of a mass experiment, and thus women who switched from the pill to the Dalkon Shield went from one experimental situation to another.

25. Matt Jenkins, "Brave New Hay," *High Country News*, June 11, 2007, 12–18.

26. Ibid.

27. Ibid.

NOTES TO CHAPTER 13

1. Adolf A. Berle and Gardiner C. Means, *The Modern Corporation and Private Property* (New York: Macmillan, 1932).

2. Robert J. Larner, *Management Control and the Large Corporation* (New York: Dunellen, 1971).

3. James Burnham, *The Managerial Revolution* (New York: John Day Co., Inc., 1941).

4. See George Melloan, "New Debate Over Corporate Governance," *Wall Street Journal*, November 11, 1986, 36; and Carl Icahn, "What Ails Corporate America—And What Should Be Done," *Business Week*, October 27, 1986, 101.

5. "American Business Has A New Kingpin, The Investment Banker," *Business Week*, November 24, 1986, 80.

6. Sarah Bartlett, "Power Investors," *Business Week*, June 20, 1988, 116–23.

7. Christopher Farrell, "The LBO Isn't A Superior New Species," *Business Week*, October 23, 1989, 126.

8. "More Than Ever, It's Management for the Short Term," *Business Week*, November 24, 1986, 92–93.
9. Charlotte Low, "Corporate Haven Hostile to Raiders," *Insight*, May 2, 1988, 56.
10. Shawn Tully, "Carl Icahn," *Fortune*, June 11, 2007, 117–124. In 2007, Icahn increased his hedge fund assets and was expected to make more noise than ever. See "House of Icahn," *Fortune*, September 17, 2007, 46.
11. See "Murdoch: Will Dow Jones be his next conquest?" *The Week*, May 18, 2007, 6; "The last press lord," *The Week*, June 1, 2007, 13; "Dow Jones: Murdoch meets the family," *The Week*, June 15, 2007, 34. In August 2007, Murdoch's deal was accepted, clearing the way for his acquisition of the company. See "Dow Jones: Murdoch closes the deal," *The Week*, August 10, 2007, 34; Allan Sloan, "The Deal," *Fortune*, August 20, 2007, 18.
12. Johnnie L. Roberts, "A Tale of Two Dynasties," *Newsweek*, June 11, 2007, 42–46.
13. "A Class (B) Act," *Business Week*, May 28, 2007, 12.
14. "Shareholders Want Chutes Closed Plus an End to Secrets, Pills, and Spills," *Wall Street Journal*, March 7, 1991, A1.
15. "Shareholders Seek to Limit Executive Pay, But None Prevail Yet," *Wall Street Journal*, May 11, 1993, A2.
16. Theodore V. Purcell, "Management and the Ethical Investors," *Harvard Business Review*, 57 (September–October 1979): 44.
17. Judith H. Dobrzynski, "An October Surprise That Has Shareholders Cheering," *Business Week*, November 2, 1992, 144. See also Kevin G. Salwen, "SEC to Allow Investors More Room to Talk," *Wall Street Journal*, October 15, 1992, C1.
18. Jena McGregor, "Activist Investors Get More Respect," *Business Week*, June 11, 2007, 34–35.
19. Ibid. See also Joan Warner, "Get Ready For A Red-Hot Proxy Season," www.forbes.com/2006/12/18/leadership-stocks-proxy-lead-govern.cx_jw_1218prox . . ., December 18, 2006, 1–3. In 2007, the Chairman of the SEC indicated that he would vote against allowing large shareholders to nominate board members, but vowed that the agency would revisit the issue the following year when the commission is back to full strength. See "Proxies: The SEC's Stopgap Solution", *Business Week*, December 3, 2007, 25. Shareholder activism also seems to be picking up in Europe. See Julia Werdigier, "Boards Feel the Heat as Investor Activists Speak Up," *New York Times*, Wednesday, May 23, 2007, C5.
20. Richard J. Barber, *The American Corporation* (New York: Dutton, 1970).
21. Murray Weidenbaum and Mark Jensen, *Introduction to the Modern Corporation and Private Property* (St Louis, MO: Washington University Center for the Study of American Business, 1990), 4.
22. Christopher Power, "Shareholders Aren't Just Rolling Over Anymore," *Business Week*, April 27, 1987, 32–33; Judith H. Dobrzynski, "Whose Company Is It, Anyway?" *Business Week*, April 25, 1988, 60–61.
23. Edward V. Regan, "Pension Funds: New Power, New Responsibility," *Wall Street Journal*, November 2, 1987, 26.
24. Larry Light, "The Power of the Pension Funds," *Business Week*, November 6, 1989, 154–58.
25. Peter Drucker, "A Crisis of Capitalism," *Wall Street Journal*, September 30, 1986, 34.
26. The Conference Board, "U.S. Institutional Investors Continue Ownership of U.S. Corporations," January 22, 2007, www.conference-board.org/utilities/pressPrinterFriendly.cfm?press_ID:3046.

27. Alan Murray, *Revolt In The Boardroom* (New York: Collins, 2007), xix.
28. "A Landmark Ruling That Puts Board Member in Peril," *Business Week*, March 18, 1985, 56–57. See also Michele Galen, "A Seat On The Board Is Getting Hotter," *Business Week*, July 3, 1989, 72–73. In January 2005, ten former board members of WorldCom agreed to pay investors $18 million out of their own pockets as part of the settlement in the accounting fraud case that involved the company. Also ten former board members of Enron agreed to pay $13 million out of their own pockets as part of that settlement. See Alan Murray, *Revolt In The Boardroom*, 39.
29. Alan Murray, *Revolt In The Boardroom*, xvii–xviii.
30. Ibid., 189–92.
31. Adam Lashinsky, "Rich Kinder Helped Himself to a Bigger Slice of his Own Company. Do You Have A Problem With That?" *Fortune*, May 28, 2007, 65–73. See also Rachel Beck, "Leveraged buyouts thrive on borrowed time, debt," *Denver Post*, May 28, 2007, 3C.
32. Murray, *Revolt In The Boardroom*, 121.
33. Richard L. Hudson, "Public Companies May Curb Disclosures To Holders on Executive Pay, SEC Rules," *Wall Street Journal*, September 23, 1983, 4.
34. Kevin G. Salwen, "The People's Proxy: Shareholder Proposals On Pay Must Be Aired, SEC to tell 10 Firms," *Wall Street Journal*, February 13, 1992, A1.
35. "Now and Then: Shareholders gain much from new pay-disclosure rules. But they also lose a little," *Wall Street Journal*, April 21, 1993, R2.
36. Lee Berton and Joann S. Lubin, "FASB Moves To Make Firms Deduct Options," *Wall Street Journal*, April 8, 1993, A3.
37. Dawn Kopecki, "Backdating: Why Penalties Are Puny," *Business Week*, June 18, 2007, 38–40.
38. AFL-CIO, "2006 Trends in CEO Pay," www.aflcio.org/corporatewatch/pay-watch/pay/index.cfm?RenderForPrint=1. According to another source, CEO pay averaged $10.8 million in 2006, 364 times the average worker's pay. This was down from 411 in 2005 and below the all-time high of 525 times the average pay set in 2000. See "The bottom line," *The Week*, September 14, 2007, 36.
39. Eduardo Porter, "More Than Ever, It Pays to Be the Top Executive," *New York Times*, May 25, 2007, A1.
40. "The bottom line," *The Week*, May 18, 2007, 36.
41. "The bottom line," *The Week*, May 11, 2007, 40.
42. Greg Ip, "Not Your Father's Pay: Why Wages Today Are Weaker," *Wall Street Journal*, May 25, 2007, A2.
43. Alan Murray, *Revolt In The Boardroom*, 197.
44. Ibid., xx–xxi.
45. Nanette Byrnes, "Cornered in the Corner Office," *Business Week*, May 14, 2007, 96.
46. Robert B. Reich, "Don't Count on Shareholders," *The American Prospect*, April 2007, 52.
47. Geoff Colvin, "A Tie Goes to the Managers," *Fortune*, May 28, 2007, 34.

NOTES TO CHAPTER 14

1. Alfred D. Chandler Jr., *The Visible Hand: The Managerial Revolution in American Business* (Cambridge, MA: Belknap Press, 1977).

2. Irving Kristol, *Two Cheers for Capitalism* (New York: Basic Books, 1978), 4–5.
3. Rakesh Khurana, *From Higher Aims to Hired Hands: The Social Transformation of American Business Schools and the Unfulfilled Promise of Management as a Profession* (Princeton, NJ: Princeton University Press, 2007), 6. This book was published while I was working on this last chapter, and I immediately ordered a copy and read it before I finished the chapter. It was extremely helpful in formulating the organization of this chapter and in providing ideas for inclusion in the chapter as the references to this book indicate.
4. Ibid., 4.
5. Ibid., 19.
6. Ibid., 271.
7. Oliver Sheldon, *The Philosophy of Management* (London: Pitman Publishing Ltd., 1923).
8. Khurana, *From Higher Aims to Hired Hands*, 297–305.
9. Ibid., 325.
10. Ibid., 324–25.
11. Ibid., 364.
12. Ibid., 379.
13. Ibid., 373. For other criticisms of investor capitalism see Clayton M. Christensen and Scott D. Anthony, "Put Investors in Their Place," *Business Week,* May 28, 2007, 108; Lawrence E. Mitchell, "The Tyranny of the Market," *Business Week,* July 30, 2007, 90; and Henry S. Givray, "When CEOs Aren't Leaders," *Business Week,* September 3, 2007, 102.
14. William A. Levi, "Ethical Confusion And The Business Community," in *Ethics and Standards in American Business,* ed. J. W. Towle (New York: Houghton Mifflin, 1964), 20–29.
15. Ibid., 27.
16. See William C. Frederick, *Corporation, Be Good!* (Indianapolis: Dog Ear Publishing, 2006), 259–260; and Robert A Giacalone and Kenneth R. Thompson, "Business Ethics and Social Responsibility Education: Shifting the Worldview," *Learning and Education,* 5 (September, 2006): 266–277.
17. Khurana, *From Higher Aims to Hired Hands*, 331.
18. Ibid., 350.
19. Ibid., 352, 348.
20. Several of these critiques have focused on the lack of a strong ethics initiative in business schools. See Diane L. Swanson and William C. Frederick, "Are Business Schools Silent Partners in Corporate Crime?" *JCC* (Spring 2003), 24–27; Ian I. Mitroff, "An Open Letter to the Deans and the Faculties of American Business Schools: A Call for Action," *Academy of Management Newsletter,* June 2004, 7–8; and Amitai Etzioni, "When It Comes to Ethics, B-Schools Get an F," *The Washington Post,* August 4, 2002, B4. For a different kind of critique of business school education that makes the case for grounding MBA programs in practical experience, shared insights, and reflection, see Jonathan Gosling and Henry Mintzberg, "The Education of Practicing Managers," *Human Resource Management and Industrial Relations,* 45 (Summer 2004): 19–22.
21. Frederick, *Corporation Be Good!*, 247.
22. Ibid., 248.
23. Khurana, *From Higher Aims to Hired Hands*, 380.
24. Ibid., 368–69.
25. Ibid., 366.

26. Giacalone and Thompson, "Business Ethics and Social Responsibility Education," 267.
27. The content of courses in the curriculum of business schools could still be science-based, depending on the nature of the course itself. Warren Bennis and James O'Toole, while critical of the scientific orientation of business schools as a whole, do not advocate throwing the baby out with the bath water. Science would still be important in providing rigor to an analysis of business problems. But the scientific base would have to be placed in the context of business as a profession and broadened to include other aspects of human and organizational behavior. Agency theory and a strictly economic view of the firm overlook such organizational phenomena as power, coercion, exploitation, discrimination, conflict and other such issues and relieve a manager of any meaningful responsibility to other members of the organization or to society as a whole. But people are not just contracting agents; they relate to co-workers in the organization and to society in a variety of ways and have a nexus of responsibilities for which the disciplines of sociology, political science, and psychology are just as important as economics and agency theory in understanding how people behave in organizations and the behavior of organizations in society. See Warren G. Bennis and James O'Toole, "How Business Schools Lost Their Way," *Harvard Business Review*, 83 (2005): 96–104.
28. It is interesting to note that the current accounting curriculum in schools of business and management is geared towards helping accounting students meet CPA requirements so that they can become a Certified Public Accountant and attain the professional status that goes with this certification. Thus these students have some exposure to professionalism that other students in the business school do not have and have to engage in continuing education to maintain this certification, including exposure to the American Institute of Certified Public Accountants (AICPA) code of ethics. Yet accounting research is dominated by the agency model, which prevents a full measure of professionalism from being imparted to these students. See Dann G. Fisher and Diane L. Swanson, "Accounting Education Lags CPE Requirements: Implications for the Profession and a Call to Action," *Accounting Education: An International Journal*, 16 (2007): 345–363.
29. A campaign was mounted in 2002 called Campaign AACSB that took aim at the Association for the Advancement of Collegiate Schools of Business (AACSB), which is the accrediting agency for the nation's business schools. This campaign sought to upgrade and strengthen ethics accreditation standards and charged that the AACSB's weak ethics standards unwillingly contributed to corporate crime and corruption by failing to mandate a required ethics course as a condition of accreditation. See Diane L. Swanson and William C. Frederick, "Campaign AACSB: Are Business Schools Complicit in Corporate Corruption?" *Journal of Individual Employment Rights*, 10 (2001–2002): 151–165; Diane L. Swanson, "The Buck Stops Here: Why Universities Must Reclaim Business Ethics Education," *Journal of Academic Ethics*, 2 (March, 2004): 43–61; and Diane L. Swanson and Dann G. Fisher, "Business Ethics Education: If We Don't Know Where We're Going, Any Road Will Take Us There," in *Advancing Business Ethics Education*, eds. R. A. Giacalone and C. L. Jurkiewicz (New York: Information Age Publishing, 2008), 1–23.
30. Albert Borgmann, "Reply to My Critics," in *Technology and the Good Life?* eds. Eric Higgs, Andrew Light, and David Strong (Chicago: The University of Chicago Press, 2000), 363.

Bibliography

Anshen, Melvin. *Managing the Socially Responsible Corporation.* New York: Macmillan, 1974.

Ayres, Clarence E. *Toward A Reasonable Society.* Austin, TX: University of Texas Press, 1961.

Barber, Richard J. *The American Corporation.* New York: Dutton, 1970.

Bell, Daniel. *The Cultural Contradictions of Capitalism.* New York: Basic Books, 1976.

Berhman, Jack N. *Essays on Ethics in Business and the Professions.* Englewood Cliffs, NJ: Prentice Hall, 1988.

Berle, Adolph A., and Gardiner C. Means. *The Modern Corporation and Private Property.* New York: Macmillan, 1932.

Bohm, David. *Wholeness and the Implicate Order.* London: Routledge & Kegan Paul, 1980.

Borgmann, Albert. *Technology and the Character of Contemporary Life.* Chicago: The University of Chicago Press, 1984.

Brockway, George P. *The End of Economic Man: An Introduction to Humanistic Economics.* New York: W. W. Norton, 2001.

Bronk, Richard. *Progress and the Invisible Hand.* London: Warner Books, 1998.

Brown, Lester. *Plan B: Rescuing a Planet Under Stress and a Civilization in Trouble.* New York: W. W. Norton, 2003.

Buchan, James. *The Authentic Adam Smith: His Life and Ideas.* New York: W. W. Norton, 2006.

Buchanan, James. *The Demand and Supply of Public Goods.* Chicago: Rand McNally, 1968.

Burnham, James. *The Managerial Revolution.* New York: John Day Co., Inc., 1941.

Cabbage, Michael, and William Harwood. *Comm Check . . . The Final Flight of Shuttle Columbia.* New York: The Free Press, 2004.

Chamberlain, Neil W. *The Limits of Corporate Responsibility.* New York: Basic Books, 1973.

Chandler, Alfred. D. Jr. *The Visible Hand: The Managerial Revolution in American Business.* Cambridge, MA: Belknap Press, 1977.

Chandler, Alfred D. Jr., and Richard S. Tedlow. *The Coming of Managerial Capitalism: A Casebook on the History of American Economic Institutions.* Homewood, IL: Irwin, 1985.

Clarkson, Max, ed. *The Corporation and Its Stakeholders: Classic and Contemporary Readings.* Toronto: University of Toronto Press, 1998.

Cortright, S. A., and Michael J. Naughton. *Rethinking the Purpose of Business.* Notre Dame, IN: University of Notre Dame Press, 2002.

DeGeorge, Richard T. *Competing With Integrity in International Business.* New York: Oxford, 1993.

Dewey, John. "Authority and Social Change." In *The Later Works, 1925–1953*, Vol. 11, ed. Jo Ann Boydston. Carbondale and Edwardsville, IL: University of Southern Illinois Press, 1987.

Dewey, John. "Ethics." In *The Middle Works*, 1899–1924, Vol. 5, ed. Jo Ann Boydston. Carbondale and Edwardsville, IL: University of Southern Illinois Press, 1978.

Dewey, John. "The Public and Its Problems." In *The Later Works, 1925–1953*, Vol. 2, ed. Jo Ann Boydston. Carbondale and Edwardsville, IL: University of Southern Illinois Press, 1984.

Donaldson, Thomas. *Corporations and Morality.* Englewood Cliffs, NJ: Prentice Hall, 1982.

Donaldson, Thomas. *The Ethics of International Business.* New York: Oxford, 1989.

Donaldson, Thomas, and Thomas W. Dunfee. *Ties That Bind: A Social Contracts Approach to Business Ethics.* Boston: Harvard Business School Press, 1999.

Durning, Alan. *How Much Is Enough?* New York: Norton, 1992.

Frederick, William C. *Corporation Be Good!: The Story of Corporate Social Responsibility.* Indianapolis, IN: Dog Ear Publishing, 2006.

Frederick, William C. *Values, Nature and Culture in the American Corporation.* New York: Oxford University Press, 1995.

Friedman, Milton. *Capitalism and Freedom.* Chicago: University of Chicago Press, 1962.

Friedman, Thomas L. *The Lexus and the Olive Tree.* New York: Farrar, Strauss, and Giroux, 1999.

Galbraith, John Kenneth. *The New Industrial State.* Boston: Houghton Mifflin, 1967.

Gewirth, Alan. *The Community of Rights.* Chicago: University of Chicago Press, 1996.

Gilchrist, John. *The Church and Economic Activity in the Middle Ages.* London: Macmillan, 1969.

Goudzwarrd, Bob. *Capitalism & Progress: A Diagnosis of Western Society.* Toronto: Wedge Publishing Foundation; Grand Rapids, MI: William B. Eerdmans, 1979.

Gray, John. *False Dawn.* New York: The New Press, 1998.

Greider, William. *The Soul of Capitalism: Opening Paths to a Moral Economy.* New York: Simon & Schuster, 2003.

Griswold, Charles L. Jr. *Adam Smith and the Virtues of Enlightenment.* Cambridge, UK: Cambridge University Press, 1999.

Hartman, Edwin. *Organizational Ethics and the Good Life.* New York: Oxford University Press, 1996.

Hassard, John, and Martin Parker, eds. *Postmodernism and Organizations.* London: Sage Publications, 1993.

Hickman, Larry A. *John Dewey's Pragmatic Technology.* Bloomington and Indianapolis, IN: Indiana University Press, 1992.

Higgs, Eric, Andrew Light, and David Strong, eds. *Technology and the Good Life?* Chicago: The University of Chicago Press, 2000.

James, William. *The Will to Believe and Other Essays: The Works of William James*, ed. Frederick Burkhardt. Cambridge, MA: Harvard University Press, 1979.

Kennedy, Allan A. *The End of Shareholder Value: Corporations at the Crossroads.* Cambridge, MA: Persus, 2000.

Kessler, David. *A Question of Intent: A Great American Battle With a Deadly Industry*. New York: Public Affairs, 2001.

Khurana, Rakesh. *From Higher Aims to Hired Hands*. Princeton, NJ: Princeton University Press, 2007.

Kristol, Irving. *Two Cheers for Capitalism*. New York: Basic Books, 1978.

Kuttner, Robert. *The Squandering of America*. New York: Knopf, 2007.

LaPiere, Richard. *The Freudian Ethic*. New York: Duell Sloan, and Pearce, 1959.

Laqueur, Walter, and Barry Rubin, eds. *The Human Rights Reader*. Philadelphia: Temple University Press, 1979.

Larner, Robert J. *Management Control and the Large Corporation*. New York: Dunellen, 1971.

Lasch, Christopher. *The Culture of Narcissism: American Life in an Age of Diminishing Expectations*. New York: Norton, 1978.

Lerner, Michael. *The Politics of Meaning: Restoring Hope and Possibility in an Age of Cynicism*. Reading, MA: Addison-Wesley, 1996.

Locke, John. *Two Treatises of Government*. Cambridge, UK: Cambridge University Press, 1988.

McCelland, David C. *The Achieving Society*. New York: The Free Press, 1961.

McKibben, Bill. *The End of Nature*. New York: Random House, 1989.

Mead, George Herbert. *Mind, Self, and Society*, ed. Charles Morris. Chicago: University of Chicago Press, 1994.

Mead, George Herbert. *Movements of Thought in the Nineteenth Century*, ed. Merritt Moore. Chicago: University of Chicago Press, 1936.

Mitchell, Lawrence E. *The Speculation Economy: How Finance Triumphed Over Industry*. San Francisco: Berrett-Koehler Publishers, Inc., 2007.

Muller, Jerry Z. *Adam Smith In His Time and Ours*. Princeton, NJ: Princeton University Press, 1993.

Muller, Jerry Z. *The Mind and the Market: Capitalism in Modern European Thought*. New York: Knopf, 2002.

Murray, Alan. *Revolt in the Boardroom*. New York: Collins, 2007.

Phillips, Kevin. *Bad Money: Reckless Finance, Failed Politics, and the Global Crisis of American Capitalism*. New York: Viking, 2008.

Polanyi, Karl. *The Great Transformation*. Boston: Beacon Press, 1944.

Shrader-Frechette, Kristin, and Laura Westra, eds. *Technology and Values*. New York: Roman & Littlefield, 1997.

Sirkin, Gerald. *The Visible Hand: The Fundamentals of Economic Planning*. New York: McGraw-Hill, 1968.

Solomon, Robert C. *Ethics and Excellence: Cooperation and Integrity in Business*. New York: Oxford University Press, 1992.

Smith, Adam. *The Wealth of Nations*. New York: Bantam Dell, 2003.

Tawney, Robert H. *Religion and the Rise of Capitalism*. Gloucester, MA: P. Smith, 1962.

Taylor, Charles. *The Ethics of Authenticity*. Cambridge, MA: Harvard University Press, 1991.

Vaughan, Diane. *The Challenger Launch Decision*. Chicago: University of Chicago Press, 1996.

Veblen, Thorstein. *Absentee Ownership*. New York: Augustus M. Kelley, 1964.

Veblen, Thorstein. *The Engineers and the Price System*. New York: Augustus M. Kelley, 1965.

Veblen, Thorstein. *The Instinct of Workmanship*. New York: Augustus M. Kelley, 1964.

Veblen, Thorstein. *The Theory of the Business Enterprise*. New York: Augustus M. Kelley, 1965.

Weber, Max. *The Protestant Ethic and the Spirit of Capitalism.* New York: Charles Scribner's Sons, 1958.

Weidenbaum, Murray L. *The Future of Business Regulation.* New York: AMA-COM, 1979.

Weidenbaum, Murray L. *Progress in Federal Regulatory Policy, 1980–2000.* St. Louis: Washington University Center for the Study of American Business, 2000.

Weidenbaum, Murray L., and Mark Jensen. *Introduction to the Modern Corporation and Private Property.* St. Louis: Washington University Center for the Study of American Business, 1990.

Wildavsky, Aaron. *Speaking Truth to Power: The Art and Craft of Policy Analysis* Boston: Little, Brown, 1979.

Index

and science, 159–169
as social institution, 141–144
and social responsibility, 18–29
and society, 142
and technology, 169–180
and trade associations, 210–211
business enterprise, 172–173
business ethics, 68–72
approaches to, 69–70
and individualism, 71, 223n38
and moral pluralism, 70–72
problems with, 69–70, 72
business schools
culture of, 1
curriculum of, 214
professionalization of, 211–215
purpose of, 212
and science, 1, 234n27
Byrnes, Nanette, 198

C
Callicott, J. Baird, 123
calling, 58
California Department of Consumer
Affairs, 43
Calorie Control Council, 161
calvinism, 57–58
Campaign AACSB, 234n29
cap and trade system, 112–114, 225n12
capital, 59–60, 209
capitalism, 84–98
and community, 16–17, 215–216
financial, 203–204
and growth, 90–93
and individualism, 9–12, 16–17
managerial, 200–204
moral foundations of, 92–93
philosophical foundations of, 4,
9–17, 75–83
and the Protestant Ethic, 56–62
and rights, 93–97
as a social system, 84–86, 97
and technology, 169, 172–175
and wealth, 86–90
carbon dioxide, 165–166, 177
carcinogen, 161
Carnegie Foundation, 202
Carter administration, 51
categorical imperative, 69–70
Catholic Church, 67–68
Caux Principles, 155
Caux Rountable, 155
Center for the Study of American Business (CASB), 51

Certified Public Accountant (CPA),
234n28
Challenger, 170–172
Chandler, Alfred, 201
changing environment of business,
18–20
Chicago Board of Trade, 113
Chief Executive Officer (CEO),
compensation of, 194–197
firings, 197–198
chlorofluorocarbons, 165
Cisco Systems, 87–88
citizen sovereignty, 47–48
Civil Rights Act of 1964, 43
Civil Rights Act of 1991, 51
classical American pragmatism, see
Pragmatism
clean air, 110–111
Clean Air Act, 112
Clean Air Act Amendments of 1990, 51
climate change, see global warming
Clients, 206–207
Clinton administration, 51, 162
codes of ethics, 2–3
Cold War, 145–146
collective bargaining, 139
Columbia, 229n18
Colvin, Geoff, 198
Committee of the Evolution of Work,
140
common other, 95
communitarianism, 223n1
community, 10, 17, 40, 224n10
and accommodation, 79
and business schools, 213
and capitalism, 16–17, 215–216
and conflict resolution, 80–83
and contracts, 12–13
and corporations, 5, 36–44, 141–
144, 208
dynamics of, 78–79, 94,96, 137
and globalization, 5, 148–149,
156–158
and governance, 199
and the individual, 16–17
and management, 199, 204, 206
and the market, 100, 102–103, 115
and property rights, 96–97
and public policy, 54–115
and natural rights, 96–97
and science, 167–169
and social responsibility, 28
and society, 13, 16, 102–103,
and stakeholder theory, 142–143